Learn VB.NET

by Chuck Easttom

Wordware Publishing, Inc.

Contents Summary

Contents

Contents

Acknowledgments

This book has been a tremendous undertaking, and I could not have done it alone. I have several people to thank for this.

First of all the people at Wordware Publishing. Jim Hill and Wes Beckwith have always been absolutely wonderful to work with. Without them, I would not be writing programming books today. I also owe a great debt to Beth Kohler. She edits the rough drafts and saves me from embarrassing myself!

I also wish to thank students who looked at rough drafts of chapters and examined source code. They allowed me to confirm that this book truly could teach the beginner how to use VB.NET.

Finally, my wife, Misty, and my son, AJ, who are always patient when I am laboring in the den for hours on a book. Their understanding allows all this to be possible

Introduction

When Visual Basic 1.0 was introduced in 1991, it revolutionized Windows programming. Before the advent of Visual Basic, programmers had to code everything by hand, the hard way. A simple task such as placing a button on the screen required some rather intricate programming. Visual Basic changed all this. It allowed the programmer to use components to build the GUI (Graphical User Interface) and then they could simply concentrate on the actual application.

Versions 2 and 3 of Visual Basic simply added some more components and a bit more functionality; however, version 3.0 was still quite limited. Most programmers simply used it for creating user interfaces or for prototyping. Version 4.0 introduced a whole new world to Visual Basic programmers. It brought the concept of classes and object-oriented programming, as well as a host of other innovations. Versions 5.0 and 6.0 continued this evolution, although Visual Basic 6.0 added several Internet programming options, as well as the ability to create your own ActiveX DLLs and components. However, in essence, the Visual Basic language had not changed a great deal since version 1.0. Code written in an older version still ran just fine, even if some of it was now superfluous.

VB.NET, however, is a radical departure from past versions of Visual Basic. I must admit that at first I thought this radical shift in programming paradigms would be a very bad mistake, until I got a chance to begin working with VB.NET. I first began working with the public beta version 1.0 and kept up with each successive beta release. What I saw amazed me. Visual Basic now has all the power and functionality of any other mainstream language including C++ and Java. It now has 100% true object orientation, inheritance, and many of the features that have made Java a great language.

This book is primarily designed to help a beginning programmer understand VB.NET. It is not assumed that you have any programming experience at all. However, an experienced VB programmer who wishes to become acclimated with the new VB.NET will also find this book useful. Each chapter contains graphics to illustrate what is happening as well as step-by-step instructions on how to write the code. The first chapter has you jump right in and develop some simple code. Then we go back and explain the theoretical and conceptual underpinnings. In my experience teaching programming, I have found that students tend to better understand concepts they have seen in action.

In this book you will learn the basics of writing VB.NET applications as well as the fundamentals of the .NET architecture. You will also be exposed to some object-oriented theory. In addition, I will show you how to access databases using ADO.NET, and how to write Internet applications with ASP.NET. By the end of the book you should have a firm grasp of VB.NET. Be sure to download the example files from www.wordware.com/VBNET as they contain fully working applications written in VB.NET. This gives you working examples to use as guides to your studies.

The first chapter dives right in and has you writing code. There is also a separate chapter that covers the actual details of the .NET architecture and how this relates to Visual Basic programming. Most of the chapters are concerned with simply showing you how to do things in VB.NET. However, certain chapters (notably Chapters 4 and 7) delve into the underlying architecture behind VB.NET. Those chapters might be a bit overwhelming for the novice programmer. The good news is that you don't have to grasp everything in them in order to use VB.NET. If you are a complete novice (new to VB and new to programming) I suggest you read them but don't worry too much. After about six months of actually working with VB.NET, come back and read them again.

There are a couple of items in this book that I don't think are in any other beginners book. The first is an entire chapter devoted to software design. There is also a chapter devoted to basic computer science. Many people come to VB from backgrounds other than computer science. These two chapters endeavor to help you "catch up" with some fundamental computer science and software engineering topics.

Chapter 1

Windows Applications with VB.NET

In this chapter, you learn about:

- Getting started with VB.NET
- Common components and their properties
- Common programming terms
- Drop-down menus
- Shortcut keys
- Naming conventions

Introduction

This chapter is designed to introduce you to the essentials of Visual Basic.NET. By the end of this chapter, you should have a basic understanding of developing a Windows application using VB.NET. This includes the use of forms, components, properties, and events. You should also be getting comfortable with the programming interface and know how to move around in the toolbar, toolbox, and drop-down menus.

Getting Started with VB.NET

When you first launch Visual Basic, you will see the following screen.

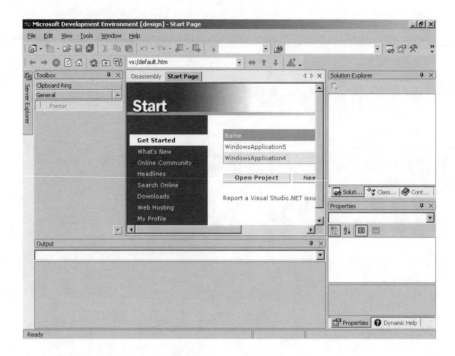

This screen is common to all the Visual Studio.NET products. In order to start a new project you will need to go to the drop-down menu at the top of the screen and click on File, New, then Project. You can also accomplish the same thing by pressing Ctrl+N on your keyboard (the Control key and the N key simultaneously).

You will then see the following screen.

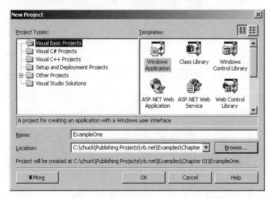

The first option you see on the left side should be Visual Basic. As I indicated before, this same environment is used for all the Visual Studio.NET products, but for the purposes of this book we will only be concerning ourselves with Visual Basic.NET projects. You will further notice that on the right-hand side you have several Visual Basic templates to choose from. For this chapter, we will focus on Windows applications; however, later chapters will introduce you to other types of Visual Basic projects.

On this screen you can also choose the name for your project as well as the location in which you place it. At the bottom of this screen you will notice a field called "Name," and just below that a field called "Location." You will notice that in our example we have named our project "ExampleOne" and placed it in a folder called "Examples\Chapter One\."

Once you have selected the project type, name, and location you will then be able to view the actual development area. This is referred to as the IDE, or integrated development environment.

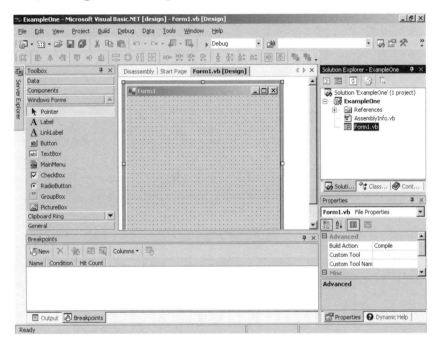

The top of the screen shows the drop-down menus and the toolbar. These contain various functions you will use when programming, such as saving, running, and debugging your program. There are a lot of interesting and useful features you will need to become familiar with in the IDE, but for the time being we are going to concentrate on getting a few simple VB.NET programs to compile and run successfully.

In the center of the screen you should see a blank form. The form is the cornerstone of Windows applications written with Visual Basic. This is what will be visually displayed to the user of your application. Beginning with version 1.0 of Visual Basic and continuing through to VB.NET, developers can simply place a variety of components directly on the form, and resize and reposition them. This makes designing the graphical user interface (GUI) much easier.

The form itself, as well as all the components you might place on it, have certain properties you can manipulate. They also have events that occur in response to user and system actions. We are going to create a few simple applications that illustrate this point. If you look on the left side of the screen, you should see a toolbox that displays all the components you initially have available. You have two methods for placing a component on a form. The first is to simply double-click on the component you wish to use in the toolbox. It will then appear in the upper left-hand corner of the currently active form. The second method is to click on the component you wish to add, then drag your mouse on the form, literally drawing the component.

The first example I am going to show you is quite simple but it is a good place to start. If you wish to follow along, you merely need to open Visual Basic.NET, start a new Windows application project, and then follow the steps provided below.

Example 1-1

For our example, place a single command button on the form, then move the button to the middle of the form. Then place a single text box directly above it. Your screen should look like the following when you are done.

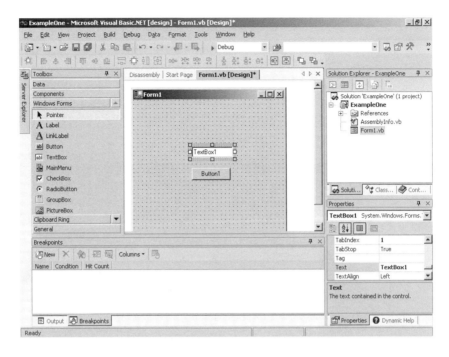

If you look to the lower right side of your screen you should see a window called Properties. If you do not see this, you can click on the form or any components on it and press F4; you should then see the Properties window. This window allows you to set the properties of the form itself or any component on the form. In order to do this, you must first select the individual component in question (by clicking on it), or you can use the drop-down box at the top of the Properties window to select any component on the form.

We are first going to set several properties of the command button.

The first property we will set is the background color. For most business applications the standard gray background is perfect; however, I want to illustrate to you what you can do with Visual Basic.NET. When you double-click the BackgroundColor property, you will be presented with three tabs. Select the one called Custom Color. Upon selecting this tab you will be shown a palette of colors. Simply double-clicking on one of the colors will change the command button's background to the color you choose. For our example, I am choosing a light blue color. You should note that just below the BackgroundColor property is the BackgroundImage property. You can use images as the background for the command button, as well as many other components.

Next we are going to set the Text property. This property determines what will display as the caption on the button. We are going to change this to read "Click Me." Obviously, there are many other properties we could set, and we will examine all of them in time. However, at this point I would like to turn your attention to how to handle user events. If you double-click on the command button, a window will open showing you the code for the button's Click event.

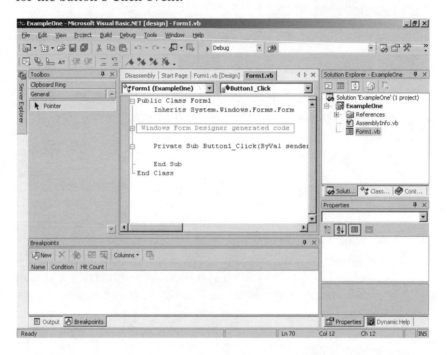

There is a lot of code here that needs to be explained, but first I would like to show you a Windows application in action. With that in mind, we are going to type in a single line of code (the line beginning with "Me.Text"):

```
Private Sub Button1_Click(ByVal Sender as System.Object, ByVal e as
        System.EventArgs) Handles Button1.Click
    Me.Text = TextBox1.Text()
End Sub
```

In order to see what our application does, you must run the program. You can do this by using any of the following methods:

- Press the F5 key.
- Press the arrow-shaped button on the toolbar (it looks like a play button on a CD player).

■   Select Debug | Start from the drop-down menu at the top of the IDE.

Whichever method you choose, when you run the example you will see a screen with our command button and our text box located on it. If you then type some text in the text box and click the command button, you will find that the caption for the form is changed to the text you put in the text box.

This simple application illustrates many of the basic principles of Visual Basic.NET. The first thing you should notice is that you can easily place any components you wish on a form and design a user interface. The next thing you should notice is that when you are developing your application (referred to as "design time") you can change the properties of any component you wish using the Properties window. Finally, you should notice that when your application is running (referred to as "run time") you can have your code written in such a way that it changes the properties of various components.

In our single line of code we did two very interesting things. First, we extracted the value contained in the Text property of the text box, then we placed that value into the Text property of the form (the "Me" keyword refers to the current form you are working with). All of this was accomplished in response to a user clicking the command button.

At this point a bit more explanation of an event is in order. When you write code in any programming language (be it Visual Basic, C, Java, Perl, etc.), you don't simply write line after line of code. You usually organize the code into logical sections that perform some action. These sections are referred to as *functions* or *subroutines*. Basically, when you place a section of code in one place with a common name to refer to that section of code, you have a function. For example, if I wish to write a function that divides two numbers, I might write something like this:

```
Public Sub Divide(Num1 as Single, Num2 as Single)
    Dim Answer as Single
    Answer = Num1 / Num2
End Sub
```

The first line of this code is referred to as the function declaration line. It contains several elements, namely the access modifier (whether it is public or private), the word "sub," the name you wish to give your function, and any parameters you want to pass to your function.

An *event* is simply a function, usually connected with some component, that is called in response to some user or system action. One example is the Click event, which is a function that is called when the user clicks on a button.

You will find that a great deal of Visual Basic code is concerned with manipulating the properties of components and responding to events. Before I begin a more detailed examination of what is occurring, I would like to show you one more example.

Example 1-2

1. Start a new project as a Windows application.
2. Place one text box and four labels on the form. Set the labels' Text properties to **blank** and the BorderStyle to **Fixed3D**.
3. Place one command button on the form.
4. Change your form's caption to read **String Stuff**.

    Now your form should look like this:

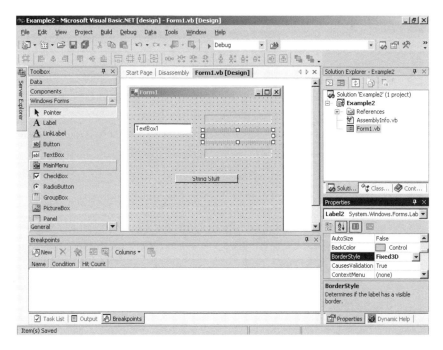

5. In the Click event of the command button place the following code:

    ```
    Dim MyString as String
    MyString = Textbox1.Text
    Label1.Text = Ucase(MyString) 'display uppercase version of the string
    Label2.Text = Lcase(MyString) 'display lowercase version of the string
    Label3.Text = Len(MyString)   'display length of the string
    ```

    Remember that the way you access the Click event is to double-click on the command button.

6. Using one of the procedures explained earlier in this chapter, run the application.

7. When the application is running, type your first name into the text box and press the command button. You will see something like the following image.

This second example has you once again manipulating the properties of text boxes and labels, both at design time and run time. It also has you returning to the Click event of the command button. The text box, label, and command button are perhaps the most ubiquitous components in Visual Basic, so it behooves us to begin our examinations with them.

Now that you have seen some simple Windows applications work in VB.NET, it is time for us to go back and examine that cryptic looking code we saw when we looked in the Click event of our command button. To refresh your memory, what you should have seen would be something like this:

```
Public Class Form1
    Inherits System.Windows.Forms.Form
    Private Sub Button1_Click(ByVal Sender as System.Object, ByVal e
        as System.EventArgs) Handles Button1.Click
    End Sub
End Class
```

The first thing you may notice is the Public Class Form1 line. You might be asking what that means. Let me explain. VB.NET has implemented a purely object-oriented paradigm (unlike previous versions of Visual Basic). What this means is that all the forms (as well as most other portions of your Visual Basic application) are really made from classes. A *class* is simply a code template for creating an object. Every component you put on a form (and, incidentally, the form itself) is an object. When you change the placement of a text box on a form and change one of its properties, what you have actually done is created an instance of the textbox object and changed one of its members.

I will go into more depth on object-oriented theory and practice in a later chapter, but for the time being it is simply necessary for you to realize that a class is a template for creating an object, and that an object has properties and methods.

So what our code example is telling us is that there is a class called "Form1" and one of the methods for that class is our button1 Click event. It is also telling us that this event takes several parameters (that are passed by the system; you don't have to write code for them). You don't have to do anything with parameters that are passed to your function or event if you don't wish to. In our case, we did not.

Common Components and Their Properties

You have already seen how easy it is to create the user interface using the components that Visual Basic.NET provides you with. There are many components you can utilize in your applications. In this section, I will describe to you, in brief, some of the most commonly used components, what they are used for, and their most important properties. I should note here that you will often hear the words "component" and "control" used interchangeably. Don't let this confuse you.

Some components are used more often than others. The form is the most basic component. It is the container in which you place all the other components. It is also what your user will see. The most important properties you will set for a form are its name (what the computer will call it), its text (what appears in the title bar that the user will see), and its back color (what color you want the background to be). You may also wish to set its border style (this determines if it can be resized by the user or not). Below are listed some other common components and the properties you will be most concerned with.

Components

Text Box

This component allows the end user to enter data. You will want to set its name (what the computer will call it), its text (the default text that initially appears when you run the program), and possibly its font if you wish a different font in the text box. You can also enter something into the Text property as a default text. Finally, you may want to set its max length property. This determines the maximum number of characters a user can type into the text box. You can also set its password character property to show a symbol in lieu of the actual password. The multiline and scroll bar properties allow you to have a text box that can handle several lines of text.

Label

Labels are used to display information to the end user, but the end user cannot change any information in the label. The properties you set in this component are the name (what the computer will call it), its text (what the user will see), and its font.

Command Button

Command buttons allow the user to click a button. A lot of the code that you write will be associated with command buttons. The properties you are most interested in are its name (what the computer will call it), its text (what the user will see), its style (whether your button will have a text caption or a picture), and its font.

List Box

A list box simply allows you to list items from which a user can choose. The property you are concerned with is the font. The items are listed using code and will be discussed later.

Combo Box

This is like a list box but you can set more options.

Picture Box

Using this component, you can place any bitmap (*.bmp), Windows metafile (*.wmf), or icon (*.ico) on your form. Starting with Visual Basic version 5.0, you can also add in JPEG (*.jpg) and GIF (*.gif) image files. All you do is set the stretch property to true (this ensures that the picture you insert will be the size of your picture box) and then use the picture property to select the picture you want to use.

Group Box

A frame is basically a container component. It is used to group other components. The property you will use most with it is its caption.

Component Properties

Font

Many components have a font property that lets you select the font for that component. Below is what you will see if you select the font property of any component:

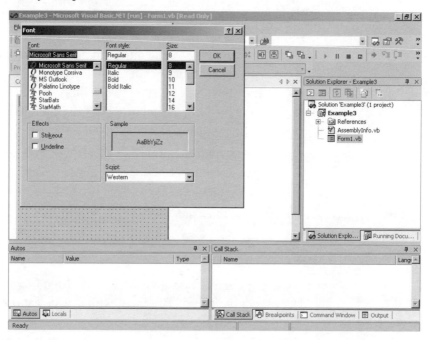

Using this screen you can easily change the font settings for most components.

A lot of the programming you do will be concerned with using code to alter the properties of some component. To do this, you write the component name you wish to alter followed by a period and the name of the property you want to change. The syntax for this is:

```
ComponentName.Property = "whatever"
```

Some specific examples are:

```
Textbox1.Text = "Howdy"
Me.Text = "This is my form"
Picturebox1.Image = "c:\folder\image.bmp"
Label1.Text = "This is a label"
```

Tip: If your code referencing a property does not work, it is most likely because you misspelled either the component or property name.

Using this basic technique, you can write code to change the properties of any component you wish. This is important to remember since much of the code you write in Visual Basic is concerned with altering the properties of various components.

Example 1-3

Let's try one more example to illustrate the use of components and properties. Start up a new Windows application. I will call mine **example3**.

Now, on that form place one list box, one text box, and one command button. In the Properties window (either select **View | Properties** or press the **F4** key) change the command button's caption to **Add Text**. Your form should look like the image below.

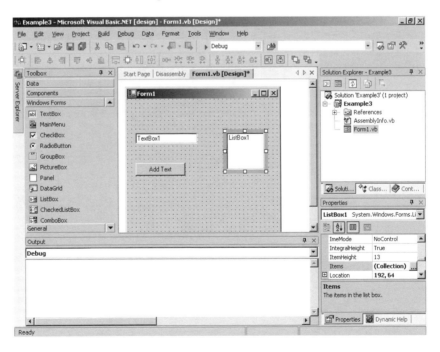

If you double-click on the command button you will get its code window. This will show you the Click event, just as we saw in the previous two examples.

In it place this code:

```
ListBox1.Items().Add(TextBox1.Text)
```

Run your program. Remember that you can do this by clicking on the Run button in the toolbar or by pressing the F5 key. Now every time you click on the command button, whatever you have typed into the text box will be added to the list box!

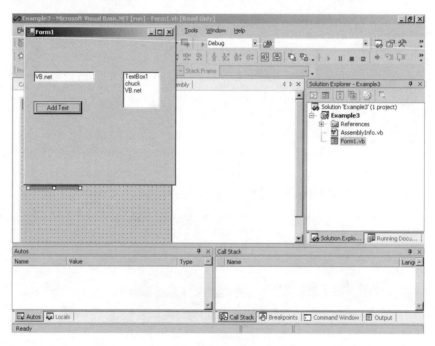

Common Programming Terms

The following is a list of standard Visual Basic and programming terms that you will need to be familiar with. In programming, proper nomenclature (or naming) is vital. You cannot understand instructions or communicate with other programmers without an understanding of proper nomenclature.

Application   A fancy word for the program you write.

Bug   An error in your program.

Code   The actual program instructions that you write.

Code module   A module of separate subroutines completely separate from a form.

Compile   The process of taking your source code and creating an executable program from it.

Components   The various objects that Visual Basic has for you to use in your graphical user interface. Examples are the text box, command button, list box, combo box, and picture box. Many Visual Basic books call these components "controls." That was the name used in previous versions of Visual Basic.

Debug   To remove errors in your program.

Event   A function that responds to an action taken by the user or the system itself. The Click event is a good example.

Form   The component on which you place other components and design the user interface.

Function   A group of related statements that perform some action.

IDE   Integrated development environment.

Project   What contains all the files in your program. It includes forms, code modules, class modules, etc. In Visual Basic.NET this idea has been expanded to the notion of the *assembly*, which also includes information about all the other items, such as DLLs, that your application may depend on.

Statement   A single line of code that performs an action.

Chapter

| *Subroutine* | A subsection of code. Events are premade subroutines in Visual Basic. |
| *Variable* | A place in memory set aside to hold data of a particular type. |

The Drop-Down Menu

The drop-down menu gives you access to several possible functions. The following is a list of the main drop-down options you see at the top of your screen and several of the suboptions along with their functions. I do not cover all the drop-down menu options here, only the ones that you as a beginner need. We will cover others later in this book.

File

New Project	Opens a new blank project for you to begin working with.
Open Project	Allows you to open an existing project. When you select this option, you will see a dialog box that you can use to browse your computer to find the project.
Close	Closes the currently open project.
Save All	Saves changes made to all the modules in your project.
Save Form	Saves the specific form that currently has focus.
Save Form As	Allows you to save a specific form under a name of your choosing and in the folder/directory that you select.
Exit	Exits Visual Basic

Edit

| *Undo* | Allows you to undo whatever action you last performed. |

Tip: The Undo option exists in most Windows programs. If you do something you wish you hadn't done, don't panic; simply select "Undo."

| *Redo* | Allows you to redo the last action performed or the action on which you used Undo. |

Cut	Removes the code or component you have selected and places it on the clipboard. You can also use the shortcut keys Ctrl+X to accomplish this task.
Copy	Places a copy of the code or component you have selected on the clipboard. You can also use the shortcut keys Ctrl+C to accomplish this task.
Paste	Inserts something that you have previously copied or cut. You can also use the shortcut keys Ctrl+V to accomplish this task.

View

Tip: I always hear at least one student in panic yelling "I can't find my project/form/code module/etc." The solution to this problem is usually to go to View and select that object.

Code	Displays the underlying code for any object that currently has focus.
Designer	Allows you to view the object of the code you are currently viewing.
Solution Explorer	Displays a window containing a listing of all files in your project.
Properties Window	Displays the Properties window. It will usually appear to the right of the IDE. You can get to it by selecting View | Properties or by pressing F4. It will display the properties of whatever component currently has focus.
Tool Box	You can use this to make your toolbox visible. The toolbox contains all the components you might use in your project. This is usually on the left side of the IDE.

Project

Add Windows Form	Adds a new form to your project. When you select this, you will be prompted as to what type of form you wish to add. You will usually select the Windows Form option, but Visual Basic has a number of premade forms you may want to use.

Add Module   Adds a blank code module.

Add Class   Adds a class module.

*Add
Component*   Adds new components to your toolbox so that you can use
                 them in your project. Visual Basic has many more
                 components than you see in your toolbox. This option lets
                 you select which components you want to be visible. If
                 you select this option you will see a window like
                 the one below from which you can choose the
                 components you want available for your project.

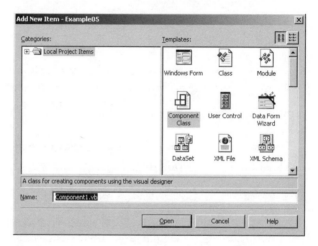

Build

This menu gives you a variety of options for compiling your project. This
will be discussed in depth in later chapters.

Debug

This menu gives you a variety of options for finding bugs in your program,
and we will discuss them at some length later in this book. For now, the
only option under this menu you should be concerned with is the Start
option. It simply causes your program to run.

Shortcut Keys

The following are a few of the most commonly used shortcut keys. You may want to memorize them.

F3	Find
F4	View an object's Properties window
F5	Run
F7	View the Code window of an object
Ctrl+Z	Undo
Ctrl+C	Copy
Ctrl+X	Cut
Ctrl+V	Paste

Naming Conventions

Microsoft has established some naming conventions that you should use when naming components. This makes for more uniform code that is easy to read. By default, each of your components will have a name like: text1, label1, command4, etc. You must go to the Name property of each component to change its name. Naming conventions simply make it much easier for another programmer to see what you are doing. Following are some examples of Microsoft naming conventions:

Component Type	Naming Convention
Text Box	TxtWhatever
Button	BtnWhatever
Label	LblWhatever
Panel	PnlWhatever
Frame	FraWhatever
Combo box	CmboWhatever
List box	LstWhatever

Using these naming conventions will make reading your code much easier. I realize that it is even easier and faster to just leave your components with the default name. While you are working on simple projects it won't really matter, but when you have to work on real-world applications, you don't really want to spend time trying to figure out that Text1 refers to the account number.

Summary

The purpose of this chapter was to give you a jump start on learning Visual Basic.NET. I wanted to introduce you to the IDE as well as common programming terms and concepts. You were also given the opportunity to begin actually writing some simple Windows applications using VB.NET. While none of these applications are likely to be the next "must have" application of the year, they did allow you to get a feel for developing Windows applications using VB.NET.

Review Questions

1. What is a GUI?
2. List two ways to run an application inside the IDE.
3. Write a line of code that will display the length of a string called "MyString" in a text box named "Textbox1."
4. What is a variable?
5. What is a statement?
6. What does the F7 key do?
7. List four components.
8. What is an event?
9. What does the F4 key do for you in the IDE?
10. What is an IDE?

Fundamentals of Programming with VB.NET

In this chapter, you learn about:

- ◆ **Programming terms**
- ◆ **Decision structures**
- ◆ **Keywords**
- ◆ **Menus**

Introduction

In Chapter 1, I introduced you to writing a few simple Windows applications with VB.NET. The point of those applications was to allow you to get comfortable with using VB.NET and the IDE. However, before we can expand your knowledge of VB.NET programming, I need to introduce you to a variety of programming concepts and techniques as they apply to Visual Basic.NET. Using these techniques, you will be able to begin to do more serious programming.

Programming Terms

I am amazed at the number of beginning programming books that never explicitly introduce the reader to some standard programming terminology. Before we get too far into this chapter, I would like to introduce you to the necessary terminology.

Variables

A variable is a place in memory set aside to hold data of a particular type. Essentially, when you declare a variable, a given number of bytes of memory are set aside to hold data of the type specified.

A variable is declared in the following manner:

```
Dim VariableName as Datatype
```

Some more specific examples would include:

```
Dim iCounter as Integer
Dim Lname as String
```

Each data type is designed to hold variables of a specific kind and for a specific purpose.

Boolean	Holds a true or false value. This is often used in programming and you will find it most useful.
Byte, Short, Integer, Long	These four data types hold whole numbers of varying size. The Byte holds the smallest size and the Long holds the largest. Examples would include numbers such as 0, 17, 450, and 98756.
Single and *Double*	These two data types hold decimal value numbers. Single holds the smaller values, and Double the larger. Examples would include numbers such as 1.098, 4444.989, and –989.88.
Char	A Char can hold a single character such as an "a" or "b" and an integer value as well.
String	As you can probably surmise, a string variable holds string values. This is simply text such as "VB.NET is cool" or "I like this book."

Date	Holds date values, such as 09/10/2001.	
Object	We will discuss objects in more depth in a later chapter, but you should know that an object variable can represent any object in Visual Basic, including classes you create, forms, and components.	
User-defined types	This useful data type is actually a compound data type you create by grouping related variables together. An example might be a user-defined type (also called a structure) used to hold information about students in a class:	

```
Structure Student
    Dim No as Long
    Dim Name as String
    Dim Address as String
    Dim Average as Single
End Structure
```

Now you can use this variable anywhere in code just like you would use any other data type.

```
Dim StudentA as Student
Dim StudentB as Student
StudentA.Grade = 97.44
StudentB.Grade = 87.33
```

The table below summarizes the various data types, the amount of memory they occupy, and the range of values they can hold.

Data Type	Size	Range
Boolean	4 Bytes	True or False
Byte	1 Byte	0 to 255 unsigned
Char	2 Bytes	0 to 65,535 unsigned
Date	8 Bytes	1/1/1 to 12/31/9999
Short	2 Bytes	−32,768 to 32,767
Integer	4 Bytes	−2,147,483,648 to 2,147,483,647
Long	8 Bytes	−9,223,372,036,854,775,808 to 9,223,372,036,854,775,807
Single	4 Bytes	−3.402823E38 to −1.401298E-45 for negative values; 1.401298E-45 to 3.402823E38 for positive values

Chapter 2

Data Type	Size	Range
Double	8 Bytes	−1.79769313486231E308 to −4.94065645841247E-324 for negative values; 4.94065645841247E-324 to 1.79769313486232E308 for positive values
String	10 Bytes + (characters in string * 2)	0 to approximately 2 billion Unicode characters
Object	4 Bytes	Any object type
Structure	Sum of the size of its members	Range-dependent data type for each member

Another important issue regarding variables is what to name them. It is possible to simply give your variables numeric or letter designations such as:

```
Dim A as String
Dim B as Single
Dim C as Integer
```

However, this presents some serious problems in that when you read the code (or anyone else reads it) you will have no idea what A is supposed to hold, or B or C. It is a much better idea to give your variables names that indicate what kind of data they will hold:

```
Dim Lastname as String
Dim GradeAverage as Single
Dim Age as Integer
```

Now it is abundantly clear to anyone reading your code what each of these variables are meant to hold, but there is still a small problem. As your code gets larger (and it certainly will as we move into more complex applications), you won't remember if GradeAverage is a Single or a Double. For this reason, many programmers preface their variable names with a one- to three-letter designation that shows what type of variable it is. For example:

```
Dim StrLastname as String    or    Dim SLastname as String
Dim SngGrade Average as Single
Dim iAge as Integer or Dim IntAge as Integer
```

Following is a table summarizing various naming conventions you may opt to utilize.

Variable	Naming Convention
Integer	IntName or iName
Long	LngName or lName
Double	Dname or dblName
Object	ObjName or oName

 Tip: Some programming languages allow you to dimension several variables on one line like this example from C that dimensions four integers:

```
Int AccountNum, IndexNum, LoopCounter, J
```

In Visual Basic this will not work. Only the first variable will be an integer; all the rest will be variants. In Visual Basic you must use this method:

```
Private AccountNum as Integer, IndexNum as Integer, LoopCounter as
     Integer, J as Integer
```

I still have one last issue to show you regarding variables, and that is scope. *Scope* refers to the range in which a variable can be used. If you declare a variable within a subroutine, function, or event, it will only be accessible inside that subroutine, function, or event. Outside of that area, the variable is out of scope and essentially does not exist.

Any variable declared in the Declarations section of the form module should also be Private. However, any variable declared in a code module that you may wish to use in more than one form should be declared public. Earlier versions of Visual Basic used the terms "Dim" and "Global" instead of "Private" and "Public." You will still see these used by many programmers and they do work, but Microsoft discourages their use. Private just means that only that level and below can use that variable. For example, a privately declared variable in an event can only be accessed within that event. A privately declared variable in a form can be accessed by events within that form.

 Note: You cannot declare a variable as public or private within an event, subroutine, or function. You must use the Dim statement.

Operators and Statements

I have already introduced you to variables, and you can think of those as the "nouns" of programming. Next I would like to introduce you to operators, which you can think of as the verbs of programming. Most of the operators are related to mathematical operations.

I trust that you are familiar with the four basic mathematical operators of addition, subtraction, multiplication, and division. However, I frequently encounter novice programmers who are not familiar with some of the other operators so I will discuss them briefly here.

The modulus operator takes two numbers and divides the first number by the second, but it only returns the remainder. The symbol for this (in all programming languages with which I am familiar) is the percent sign (%). For example, if I write:

```
Dim Answer as Integer
Answer = 5 % 3
```

The value placed in Answer will be 2, since 5 divided by 3 yields 1 with a remainder of 2. This operator can be useful in determining if any given variable holds an even number. If any variable modulus 2 is 0, that number is even.

Some beginning programmers are also unfamiliar with concatenation. This is the process of taking two strings and simply linking the second to the end of the first. The symbol for this is the ampersand (&).

In some programming languages (such as C, C++, and Java) a single equal sign indicates assignment. In other words, take the value on the right side and place it into the variable on the left. And a double equal sign (==) is the evaluation operator. It asks, "is the variable on the left equal to the value on the right?" In Visual Basic, the single equal sign acts as both the assignment and the evaluator, depending upon the situation.

These operators are summarized in the table below.

Operation	Operator	Example
Evaluator — Evaluates if two items are of equal value	=	If iaccount = 49898
Assignment — Assigns a value to a variable	=	SngBalance = 345.98

Operation	Operator	Example
Addition	+	SngBalance = sngBalance + 299.44
Subtraction	–	SngBalance = sngBalance – 29.98
Multiplication	*	DblAnswer = 393 * 22.99
Division	/	DblAnswer = sngNumber / 33.43
Modulus	%	DblRemainder = 5 % 4
Concatenation	&	StrNew = strold1 & strold2

Now that I have shown you variables (nouns) and operators (verbs), I should probably show you complete statements (sentences). You have actually already written several statements. A statement is merely a line of code that performs some action. Any action at all, in fact. All of the following are statements:

```
Dim Answer as Integer
Answer = 5 + 4
If Answer > 3 then
```

The first performs the action of declaring a variable. The second performs the operations of addition and assignment. The third example evaluates the value of a variable against a given value. All three perform an action.

Functions and Procedures

A *function* is simply a block of code that can be called to perform some type of action. Another way of defining a function would be to call it a group of related statements grouped together under a common name that can be called as a unit. A *procedure* is simply a function that does not return any value. If we think of variables as nouns and statements as sentences, functions would be chapters.

Note that in other programming languages there is often no distinction between functions and procedures (also called subroutines).

The basic structure of a function is that it begins with a declaration line, which tells you a great deal about the function. Then we have all the statements that make up the function. Finally, the function is terminated. Here is a generic example of the declaration line of a function:

```
Access modifier function name (parameters) as type
```

The access modifier simply tells us who can access this function. If that modifier is private, only other functions in the same class can access it. If it's public, it can be called from outside that class. There are other access modifiers that we will discuss later in this book. The function name is any name you wish to give the function. It's a good idea to give it a name that reflects what it is going to be accomplishing. Then, inside parentheses there are the parameters. Parameters are simply variables you wish to pass to the function. Consider them raw materials for the function to work with. The "as type" segment at the end simply tells us what type of value the function will return.

Here is an example of a function:

```
Public Function Divide_Integers(iNum1 as integer, iNum2 as integer)
      as Single
   Dim Answer as Single
   Answer = iNum1/iNum2
   Return Answer
End Function
```

You see we have a group of related statements, three to be precise. They all work together to perform the task of dividing two integers, and they are grouped under the common name Divide_Integers. Now, if I wish to call this function from somewhere else in my code, it's really simple:

```
Dim SomeValue as Single
SomeValue = Divide_Integers(12,5)
```

That's all there is to it.

Note that in previous versions of Visual Basic, to return a value of a function you set the name of the function equal to the value you wished to return. In Visual Basic.NET, you can still use this method or use the Return keyword to return a value from a function. I highly recommend that you use the Return keyword. This is the method used in most programming languages and Microsoft will eventually phase out the older method.

There are two other keywords with function parameters: Optional and ParamArray. The Optional keyword is used for parameters that are not required when calling a function. It is important to remember two things about optional parameters. First, when a parameter is declared as optional, all parameters after it must also be optional. You cannot have an optional parameter and after it have a required parameter. You must also supply a default value for the optional parameter. If this parameter is not specified, the default value is used when the function is called. Let's look at an example:

```
Function Multiply(ByVal Num1 as Integer, ByVal Num2 as Integer,
        Optional ByVal Num3 as Integer = 1) as Integer
    Return Num1 * Num2 * Num3
End Function
```

In this example, you only have to pass in values for Num1 and Num2. If you don't provide a value for Num3, it defaults to 1. Let's look at two calls to this function:

```
i = Multiply(2, 3)
i = Multiply(2, 3, 4)
```

In the first call, no optional parameter is provided, and the function returns the value 6. In the second call, the value 4 is provided, and the function returns the value 24.

Now let's take a look at how to use ParamArray. You can only use this keyword as the last parameter and with only one parameter. This means you can only have one ParamArray per function. This keyword allows the function to be called with any number of arguments. The limitation is that all values must be passed by value. Let's modify our Multiply function to use ParamArray:

```
Function Multiply(ByVal ParamArray Args() as Integer) as Integer
    Dim iCount as Integer
    Dim Answer as Integer = 1
    For iCount = 0 to Args.Length() - 1
        Answer = Answer * Args(i)
    Next
    Return Answer
End Function
```

Notice that the Args array is an object and that we have used the Length property to determine how many arguments were passed into the function. We then used a For loop to multiply all of the arguments together and return the result. If some of this seems a bit odd, don't worry. We will be discussing For loops later in this chapter.

Comments

One critical item to introduce you to is the comment. A *comment* is a line that the computer will ignore but that another programmer viewing your source code can read. Comments are vital to good programming. They allow people reading your code to get an idea of what you were thinking when you wrote the code. You can put a comment anywhere by simply placing an apostrophe before the line such as:

```
' This is a comment
```

Commented lines will appear in green in the IDE. Actual keywords that Visual Basic recognizes will show up in blue and errors will be in red.

Note: It is absolutely vital that you use comments in your code. Comments can explain to other programmers what you intended to accomplish. As a rule there is no such thing as too many comments in your code. Here are some examples:

```
Dim X as Integer                     'this X is simply used as a loop counter
Let iAcct = left(iAccountNum,4)'get the first 4 digits of iAccount Num
                                     ' and put them in the variable "iAcct"
```

From here on, I will use comments in my code examples so that you can become acquainted with commenting.

Decision Structures

Frequently, you will need to execute different sections of code depending on some condition. The mechanisms by which you accomplish this are referred to as decision structures. A decision structure is simply a section of code that will evaluate some value and take different action based on what that value is.

If-Then

If-Then statements are perhaps the most common method by which your program can make decisions based on either the conditions existing or on user input. Let me first give you a generic example, and then I will use a specific example:

```
If some condition exists then
     Do this code
 End If
```

A specific example would be:

```
If Textbox1.Text = "Howdy" then
    Textbox1.Text = "Hi back at ya"
End If
```

Basically, this code looks at the text in the textbox1 component and checks its value. If that value is "Howdy," it changes the text to say "Hi back at ya." If not, it simply proceeds with the rest of the program.

Another example would be:

```
If MyAge > 21 then
      Textbox1.Text = "come on in"
 Else
      Textbox1.Text = "Sorry, you are not old enough to enter"
 End If
```

The concept is simple and is found in all programming languages. If some condition is true, execute the specified code.

Of course, you may have a need for more options in your If-Then loop. This is where the Else and Else-If statements come in. You could rewrite the above loop like this:

```
If MyAge < 21 then
    Textbox1.Text = "Sorry, you are not old enough to enter"
ElseIf MyAge < 65 then
    Textbox1.Text = "come on in"
Else
    Textbox1.Text = "you get a seniors discount"
End If
```

Example 2-1

Let's try placing a text box and a button on a form. Your form should look much like what you see in the following image.

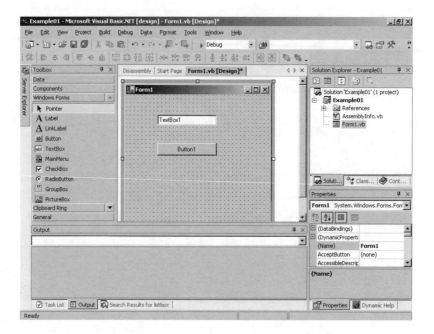

Given that we have discussed proper naming conventions in this chapter, we will rename the button, the form, and the text box to something more appropriate. Using the Properties window, change the text box name to **txtgreeting** as you see in the following image.

Then change the button's name to **btngreet**. In the button's Click event, place the following code:

```
If Txtgreeting.Text = "AM" then
      Txtgreeting.Text = "Good Morning"
Else
      Txtgreeting.Text = "Good Afternoon"
End If
```

You can continue to add many Else-If statements if you so desire, but remember that too many will make your program hard to read.

Select Case

When you are faced with multiple choices, an If-Elseif-End If scheme can get very convoluted. For that purpose we use the Select Case statement. Most programming languages have some construct similar to Select Case.

Assume you have some variable called TempValue and it is an integer. Depending on the value of that integer, you wish to take some action.

```
Select Case TempValue

    Case 1
                ' Place code here
    Case 2
                ' Place code here
    Case 3
                ' Place code here
    Case 4
                ' Place code here
        Case Else
End Select
```

If TempValue is 1, the first case will be executed and the others ignored. If, however, it is 3, then Case 3 will be executed and the others ignored. You can have a virtually unlimited number of cases. Essentially, the Select Case is looking at the value in TempValue and if it is 1, Case 1 is executed. If the value is 2, Case 2 is executed. We have a case for each and every value we expect to get. The Case Else statement is a catchall for any other value we might get.

Unlike many other programming languages, which limit you to whole numbers as the basis for a Select Case, Visual Basic allows you to make switches based on strings as well as numeric values.

Loops

It frequently becomes necessary for you to execute a given segment of code repeatedly until either a certain number of executions have been completed or some condition has been met. The way you accomplish this in code is through some type of loop. A loop will simply keep executing the same code segment until the right conditions have been met for it to cease execution.

For Loops

For loops are very common and exist in all programming languages (at least all that I have ever seen). The basic structure of a For loop is as follows:

```
For somevariable = somestartingpoint to somestoppingpoint
    ' code to execute goes here
next somevariable
```

A more concrete example would be:

```
Dim iCount as Integer
For iCount = 0 to 10
    Textbox1.Text = iCount
Next iCount
```

This code will loop from zero to ten, and place the current value into Textbox1 on each loop.

Do Loops (Do-Until and Do-While)

The Do-While and Do-Until loops can be very useful. Unlike the For loop, which will execute a set number of times, the Do loop executes until some condition is met. To illustrate this concept, I will simply rewrite the previous For loop as both a Do-Until loop and a Do-While loop, so you can see how each of these different loop structures can be used to accomplish the same goal.

```
Do until iCount = 10
    Textbox1.Text = iCount
    iCount = iCount + 1
Loop
```

Alternatively, I can write the loop like this:

```
Do while iCount < 10
    Textbox1.Text = iCount
    iCount = iCount +1
Loop
```

Each of these loop structures accomplishes the same goal. Which one you use will depend on a combination of the problem you are attempting to overcome and your own personal inclinations.

With-End Loops

The With-End loop is a bit different than the other loop structures I have shown you. It does not progressively execute a section of code a given number of times or until some condition is met. Instead, it allows you to reduce the amount of code you must write in order to utilize multiple properties and methods of a given object. For example, you might wish to set several different properties of a button. You could do this in the following manner:

```
Button1.Text = "something"
Button1.Flatstyle = Popup
Button1.Visible = true
```

You might notice in our example you are continuously writing "Button1," which gets a bit redundant. This is where the With-End loop comes in handy.

```
With Button1
    .Text = "something"
    .Flatstyle = Popup
    .Visible = true
End With
```

Essentially, the With-End loop allows you to access all the properties and methods of any given object without having to continuously rewrite the object's name.

The Message Box

The message box is a wonderful tool available to you in Visual Basic. With it, you can give the user a tremendous amount of feedback and you can get responses. To use the message box function, you must first declare an integer variable to hold the response code from your message box. It is a good idea to name it something like iMessage or iResponse.

You declare the message box function in the following manner:

```
iMessage = MsgBox("your message", buttons, "Your title")
```

This code simply has instructions to make a message box using the built-in msgbox function. Give it whatever message you decide, the buttons you want, and your title. Whatever button the user presses will return a code to the variable iMessage. Now for the really great part: you don't have to memorize any numeric codes. In version 4.0, Visual Basic began implementing names for you to use. For example, if you only want an OK button, then in the above code place "VBOKOnly" where I have the word "buttons." If you want a Yes button and a No button, place "VBYesNo" where I have the word "buttons."

If you want a complete listing, look up "msgbox" in the Help files. The most common names, however, are VBOKOnly, VBYesNo, and VBOKCancel. Also, when you begin typing in the message box code, the list of available button types will be shown to you.

When the user clicks a button, it will return a code to your variable iMessage that will indicate what button was pushed. For example, you can put in an Exit button to see if the user really wants to exit. Place this code in the Click event of a button with the caption "Exit":

```
Private iMessage as Integer
iMessage = MsgBox("Are you sure you want to quit?",vbyesno, "Exiting")
If iMessage = vbyes then          'if the user types in the word end
                                  'then stop the program
        End
End If
```

There are many settings you can use with the message box function in order to control what buttons are displayed and how they behave. The following table summarizes the settings and their use.

Settings	Description	Message Box or Return Value
AbortRetryIgnore	This value means the message box will display three buttons: Abort, Retry, and Ignore.	Message box

Settings	Description	Message Box or Return Value
ApplicationModal	This means the message box will be application modal. The user will not be able to click on anything else in the application until the message box goes away.	Message box
Critical	This will display the critical icon.	Message box
Default button1	This will make the first button the default button.	Message box
Default button 2	This will cause the second button to be the default button.	Message box
Exclamation	This will cause the exclamation icon to be displayed in the message box.	Message box
Information	This will cause the information icon to be displayed in the message box.	Message box
OKCancel	This will display the OK and Cancel buttons in the message box.	Message box
OKOnly	This will display only the OK button.	Message box
RetryCancel	This will display Retry and Cancel buttons in the message box.	Message box
SystemModel	This means the user cannot click on anything else in the system until the message box is dismissed.	Message box
YesNo	This will display Yes and No buttons in the message box.	Message box
YesNoCancel	This will display Yes, No, and Cancel buttons in the message box.	Message box
VBYes	This indicates that the user selected the Yes button.	Return value
VBNo	This indicates that the user selected the No button.	Return value
VBRetry	This indicates that the user selected the Retry button.	Return value
VBCancel	This indicates that the user selected the Cancel button.	Return value

Input Box

The input box is very much like the message box except that it prompts the user to input data. I don't see this function used that much, but I have personally found it to be very useful. Here is an example:

```
Dim s_Name as String
s_Name = InputBox("Please Enter Your Name")
```

You can expand the call using more variables. The three most commonly used parts of the input box are prompt, title, and default value.

Keywords

Keywords are programming terms that Visual Basic recognizes as a command. You can also think of them as commands. Visual Basic has many such words that can be used to execute various built-in functions. The following are several of these functions that you will need, along with an example of each.

Len   If you want to get the length of some variable or text, you can use the Len command. For example:

```
iLength = Len(txtname)
    'this will take the length of the text in
    'txtname and place it in the variable iLength
iLength = Len(iAccount)
    'This will take the length of the variable
    'iAccount and place it in the variable iLength
```

Hide   This makes whatever you are referring to invisible. For example:

```
FrmOrders.Hide
```

The form is still loaded but not visible.

Show   This shows something that is hidden. If you use it in conjunction with a form that is not loaded, it will first load the form then show it.

```
FrmOrders.Show
```

Ucase   What if you wish to compare two values but you don't care if their case matches (lower- or uppercase)? You can compare the uppercase values of both.

```
If Ucase(sSearchValue) = Ucase(txtLastName) then…
```

You can also compare the lowercase values using the same technique with the keyword Lcase.

SetFocus   This tells the program to change focus to another control. You might place something in your CmdAddNew button that sets focus to the first text box on your form:

```
CmdAddnew_Click()
   TxtFirst.setfocus
```

Date   This simply returns the current system date.

```
Let Txtdate.Text = Date
```

Time   This returns the current system time. You can display this to the user with the following code:

```
Let Lbltime.Text = Time
```

Format   This allows you to change the format of any variable, text box, or label.

If I want the date to be yymmdd, I use the format command like this:

```
Let Txtdate.Text = Format(date,"yymmdd")
```

As you can see, I place an open parenthesis after the format command then I tell it what I wish to format. In this case, that is "date." In the quotation marks, I tell it how to format the date. We can also format numbers. For example, if you want a number to appear as a dollar amount:

```
Let TxtMyNumber = Format(TxtMyNumber,"$###,###.##")
```

Your number will show a dollar sign, six digits, a decimal point, and two additional digits.

Following are some examples of Date formats and their outputs:

Format	Output
Format(Now, "m/d/yy")	1/21/98
Format(Now, "dddd,mmmm,dd,yy")	Wednesday, January 21, 1998
Format(Now, "d-mmmm")	21 Jan
Format(Now, "mmmm-yy")	January 1998
Format(Now, "hh:mm am/pm")	08:45 AM
Format(Now, "h:mm:ss a/p")	7:15:04 a
Format(Now, "d-mmmm h:mm")	3-January 7:18

Shell

This is a very useful keyword. Using the Shell command, you can start other programs. Look at this example:

```
Private lShell as Long
lShell = Shell("c:\path\name.exe",1)
```

This tells the computer to take the path name and start the program name.exe in standard mode (1) and return its Windows handle to the variable entitled lShell.

 Tip: You must use a Long in 32-bit operating systems like Windows 95, 98, or NT because they return a Long Windows handle. Windows 3.1 was 16-bit and returned an Integer handle.

App.activate

This statement allows you to activate a program that is already running. You can either activate a program by using its name as it appears in the toolbar or by using the Windows handle returned to lShell. For example:

```
App.Activate lShell
```

or

```
App.Activate "MS Word"
```

Sendkeys

After you have used app.activate you can send keystrokes to a program. For example, if you have activated the Notepad.exe, you can then enter the code:

```
Sendkeys "My Dog Has Fleas"
```

and that phrase will appear in Notepad!

Left

This command allows you to get the left portion of a string. For example, if you want to get the left three characters in a text box you can use this code:

```
Private sMyString as String
sMyString = left(TxtMyText,3)
```

This will place the leftmost three characters of txtMyText into the string sMyString. So, if the text box txtMyText had the word "Hello" in it, sMyString would now have "Hel" in it.

Right	This is very similar to the Left command, except that it returns the right side characters requested. For example:

```
Private sMyString as String
sMyString = right(TxtMyText,2)
```

would result in "lo."

Trim	This command will remove all blank spaces from a string. For example:

```
MyString=trim(Textbox1.Text)
```

Ltrim	This command will remove all trailing spaces from the left side of a string.

This is by no means an exhaustive look at the built-in functions you have available to you in Visual Basic. It is meant simply to introduce you to some common commands that you are likely to need.

Example 2-2

In this example, we are going to combine many of the coding techniques you have covered so far in this book with the mathematical functions you have just learned to create a Windows calculator.

1. Create a new project with a single form.

2. Change the form's text to **VB Calculator.**

3. You are going to place two control arrays of buttons on the form. You will place the buttons on separate group components. This will be your first time using this component. Its purpose is simply to group other components into logical places. Each frame will have its Text property set to **blank.**

At this point your form should look like the following illustration.

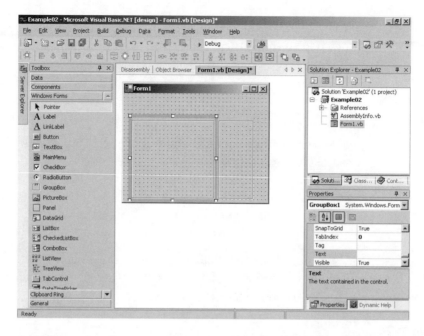

First create ten buttons (0 through 9). Make sure that the text for each of the numeric buttons matches the button's array index. Then, on a separate frame, create a second set of six buttons (+, −, *, /, ., =).

4. Next, place a label across the top of your form and set its text to **0**. Set its border style to **fixed single** and its background color to **white**. Its alignment should be set to **right justify**. Assign it the name **display**. At this point, your form should look like the following.

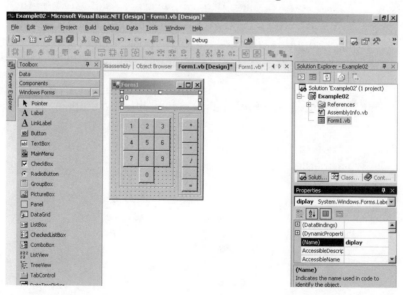

5. Now that we have created our graphical user interface (GUI) we have to add the code so that our calculator will actually accomplish something. In the general declarations section of the code for the form, place the following declarations.

```
Dim FirstNum as Single
Dim SecondNum as Single
Dim Answer as Double
Dim Operation as Integer
Const PLUS = 0
Const MINUS = 1
Const MULTIPLY = 2
Const DIVIDE = 3
Const DECPOINT = 4
Const EQUALS = 5
```

Note: The keyword Const simply identifies a constant. A constant is a value that cannot change.

6. The next step is to add appropriate code to each of the numeric buttons.

```
Display = Display.Text & "button number"
```

So Button1 will have:

```
Display.Text = Display.Text & "1"
```

Button2 will have:

```
Display.Text = Display.Text & "2"
```

And so on through all ten buttons.

7. Now we need to add some code in the Click event of the function buttons. What our code will do is capture the current value in the display, convert it to a single value (decimal point), and then set a flag indicating what mathematical function is going to be performed. When the equal sign button is pressed, the flag that had previously been set will be read to determine what mathematical operation is to be performed.

The addition button needs the following code:

```
Firstnum = Val(Display.Text)
Display.Text = "0"
Operation = PLUS
```

Next, we place this code in the Click event of the minus button:

```
Firstnum = Val(Display.Text)
Display.Text = "0"
Operation = MINUS
```

The multiplication button will have this code:

```
Firstnum = Val(Display.Text)
Display.Text = "0"
Operation = MULTIPLY
```

The following code will be put into the division button:

```
Firstnum = Val(Display.Text)
Display.Text = "0"
Operation = DIVIDE
```

The decimal point button is much like the numeric buttons:

```
Display.Text = Display.Text & "."
```

The equal sign button will read the previously set flag as well as the first number that was entered. It will then do the appropriate math with the two numbers entered.

```
Secondnum = Val(Display.Text)
Do_Math
```

8. Finally, for the subroutine Do_Math that we referenced above, enter the following code into the general declarations section of your form module.

```
Public Sub Do_Math()
    Select Case Operation
            Case PLUS
                Answer = Firstnum + Secondnum
                Display.Text = CStr(Answer)
            Case MINUS
                Answer = Firstnum + Secondnum
                Display.Text = CStr(Answer)
            Case MULTIPLY
                Answer = Firstnum + Secondnum
                Display.Text = CStr(Answer)
            Case DIVIDE
                Answer = Firstnum + Secondnum
                Display.Text = CStr(Answer)
        End Select
End Sub
```

This example has brought together the declaration of variables, creation of procedures, use of components, and the use of the Select Case statement. It has also introduced two new Visual Basic functions. The first, Val, takes a string argument and returns the numeric value. The second, CStr, does exactly the opposite, taking the numeric value and returning a string.

Menus

Most Windows applications have drop-down menus that allow the user to make various selections. Usually the drop-down menu is offered in addition to the toolbar or buttons, rather than in lieu of them. Fortunately, creating drop-down menus in VB.NET is a very simple matter.

In previous versions of Visual Basic there was a drop-down menu in the IDE that allowed you to create menus for your application. The problem with this approach was that it could be difficult to tell which form was being associated with what menu. Now, in VB.NET, the menu is a component in your toolbox.

Example 2-3

This example is simply going to create a series of drop-down menus on a single form that will perform some simple action.

1. Start a new project of the Windows Forms type.

2. In the toolbox, locate the main menu component and place one on your form in the upper left corner. Type **File** directly on the menu.

3. You will notice that another menu has appeared to the right and below the one you just typed in.

4. In the menu item just below the one you labeled File, change the caption to read **Exit**.

5. Double-click on the Exit menu item and place the following code there:

```
Dim iMessage as Integer
iMessage = MsgBox("Are you sure you want to exit",
    vbYesNo, "Confirm Exit")
If iMessage = vbYes then
    End
End If
```

When you run this application you will be able to click on the File menu and the Exit menu will drop down below. This is fairly simple and direct. You can have as many submenus as you like, and you can have submenus for the submenus. Each menu has certain properties you can set to alter its behavior should you so desire.

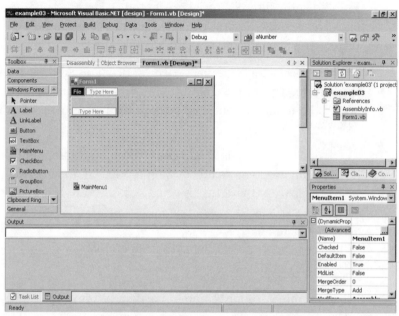

Property	Description
Checked	Whether or not this menu item has a check mark by it.
Radio Check	Whether or not this menu item behaves like a radio button.
Shortcut	Any shortcut key that will also trigger the Click event of this menu item.
CtlparText	The text the user will see.
Visible	This property determines if the menu item is visible at run time.

With these properties you can enhance the appearance and the behavior of your menus. Since most professional applications include menus, it is recommended that you use them and become familiar with how they work.

Summary

In this chapter, I took the foundation we laid in Chapter 1 and built upon it. By now you should be getting quite comfortable with the basics of writing Windows applications using Visual Basic.NET. If you are not totally comfortable with all the material presented so far, it is imperative that you go back and review the first two chapters of this book. Without this knowledge you will be unable to continue with the rest of the book.

Review Questions

1. What does the Val() function do?
2. What does the Ucase function do?
3. What is the purpose of the Format function?
4. List four VB.NET data types.
5. List four VB.NET operators.
6. What is the purpose of the modulus operator?
7. What is a parameter?
8. What are the three parts to the message box function call?
9. What is a function?
10. What is the purpose of a Select Case statement?

Object-Oriented Programming

Introduction

The term "object-oriented programming" tends to bring fear to the hearts of novice programmers. The concept seems difficult to understand, and the new jargon makes it look quite mysterious. However, you have been doing object-oriented programming since you started working with this book. An object is simply a thing with properties and methods. In programming, a class is just a template for creating objects. When you place a text box on a form and change one of its properties, what you have actually done is created an *instance* of the textbox object and changed one of its properties.

As I said in Chapter 1, it is important to realize that you deal with objects every single day. The car you drive is an object. It has properties such as size, shape, color, etc. It also has methods such as accelerate, brake, etc. You don't have to know how a car works, you just have to know how to call its methods. That is how an object works in programming.

You can create a text box, manipulate its properties, and utilize its events without having the slightest idea how a text box is made. This is often referred to as the "black box" approach. You can utilize the black box without knowing how it works inside. You just have to know what data to feed it. You do this with a car every day. You can turn on the ignition, accelerate, brake, etc., all with only a vague idea of what the internal mechanisms behind these methods are.

Programming Terms

Before I move forward into showing you how to create your own objects using Visual Basic.NET, I would like to introduce you to a little object-oriented terminology:

OOP	Object-oriented programming.
OOD	Closely related to OOP, this term means object-oriented design.
Instance	The current incarnation of your object's template. For example, if there were a general class called "car," you would own a car as a specific instance of the Car class.
Class	A special kind of code module that you use to make your own objects. It is a template for objects you create.
Encapsulation	This is probably the single most important part of object-oriented programming. It basically refers to the fact that an object stores both data and the methods to manipulate that data in the same place. This way, you deal with both functions and data simultaneously and all the relevant code is in a single place.
Inheritance	The ability to make classes from other classes. When one class inherits from another, it receives all the public and protected methods and properties of that class. Private methods and properties are not inherited. The class that is being inherited from is often called the parent or base class. The class doing the inheriting is usually referred to as the child or subclass.
Multiple inheritance	An arrangement in which a class can inherit from more than one parent class. This feature is not available in VB.NET (nor in Java for that matter) but is available in Visual C++.

Polymorphism The ability to define a new object based on an existing object, and then simply altering the new object. When you inherit a class, you can either keep the methods you inherit as they are, or you can override them and change them. The word "polymorphism" literally means there are many forms.

New This keyword denotes a new instance of an object. For example:

```
Dim MyClass as new OriginalClass
```

This will allocate the appropriate amount of memory, then use the class OriginalClass as a template for creating an object called MyClass. You can then call any public methods or properties of this class. A method is simply another name for a function that is a part of a class.

Interface An interface is a lot like a class. It has methods, but those methods have no code in them.

Classes

Let's begin by talking about classes, since that is how you do object-oriented programming. The simplest definition I can think of is that a class is a template for creating objects. In Visual Basic, a class is a special kind of code module. Any subroutines or functions that you add will be your class's methods. Any variables you add that are accessible from outside the class are called properties.

In order to add a new class to a Visual Basic.NET project you simply go to the drop-down menu and choose Project | Class. This will give you a blank class code module you can then fill in with your own code.

When you first add a class to your project, it will have a declarations section and a class section. Under the general declarations section you will declare any variables (properties) of your class that you might need. All variables should be declared as private. One of the reasons you use a class is to protect data. The variables should only be accessible via methods (subroutines and functions). Using this approach allows you to validate the data before actually setting it into a variable. For example, if you have a class that handles employee records with a property called Salary, instead of making the Salary variable public, thus allowing anyone to directly set the salary, you would want to create special methods (which I will show you later in this chapter) to set the property. Then in those methods you can see that the new salary meets any parameters you need to check. Such parameters might include making sure the salary is not ridiculously high or low. This is the embodiment of encapsulation.

Class modules are the only modules in VB.NET (even the form is really an instance of the Form class). However, all the previous versions of Visual Basic included standard code modules. That means it is highly likely you will see these, so let me take a brief moment to explain the difference. Class modules are different from standard modules primarily in the way their data is stored. There's only one copy of a standard module's data, since you cannot create separate instances of a standard module. This means that when one part of your program changes, such as a public variable in a standard module, and another part of your program subsequently reads that variable, it will get the same value. This means that the standard code module's variables are global and that any change done to them is made for the entire application.

Class data, on the other hand, exists separately for each instance of the class. Each instance of a class is a separate entity. Remember that the class module itself is simply a template for the class objects you create. Therefore, if you have more than one instance of a class module, a change in the data of one module has absolutely no bearing on the data in other class modules.

The usual way to access the variables in your class is via Get and Set properties. These are simply specialized functions with the explicit purpose of giving you access to the class's data. Set properties are used to change the value of a class variable. Get properties are used to retrieve the value of a class's variable. The following table summarizes the two property types.

Property	Description
Get	The Get property is used when you want to get the value of a property (variable).
Set	The Set property is very much like the Get property, but is used with object variables.

Note: In earlier versions of Visual Basic there was a Set and a Let property.

You will also note that as soon as you create a class, it already has blank New and Finalize methods. The New method is where you put any code that is required as soon as your class is initialized. The Finalize method is where you put "cleanup" code, to be executed when you dispose of the object you create from this class.

The New method is essentially what other programming languages refer to as a constructor. A *constructor* is a function that is executed automatically when an instance of a class is created. It is a useful place to put any code that must be executed in order to make the class fully functional. Perhaps the best way to illustrate the utilization of a class is by example.

Example 3-1

1. Start a new Windows application project.

2. From the drop-down menu select **Project | Add new class**.

3. In the class module you have just created, place the following code:

```
Public Class Class1
    Private iAge as Integer
    Private sName as String
    Private sJobTitle as String
    Private sSalary as Single
    Public Sub New()
        ' Set default values for all of the
        ' data in this class
        iAge = 30
        sName = "John Doe"
        sJobTitle = "Programmer"
        sSalary = 40  ' Hourly salary
    End Sub
    Public Property Age()
        Get
            Return iAge
        End Get
        Set(ByVal Value)
            iAge = Value
        End Set
```

```
        End Property
        Public Property Name()
            Get
                Return sName
            End Get
            Set(ByVal Value)
                sName = Value
            End Set
        End Property
    Public Property JobTitle()
            Get
                Return sJobTitle
            End Get
            Set(ByVal Value)
                sJobTitle = Value
            End Set
        End Property
        Public Property Salary()
            Get
                Return sSalary
            End Get
            Set(ByVal Value)
                sSalary = Value
            End Set
        End Property
        Public Function ComputePay(ByVal HoursWorked as Single) as Single
            Dim Answer as Single
            Answer = sSalary * HoursWorked
            Return Answer
        End Function
    End Class
```

4. On the form module, place four text boxes and two buttons. Also place one label to the left of each of the text boxes, labeling the content of each box. The first text box should be labeled **Name**, the second **Job Title**, the third **Hourly Wage**, and the fourth **Pay**. One text box should have its text field set to **Compute Pay** and the second to **Save Changes**. Your form should look like the following:

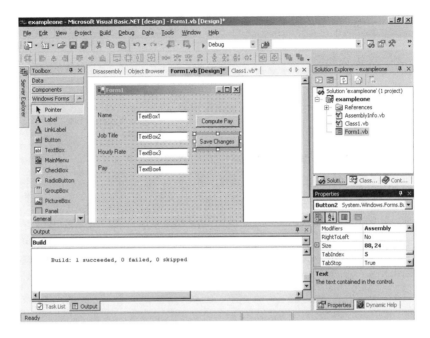

In the Form Load event of this form place the following code:

```
Textbox1.Text = Employee.Name
Textbox2.Text = Employee.Age
Textbox3.Text = Employee.Salary
```

5. At the very beginning of the Form1 class place this code:

```
Dim Employee as new Class1()
```

It should appear immediately after this code:

```
Public Class Form1
    Inherits System.Windows.Forms.Form
```

Note: If you run your application at this point, the default values that we set in the constructor function of Class1 will be displayed in the first three text boxes.

6. Place the following code in the button with the caption "Compute Pay."

```
Dim Hours as Single
Dim Pay as Single
Hours = CSng(TextBox4.Text)
Pay = Employee.ComputePay(Hours)
MsgBox("The pay for this employee is " & CStr(Pay))
```

Chapter 3

7. Place the following code in the Click event of the button with the caption "Save Changes."

```
Employee.Name = Textbox1.Text
Employee.JobTitle = Textbox2.Text
Employee.Salary = Textbox3.Text
```

8. In the form's Finalize event place this code:

```
Set Employee = Nothing
```

In this example, we create a class with four private variables. We then use the public properties Get and Set to access those variables. We also include a method called ComputeSalary. Then, from the form module we create an instance of this class and utilize its properties and methods. This illustrates several key points in object-oriented programming:

■ The data regarding an employee, such as salary, and the methods that manipulate that data, such as ComputeSalary, are contained together in a single class. This is the very essence of encapsulation.

■ We utilize a constructor method to give default values to our class's properties.

■ We instantiate the class, utilize it, then destroy it.

In our example, we did not directly utilize inheritance, but via inheritance, we could make any number of classes that inherit from Class1. Remember that when one class inherits from another, it gets all the public and protected properties and methods of the parent class.

Events

You might have noticed that other classes (such as the Form class) have events associated with them. Remember that an event is simply a function that is executed in response to some user action, such as clicking a mouse. You can create your own events for your Visual Basic classes.

Consider Example 3-2. We are going to hypothesize that our employer wants to make sure that no salary is raised beyond a certain limit. With this in mind, we are going to add an event to our class, and trigger that event whenever someone attempts to raise a salary beyond this cutoff point.

Example 3-2

1. We begin by exactly duplicating the code for Class1 in Example 3-1.

2. Add this event declaration right after declaring the four private variables.

   ```
   Public Event SalaryLimitExceeded(ByVal Salary as Single)
   ```

3. Change the Set property of the Salary property to look like this:

   ```
   If sSalary > 75 Then
       RaiseEvent SalaryLimitExceeded(Value)
   Else
       sSalary = Value
   End If
   ```

Now, in the Form1 class where you create the instance of Class1, we are only going to add one small piece:

```
Private WithEvents Employee as Class1
```

The WithEvents keyword causes blank event functions to be generated for all of the events that are declared inside that class. If someone attempts to raise an hourly rate beyond 75 dollars, they will not be able to and an event will be triggered. You can then write code for that event just as you do for other events like the Click event of a button.

Access Modifiers

All variables and all functions have access modifiers. You have already seen public and private used in previous chapters. Let me refresh your memory concerning these two. The public access modifier means that this variable or function can be accessed from outside the module it is in. The private modifier means that the variable or function cannot be accessed from outside that module. When you inherit a class, you will not inherit the private variables and functions. This brings us to the subject of protected variables and functions. A protected variable or function works just like a private one, except that it can be inherited.

It is customary to have all variables in a class as private or protected. The only way you should be able to access the variables is via public functions such as Get and Set. In this way you can do some validation of the data prior to storing it in a variable.

Chapter 3

Inheritance

This is perhaps the most powerful feature that has been added to VB.NET. Inheritance is literally the process whereby one class inherits all the public and protected variables and functions from another class. This keeps you from having to rewrite code. You can inherit the functions you need from an existing class, then simply add on additional functionality.

In Visual Basic.NET, inheritance is easy to accomplish. It only requires two simple steps. The first step is to make sure that the namespace that contains the class you wish to inherit has been imported. For example, when you wish to access some of the VB.NET classes for file manipulation, you import system.io. The second step is done immediately after the initial declaration line of the class:

```
Class SomeClass
    Inherits MyClass
```

You simply tell Visual Basic what class you wish to inherit. Remember that if you don't import the namespace that contains the class you wish to inherit, the code that is attempting to do the inheritance will fail.

Collections

Collections are basically object-oriented arrays. Visual Basic has several built-in collections. The forms collection contains a reference to all the forms in a project and the controls collection contains a reference to all the controls on a given form. For example, if you wanted to disable all the text boxes on a given form you could use the controls collection like this:

```
Private Sub Disable_Text()
Dim I as Integer    'used as a counter
Dim C as Control    'use c as the generic control object
For each C in controls
    If typeof C is textbox then
            C.enabled = false
    End If
next C
```

You can also create your own collections by simply dimensioning a collection variable then adding stuff to it:

```
Dim myCollection as new Collection
```

Now add items to your collection using the add method:

```
myCollection.add somevariable
```

Now, you may ask why you would use a collection instead of an array. The answer is that a collection is far more flexible. In an array, all the elements must be of a single data type. You can have an array of Integers, an array of Strings, or an array of Doubles, but you cannot have a single array that contains more than one type of variable. A collection can contain diverse types of variables. Let's look at another example.

```
Dim EmpCollection as new Collection
Let sName = "Employee Name"
Let iNum = 3848457
Let sPhone = "1-555-555-5555"
EmpCollection.add sName
EmpCollection.add iNum
EmpCollection.add sPhone
```

This added flexibility makes the collection a far better alternative to the array. In the real world, it is often necessary to use several different data types. In my personal programming, I now only use arrays with controls; in code, I use only collections.

Shared Members

In previous versions of Visual Basic, any functions that did not require the creation of an object were placed into standard modules. Visual Basic.NET implements this functionality by allowing you to create shared members in your classes. Shared members are methods of a class that can be called without actually creating an instance of the class.

When you add a shared method to a class, the method is accessed directly rather than through an object instance. A common use for shared methods is a utility class. In the following example, we create a utility class called MathStuff with a shared method Square:

```
Public Class MathStuff
    Shared Function Square(ByVal num as Integer) ss Integer
        Return Num * Num
    End Function
End Class
```

To use the Square function that we just created in the Math class, you don't need to create an instance of the MathStuff class. We can call the function directly from the MathStuff class as follows:

```
Dim Answer as Integer
Answer = MathStuff.Square(7)
```

It is important for you to notice that no object of type Math was created. The Square method was called directly, just as it would have been called from a standard module in previous versions of Visual Basic. This technique can be quite useful. However, from my point of view, it is cleaner coding to simply use classes in the usual way, creating instances of them. I included this technique here simply because I would be remiss as an author if I did not share this knowledge with you.

Interfaces

An *interface* is a template for class members. An interface simply gives you a framework for a class. It defines the methods of the class but not the implementation. In previous versions of Visual Basic, you could only create an interface by creating a class with all the methods left empty and then implement it. The process is cleaner in Visual Basic.NET. You can explicitly create interfaces using the Interface keyword. You can also implement interfaces using the Implements keyword. This is very similar to the way interfaces are created in other languages, such as Java. Interfaces allow you to design the interaction between components before you actually develop them.

Summary

This chapter is not meant to be an exhaustive coverage of object-oriented theory or programming. Entire volumes have been written on those subjects. However, if you carefully study this chapter you should have the rudimentary understanding of object orientation required to follow the rest of this text, and to successfully utilize Visual Basic.NET. It is imperative that you fully understand the concepts in this chapter. Since Visual Basic.NET is now totally object oriented, you will have great difficulty proceeding without a firm understanding of this chapter.

Review Questions

1. What does the term "encapsulation" mean?

2. What is a term for a class that is being inherited from?

3. Can you inherit private functions?

4. What is a method?

5. What is an access modifier?

6. What is the purpose of the protected modifier?

7. What is the purpose of a Set property?

8. What does the WithEvents keyword do?

9. What is the code to raise an event?

10. What is the code to create a new event?

Chapter

The .NET Architecture

In this
chapter, you
learn about:

♦ **The Virtual
Execution
System**

♦ **Language
fundamentals
of VB.NET**

♦ **Drawing**

♦ **Printing**

♦ **Data types
and the
Common Type
System**

Introduction

So far, I have focused simply on how to get things done in
VB.NET. Now that you have had an opportunity to work
with VB.NET, and to get comfortable with it, it's time to
introduce you to the architecture behind it all. This chapter
is essential for those readers wishing to truly master
VB.NET. However, for the casual programmer or hobbyist,
a simple, quick familiarization with these concepts will be
sufficient.

VB.NET is a radical departure from previous versions of
Visual Basic. In previous versions of Visual Studio, each
different development tool (Visual Basic, Visual C++, etc.)
had a separate run-time environment. With .NET all the
development tools share a common run-time environment.
This environment is referred to as the Common Language
Runtime (CLR). This means that Visual Basic has access
to the same powerful features that Visual C++ does. It
also means that Visual C++ programmers have access to
the many easy-to-use tools that Visual Basic programmers
have grown to expect.

In .NET, the CLR controls or manages the execution of a
program. When you develop code using VB.NET, the code
will be compiled for use under the control of the CLR. This
design strategy is referred to as managed code. The

Common Language Runtime (CLR) is the foundation of the entire .NET platform. The table below illustrates the basic architecture of .NET.

Component	Description
Common Type System	Provides support for various types and operations on those types.
Metadata	Defines the references and types used in the Common Type System.
Virtual Execution System	Loads and runs programs written for the CLR, uses metadata to execute the managed code, and performs garbage collection.

In the previous chapter, I introduced you to the concepts of object-oriented programming. These concepts are vital to understanding the .NET architecture. In previous versions of Visual Basic, object orientation was quite limited. First of all, the object orientation in previous versions of Visual Basic was not complete. The most obvious missing piece was the lack of inheritance. Another difference is that in previous versions of Visual Basic, the object orientation was optional. You could write programs in Visual Basic 6.0 without ever seeing a class module or any object-oriented programming. This has all changed with VB.NET. The new .NET architecture is purely object oriented. As you saw in Chapters 1 and 2, even your form is really a form class. The various methods for components on your form are now public methods added to that form class. You cannot do any .NET programming without object orientation.

Every object is now inherited from a single class called the System.Object class. Almost all of the system functionality is included in the System namespace. All tasks are available from within the System namespace. The System namespace also contains the various data types. This feature allows a common type system for all .NET programming languages. This makes passing data between components developed in different languages (such as Visual C++ and Visual Basic) much easier.

Virtual Execution System

The Virtual Execution System is a fundamental part of the new .NET architecture. This system handles the execution of applications as well as memory management. Your application is actually being run by the Virtual Execution System, rather than being run by the operating system directly.

The CLR provides an execution engine that creates what is known as the Virtual Execution System (VES). The VES is what handles and maintains all of the code. The VES loads managed code at run time and, by inspecting the metadata of that code, performs all of the required tasks. Some of the more important tasks are:

- Converting MSIL code into native code
- Garbage collection
- Security services
- Profiling and debugging services
- Thread management

Code written in VB.NET, or any of the .NET languages, is actually converted to native code at run time by the VES. This means that it is at least possible for any operating system to support the VES, and therefore be able to run Visual Studio.NET code.

One of the most important innovations in the new .NET architecture is the addition of garbage collection. Garbage collection means that the Virtual Execution System monitors memory and object usage, and, when appropriate, removes objects from memory. This relieves the programmer of having to directly monitor memory, remove objects from memory, and manage object allocation and deallocation.

Component Architecture

Reusable code in the form of distributable components has been a critical factor in the success of Visual Basic. One of the best features of Visual Basic 6.0 was that it allowed you to easily create ActiveX DLLs and components. Similar component creation capabilities exist in VB.NET. However, the means of effecting the creation of these reusable components is quite different in Visual Basic.NET than it was with COM.

Chapter 4

Assemblies

One of the primary architectural changes that affects component creation is the use of assemblies. In Visual Basic.NET, when you create a new application or reusable component you also create an assembly for it. Assemblies are reusable, self-describing packages that are self contained. Everything you need to run that application is contained or described in the assembly. This means that if you use a particular dynamic-link library (DLL) with one assembly, and a different version of that same DLL is used with a different application, there will be no conflict. Each assembly contains an assembly manifest that contains all the information describing the contents of the assembly. For those of you who have used Visual Basic 6.0, this is a big change. With traditional COM (Component Object Model) components, all information about the component was kept in the Windows registry. With the new .NET architecture, information about any component or application is kept in the assembly manifest. This makes installing and uninstalling much easier. The assembly manifest contains the following information describing the assembly itself:

- The assembly's identity. This may include the assembly's name, as well as a version number.

- A file table, which describes all of the files that make up the assembly, including other graphics files (.gifs, .jpgs, etc.), text files, and even other assemblies.

- An assembly reference, which lists all external dependencies, such as DLLs and other files that your assembly requires in order to execute.

The Common Language Runtime can then use the information contained within the assemblies at run time to determine what dependencies the application may require and where to look for those dependencies.

Metadata

Metadata is simply binary information that describes just about every aspect of your code. It contains information about every type defined and referenced within your assembly.

Managed Code

Simply put, managed code is code that runs within and is managed by the CLR. All .NET languages will produce managed code that will run under control of the CLR.

As I previously told you, all code in Visual Studio.NET uses a Common Language Runtime. The implications of this are twofold. The first implication is that all the languages producing managed code can interoperate with one another. For example, you write a class in Visual Basic that can be inherited inside a Visual C++ application and vice versa. If you recall, all of our examples in Chapters 1 and 2 included an import statement. All the classes we looked at (primarily the form classes) began with an import statement. The import statement allows you to import already existing assemblies. Many of these assemblies are built into Visual Studio.NET. If you wish to use a class created in any assembly, regardless of the language used to create the assembly, simply import the namespaces you wish to use and start working with the classes they define. I must say that I found this to be one of the greatest innovations in Visual Studio.NET.

This feature means that you can literally use Visual C++ code inside Visual Basic and vice versa.

Garbage Collection and Object Management

Garbage collection is a new feature for Microsoft development tools, but Java programmers will be quite familiar with it. Essentially, any programming language that utilizes garbage collection is one that manages its own memory. The garbage collector is routinely monitoring the system to see if there are any unused objects still in memory. If it finds any, it destroys the object and releases that memory. This can be a great asset, as it can prevent memory leaks.

Microsoft's implementation of garbage collection utilizes generational garbage collecting. A generational approach categorizes objects on the heap into sections called "generations." The idea behind this is that the longer an object "stays alive," the older the generation it exists in becomes and the more likely that object is to be required by the application. Objects that have been running for some time are assumed to be more important to the application than objects that have just been created. Research and experience shows that this is the usual trend. Currently, garbage collection under the CLR supports only three levels of generations: 0, 1, and 2. Generation 0 is where new objects are placed, generation 1 is for those that have survived a single collection, and generation 2 is for those that have survived two or more collections. Garbage collection performs a collection when generation 0 becomes full. It can then decide if it should perform a collection on all the objects on the heap or just the newer ones located within generation 0. For applications that may contain many objects in generations 1 and 2, this can greatly reduce the overhead encountered during a collection. This method is significantly different from the mark sweep algorithm implemented by most Java compilers.

When a process is first initialized, the CLR reserves some contiguous space in memory for the process. This space in memory will be used to manage the entire process. This is the managed heap. When objects are created via the New keyword, they are placed onto the heap. This process continues until there is not enough memory left on the heap to allocate memory for the next object requesting resources. At this point, a collection must be performed. The garbage collector then applies its algorithm for determining which objects are no longer in use on the managed heap and clears them accordingly.

In previous versions of Visual Basic, the programmer was responsible for destroying all objects; therefore, the process of object deallocation was clearly defined. When writing classes, a programmer wrote code in the Terminate event of the class in order to perform any cleanup necessary when that object was destroyed. With the introduction of garbage collection, this has changed. Now programmers are utilizing a language that implements *non-deterministic finalization*, which means that we cannot predetermine the exact time when the finalization for an object will occur. The finalization will occur when the garbage collector sees fit to finalize the object. In fact, the Terminate event no longer exists and has instead been replaced by the Finalize event. The Finalize event does not offer the same functionality as the Terminate event, though both events fire when the object is released from memory.

Since the Terminate event no longer exists and the Finalize method will be called at an undetermined time, many programmers choose to create Close or Dispose methods to ensure that their classes perform proper cleanup immediately.

It is recommended that you use Close if you want to allow the object to be able to be reopened or reused in future operations. You should utilize a Dispose method if you do not wish the object to be reusable in a future operation. The Dispose method is called to completely destroy your object. This is the same as setting an object to Nothing in previous versions of Visual Basic.

Now that I have shown you some of the architectural basis for VB.NET, it is time to begin discussing some of the language fundamentals.

Language Fundamentals of VB.NET

Event Handling

Event handling has changed in Visual Basic.NET. One change has been the new concept of delegates. Delegates can be thought of as function pointers that are typesafe. A function pointer is literally what the name suggests, a pointer to a function. This has been a technique used in other programming languages for some time, but is just now available to Visual Basic developers. All events will be handled using delegates. For the most part, Visual Basic.NET will create all the delegates you need, but you will now have the power to override some event handlers. You can still create your own custom events as in previous versions of Visual Basic.

Error Handling

Errors are going to occur in applications. That is simply a fact of life. Even if you could write perfect code, errors would still occur. For example, if you ask a user to enter the name of a file, and he enters an erroneous name, you will get an error. Another good example is division by zero. If you ask a user to enter two numbers to divide, and she provides zero as the second number, your application will generate an error. Previous versions of Visual Basic had a rather odd method of error handling not found in any other programming language. Visual Basic.NET utilizes the same type of error handling as Java and C++. Let's look at division as we did in Chapter 2 and add some error handling to it.

```
Dim Answer as Single
    Try
        Answer = Firstnum / Secondnum
        Catch Err as Exception
```

```
        MsgBox("Error printing file: " & err.ToString)
    End Try
```

The Try block is referred to as a guarded space. This means that should any exception occur inside that code section (such as division by zero), the code will stop executing and jump to the matching Catch block. Think of the Try block as literally meaning "try this code."

The Catch block will "catch" any exception the Try block generates. If no error is generated, the code inside of the Catch block will never be executed. When an error is generated, there is an error class that tells you about that error. The main or primary error class is the Exception class. This is why the first line of the Catch block also creates an instance of the Exception class with "Err as Exception." This class has several useful methods, one of which is the ToString method. This method generates a text message describing the error that has occurred.

System Namespace

With VB.NET, Microsoft has introduced the idea of namespaces. Namespaces organize all of the objects that are defined within an assembly. The assembly can contain multiple namespaces, which can, in turn, contain other namespaces. Under VB.NET, all objects derive from the System namespace. The System namespace contains the classes that define most of the common data types, events, interfaces, and exceptions. All other objects derive from the System.Object class, which, in turn, derives from the System namespace. Most of the classes you write will inherit from System.Object rather than directly from System.Namespace.

File I/O

A commonly encountered programming task is working with files, and often text files. Over the years, Visual Basic has gradually been evolving into a better and better file access methodology. In VB.NET, file I/O is encapsulated in the System.IO namespace.

Consider the following example.

Example 4-1

1. Open a new Windows application project.

2. Place a single button on the form.

3. In the Click event of that command place the following import statement before the Public Class Form1:

    ```
    Imports System.IO
    ```

    Then place the following code into the Click event function:

    ```
    Dim MyFile as FileStream = New FileStream _
    "C:\vb.net\examples\chapter 04\example1\mytext.txt", FileMode.Open,
            FileAccess.Read)
        Dim MyStream as StreamReader = New StreamReader(MyFile)
        MsgBox(MyStream.ReadLine)
        MyFile.Close()
        MyStream.Close()
    ```

Note: You will need to replace the above path with the actual path to your code. The downloadable companion files, available at www.wordware.com/VBNET, contain the entire project and the sample text file.

As you can see, the first step in the process is to import the System.IO. Within the System.IO namespace are the two classes we are using in the example, namely FileStream and StreamReader. The FileStream class allows us to open a stream to a file, and the StreamReader class allows us to read from that stream. With these two classes you can easily open any standard text file, read from it, write to it, and even create a new one.

Drawing

In previous versions of Visual Basic, if you wished to do any graphics programming, you had to work with the Windows Graphical Device Interface (GDI) API. Visual Basic.NET provides a number of very useful classes that encapsulate all of the functionality of the Windows GDI API. You can have access to these classes by importing the System.Drawing namespace. The new functions provided in this namespace have often been referred to as the GDI+ functions. The Graphics class in the System.Drawing namespace is where most of the important functionality is located. Let us consider a relatively simple example.

Example 4-2

1. Start a new Windows application project.

2. Place a button on the form. Change its name to **btndrawline** and its caption to **Draw Line**.

3. Place two other buttons on the form named **btndrawcircle** and **btndrawrec**. Give them the captions **Draw Ellipse** and **Draw Rectangle**.

   Your form should look like the one in the following picture.

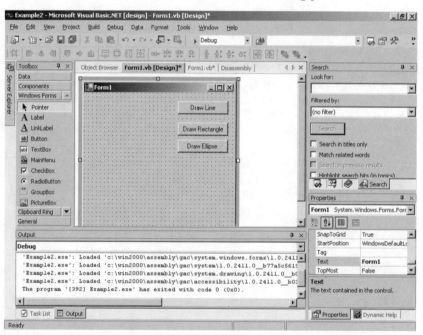

4. In the btndrawline Click event, place this code:

```
Dim G as Graphics = Me.CreateGraphics()
G.DrawLine(New Pen(Color.Blue), New Point(10, 10), New Point(50, 75))
```

   In btndraw circle, place this code:

```
Dim G as Graphics = Me.CreateGraphics()
G.DrawEllipse(New Pen(Color.Purple), New RectangleF(60, 40, 40, 40))
```

   In btndrawrec, place this code:

```
Dim G as Graphics = Me.CreateGraphics()
G.DrawRectangle(New Pen(Color.Red), New Rectangle(75, 75, 100, 100))
```

If you run this example, you will see that each button you have added creates a different basic graphics component. There are several drawing methods associated with the System.Graphics class that you can use to create graphics for your applications. If you have never used previous versions of Visual Basic, let me assure you that these methods are much easier to use than previous methods.

These examples introduced you to the DrawRectangle, DrawLine, and DrawEllipse methods of the Graphics class. The Graphics class has many other drawing methods including:

- DrawArc
- DrawBeziers
- DrawCurve
- DrawClosedCurve
- DrawIcon
- DrawPolygon
- DrawString

Each of these drawing methods can be quite useful in rendering graphics in your applications.

Printing

The Printer object has been replaced by the System.Drawing.Printing namespace, which is contained within the System.Drawing namespace. As I have previously mentioned, a namespace can contain other namespaces, and this is a good example of that. Let us consider an example that illustrates the basic concepts in printing.

Example 4-3

1. Create a new Windows application. Place a single button on the form and change the button's Text property to read **Print Doc**.

   It should look like the following image.

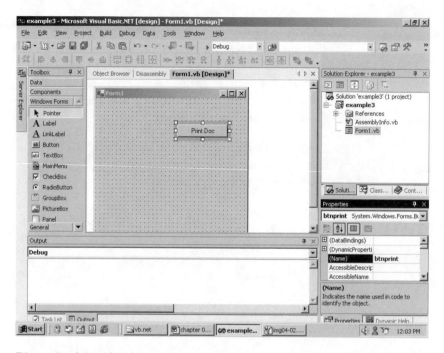

2. Place the following import statements before the line of code that says "Public Class Form1."

```
Imports System.Drawing
Imports System.Drawing.Printing
```

3. Place this line right after the line "inherits System.windows.forms.form."

```
Private WithEvents oPrint as PrintDocument
```

4. Place the following code in the button's Click event.

```
Try
    oPrint = New PrintDocument()
    oPrint.Print()
Catch Err as Exception
    MsgBox("Error printing file: " & err.ToString)
End Try
```

If you look in the left drop-down box in the top of the code view of your form, you will notice that after you placed the code "Private WithEvents oPrint As PrintDocument," an oPrint object appeared on the left side. If you go to that object's code, you will find that it has a PrintPage event.

In that event, place the following code:

```
Try
    e.Graphics.DrawString("Print test", New Font("Arial", 10),
        New SolidBrush(Color.Black), 100, 100)
Catch Err as Exception
    MsgBox("Error: " & err.ToString)
End Try
```

Now you have the basic code required to print out a document to your printer. If you run this application, it will print a test page to your default printer.

Data Types and the Common Type System

I have previously mentioned the fact that .NET languages can be used in conjunction with each other. You can inherit a class made with one .NET language in a different .NET language. One of the .NET architectural features that makes this possible is the Common Type System (CTS, also referred to as the Universal Type System). The CTS provides for data types that are universal across the various .NET languages.

The CTS defines the rules that the various .NET language compilers must implement. The fact that each .NET language must treat types in a consistent manner is the basis on which the CTS exists and allows for objects created in the different languages to correctly interact with one another. The .NET platform provides a programming model that is based on the CTS. As I have already mentioned, everything derives from the System.Object class. Some data types (namely String and Array) inherit directly from System.Object, and some inherit from other classes that have inherited from .NET. The adjacent chart shows the relationship between various classes and data types.

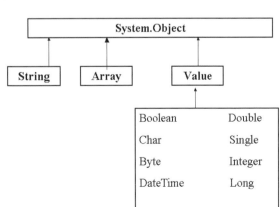

Typecasting is the process of changing the data type of a given variable. This is a very common practice in all programming languages. The ability to convert values from one type to another is essential to the usefulness of any programming language. At times, you may be getting data from somewhere in one data type, but need to use it in a different context from within your code. A good example of this is when you extract data from a text file. When you read data from a text file, it is most likely read in as a string. However, you may need to read in numeric values. To do this, you will have to convert them to numeric values after you have read them in.

VB.NET still supports all of the explicit type conversion functions that existed in previous versions of Visual Basic, such as CStr, CDbl, CSng. In case you have never used Visual Basic before, let me give you a brief introduction to using these functions. If, for example, you have a string called MyString that contains "123.45" and you wish to convert that to a Single, you would use the following code:

```
Dim Num as Single
Num = CStr(MyString)
```

This is a fairly simple way to convert data types and will serve most of your data type conversion needs. However, you should also be aware that all of the primitive data types in Visual Basic.NET now have an associated wrapper class. These wrapper classes have a number of properties and methods you can use, including methods for type conversion. Let me illustrate how you would accomplish typecasting with these wrapper classes:

```
Dim I as Integer
Dim MyString as String
MyString = "12345"
I = MyString.ToInt32
MsgBox(i)
```

In this example, I am using the String object's intrinsic type conversion method, ToInt32, to convert the string to a 32-bit (4-byte) integer. It is important to note that integers are 32 bits by default in VB.NET. (They were 16 bit in previous versions of Visual Basic.) You can even wrap all this code up in a single line:

```
Dim I as Integer = New String("12345").ToInt32
MsgBox(I)
```

As you might have guessed, there are conversion methods to convert to any of the primitive data types.

Summary

In this chapter, I have shown you the basics of the underlying architecture behind .NET programming. You have been introduced to the Common Language Runtime, data types and data type conversion, garbage collection, and some commonly used classes found in Visual Basic.NET. This knowledge, coupled with the information provided in the preceding three chapters, should provide you with a solid foundation for continuing to learn Visual Basic.NET.

Review Questions

1. What is generational garbage collection?

2. What class do VB.NET primitive data types inherit from?

3. List three methods of the Graphics class.

4. What is an assembly?

5. What is typecasting?

6. What is metadata?

7. What package must you import in order to utilize the File and FileStream classes?

8. What is the purpose of the Common Type System?

9. What method of a class do you utilize if you wish to destroy that class?

10. What method of a class do you use if you wish to finalize the class, but still have it eligible for reuse?

Introduction to Database Programming

Most business programming is, at some level, database programming. What is an employee control program but a database program? What is a point-of-sale or inventory control program but a database program? In order to do the exercises in this chapter, you need to be able to create a table in Access or in the Data Manager. If you know how to do this you can skip the "Introduction to Databases" section. If not, the following section will provide you a quick introduction to database concepts and to Microsoft Access.

Introduction to Databases

This section is designed to give you a very brief introduction to creating tables using Microsoft Access. Access is one of the most popular relational database systems on the market today (at least for small to medium-sized databases). But first let me define some database terms.

Field	A particular piece of data like last name, address, phone, etc. In SQL Server or Oracle, this is referred to as a "column."

Record   All the fields for a particular entry. For example, all the fields that make up a single employee's file are a record.

Table   Related records stored together. For example, all the records of all the employees might be stored in an "Employee" table.

Database   Related tables stored together. For example the Employee table, Inventory table, and Finance table might be stored together in a common small business database.

The *Relational Database Management System* (RDBMS) refers to data that is related. Let's say you have a database that includes employee data. For each employee you would want a job description. But what if you have 20 people with the same job description (20 Visual Basic programmers, for example)? Do you really want to rewrite the job description 20 times? In the relational database model you simply have a table of job descriptions, and each employee's record in the Employee table is related or linked to their job description. This drastically reduces the amount of overhead a database requires. It also makes for a very logical layout to your database.

This method of storing data is different than the previously used flat file. A flat file simply stores information one record after another. A text document is an example of a flat file. There is no relationship between records or fields. This makes for an inordinately large data file and one that has a lot of duplication. It is also quite difficult to perform searches in such a file.

Creating a Database and Tables

To create a database in Access, you first open Access. You will see a dialog box like the one shown below.

For our purposes, choose the first option, Blank Access database, and click OK. (Note: You could choose the database wizard to have Access create an entire database for you!) You will then be asked where to create that database and what to name it. This is the dialog box you will see:

Click the Create button and a new database will be created according to your specifications.

Tips: In case you are not familiar with dialog boxes, here are some tips:

- The Look in drop-down allows you to change directories and drives searching for files.

- The small folder button to the right of that drop-down box will allow you to go up one level in the directory structure.

- The large white box in the middle of the dialog box will display files and folders that are in the location you are viewing.

- The small box towards the bottom that says "File name" is where you place the name of your file.

- The small box that says "File Type" is where you can select a variety of file types.

This dialog box is the same for opening files or saving them. The only difference will be the two buttons on the right and the caption at the top. If you are saving files, the two buttons will be Save and Cancel and the caption will be Save As. If you are attempting to open files, the two buttons will be Open and Cancel and the caption will be Open.

To create a new table, select Create table in Design view.

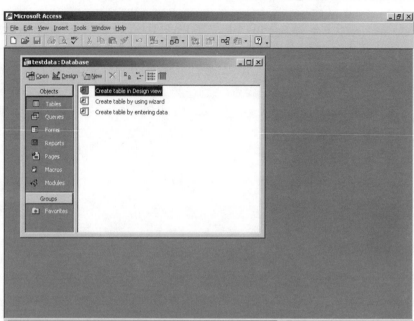

You are now looking at a grid for designing a database table.

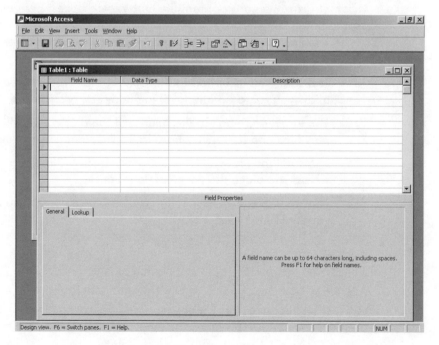

Put in the names of the fields you want to include and what data types you want the fields to hold. When you have added in all the fields you need, you can close Access. Note that each field needs a name and data type. The description is optional, but is a good idea.

MS Access will allow you to do a number of interesting things with database design. Unfortunately, a thorough coverage of Access is not within the scope of this book. However, if you intend to truly maximize your Visual Basic programming skills, I strongly recommend that you become at least moderately familiar with Microsoft Access. Some recommended books on MS Access are listed in Appendix B.

It is also important to remember that Access 2000 has a number of wizards that automate the process of developing tables, queries, or even entire databases.

Database Practice

Continuing with the table we created in the previous paragraphs, we will now create the following fields: Last Name, First Name, Street Address, City, State, Zip Code, Phone Number, and Email. You can also either add a field here, such as Entry Key, and then right-click on it and select Primary Key, or you can wait until you close the design view and be prompted to let Access create a primary key for you. A primary key is a unique field used to uniquely identify each record in the database. We will use this table later in this chapter when we write Windows applications that connect to this database. Your table should look something like this:

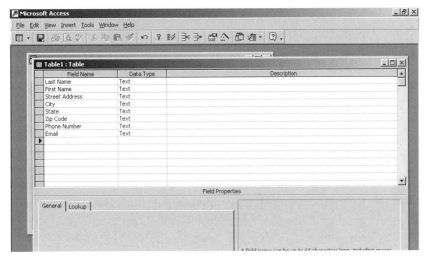

When you close the design window you will be asked to give your table a name. Call your table Contacts. After you have saved it, double-click on the table to open it, and add in one or more sample records.

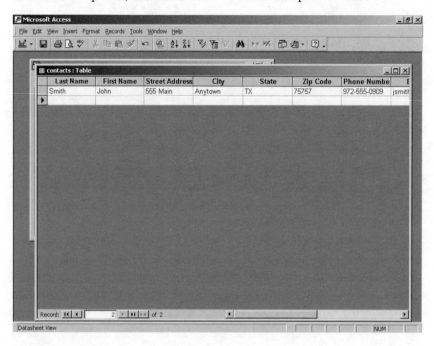

SQL

Before we go any further into database programming, it is necessary to introduce you to SQL, or Structured Query Language. This is basically the language of databases. You can use Visual Basic to write SQL statements. For example:

```
Dim sSQL as String 'used to hold the sql statement
sSQL = "SELECT * FROM [MYTABLE]"
Let Data1.RecordSource = sSQL
Data1.Recordset.Refresh
```

This statement will select all files from the table.

What we did here is take a string variable and set it equal to an SQL (pronounced S-Q-L or sequel) statement. We then set the data control's RecordSource property equal to that SQL statement. The brackets are used to denote a table within the database. The asterisk (*) symbol is computer shorthand for "everything." So basically we told the data control to give us all the files in the table named "MyTable." The capitalization is not absolutely necessary, but is a frequently used convention.

Before we go any further, you should realize that the Structured Query Language is not a part of Visual Basic. That's why we have to put SQL statements in a string. It is the language used by relational databases. Most relational databases utilize SQL, not just MS Access. It is a good idea to become very comfortable with SQL since it is used by MS SQL Server, Oracle, MS Access, SYBASE SQL Anywhere, and many other relational database systems.

More often you will have a complex SQL statement with clauses like:

```
"...WHERE [state] =California"
```

The basic format for this is:

```
"SELECT [field1],[field2],.... FROM [sometable] WHERE [somefield]
    = SomeCriteria"
```

The Where clause denotes some condition. Basically, you are saying that you want all the specified fields if a certain criteria is met.

For SQL, you will have to declare a string variable (most people just call it strSQL) and then you will assign SQL statements to that variable. You can then assign the SQL statement's value to whatever data access object you are using, be it a data control or a Recordset object. For example:

```
SELECT: strSQL = "SELECT Publishers.[Company Name], Publishers.State
        FROM Publishers WHERE Publishers.State ="
strSQL = strSQL & Chr(34) & txtVariable & Chr(34)
Data1.RecordSource = strSQL
Data1.Refresh
```

Note: Chr(34) inserts quotes into your string. You have to do it this way because if you try to literally place a quote into a string, the quote will terminate the string!

Please notice several things about this statement:

■ You can have lines added to each other by making the next line of SQL:

```
SQL = SQL + "...."
```

- You can add in a variable contained within a text box. This is vital as this is how you will most often do searches.
- Once you have built your SQL statement you merely have to set an object equal to it. You can set Recordset objects or data controls equal to an SQL statement.

You can also build a variable into your SQL statement like this:

```
"SELECT * FROM [Employees] WHERE [State] = '" & sState & "'"
```

The above statement will let you select the company names of publishers from a database based upon the state the company is in. (For example, you can select all the publishing companies in Texas.) Also notice that we used two different examples of including a variable in an SQL statement. In the first example, we used ASCII character codes (Chr(34)) to place in the proper quotation marks, and in the second example we used a combination of single quotes ('), double quotes ("), and the ampersand (&) to accomplish the same goal. This is just another reminder that there is often more than one way to accomplish a desired task.

ORDER BY: This statement simply orders the records based on a particular field you wish to order by. Here is an example:

```
strSQL = strSQL & "ORDER BY[Publishers.State]"
```

This statement says to sort the records returned by our SQL query by the state of the publisher. I frequently use this statement simply to arrange data in a particular manner. For example, I might add this statement to an employee database:

```
strSQL = strSQL & "ORDER BY [Employee ID]
```

This way all the records are now in order by employee ID number. I use this statement a lot since it is the quickest and easiest way to sort records. In some cases I will create drop-down menus or command buttons that each sort by a different criteria. Using the Order By statement in this way, I let my users sort their data in any fashion they wish.

INNER JOIN: What if you want to search more than one table for the publisher's records? SQL offers the INNER JOIN statement:

```
SELECT Publishers.[company Name] FROM Publishers
INNER JOIN Titles ON Publishers.PubID = Titles.PubID
```

This statement just says to get all the company names of publishers from either the Publishers table or the Titles table, if the publisher IDs match!

DISTINCT: What about duplicate records? In the previous examples, the same record may be duplicated many times. One way around this is to simply add the DISTINCT statement to your SELECT statement such as:

```
strSQL = "SELECT DISTINCT..."
```

I have just covered the SELECT, INNER JOIN, and DISTINCT statements. While there is certainly a great deal more to SQL, this will give you a start. You will probably use the SELECT statement on a regular basis. Consider the ORDER BY statement a good way to sort the records in your data control in any way you wish.

 Tip: Always double-check the spelling of your SQL statements. A single misspelling will cause it to not work.

A Brief History of SQL

SQL, or Structured Query Language, is the language used to talk to relational databases. The relational database model for database design was invented by Dr. E.F. Cobb in 1969 and published in *Computer World* in 1985.

SQL was first implemented in 1974 at IBM's San Jose Research Laboratory. SQL is essentially a non-procedural language that uses English-like words to talk to a database. The American National Standards Institute (ANSI) is continually updating its versions of SQL standards.

This is just a brief working introduction to Structured Query Language. It should get you up and running so that you can use SQL in your programs. I strongly suggest that early on in your programming career you make a point of learning more about SQL. You can find some good resources for SQL and other programming topics in Appendix B.

The Basics of Data Binding

Data binding refers to the process of setting properties of one or more form components so that they are connected directly to a field or fields in a database recordset. Windows forms utilize ADO.NET in order to accomplish this, but with data binding, you do not need to write the code that connects to and communicates with the database.

Chapter 5

Windows forms allow you to bind easily to just about any structure that contains data. This means that you can use ADO.NET to bind to traditional databases, such as Microsoft Access, Microsoft SQL Server, and Oracle. It also means that you can bind to the result of data read from a file, contained in other components, or even stored in an array.

There are two types of bound components. These types are simple and complex. Simple data binding occurs when a single component (such as a text box) is bound to a single field. Complex data binding allows you to bind more than one field to a control. A good example of this is the data-bound grid, which displays an entire recordset.

A Basic Data-bound Application

For this example, we are going to rely on the database table you created in the beginning of this chapter.

Example 5-1

1. On the toolbox there is a tab labeled Data. On that tab you have several options. Select the **Data** tab, then select the **OLEDatabaseAdapter** option. This should be the third option from the top.

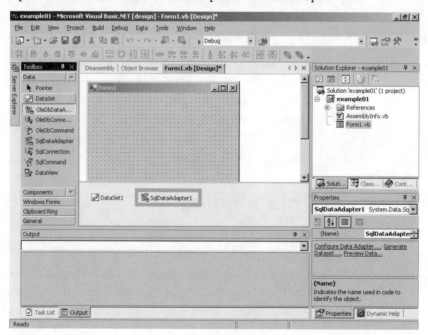

When you place this on the form you will immediately launch a wizard that will walk you through all the steps required to connect to a database.

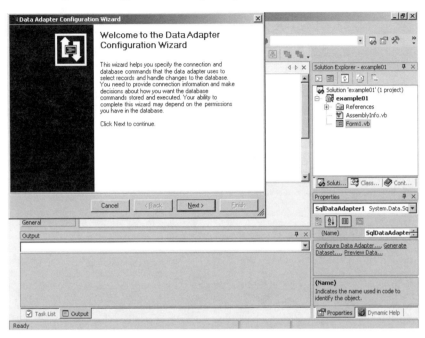

2.   On the second screen of the wizard select the **New Connection** button. You will then be shown a window like the one below:

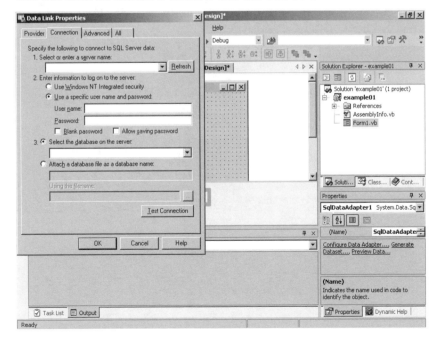

3. Choose the Provider tab so that you can select the settings for an MS Access database. By default, the wizard initially displays the Connection tab, which has settings for an SQL Server database. Select **Microsoft Jet 3.51 OLE DB Provider** and click the **Next** button.

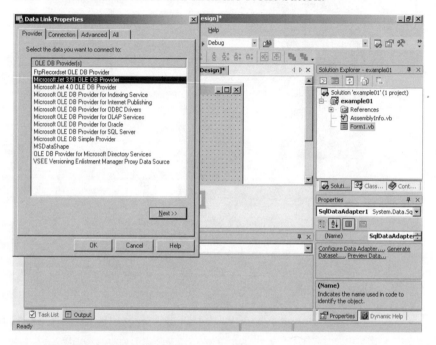

4. On this screen you will click on the button to the right of the Select or Enter database name field.

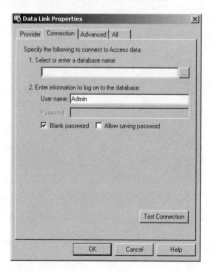

5. This will take you to a dialog box that you can use to browse your PC's drives. Locate the database you made at the beginning of this chapter and select it. Once you have selected your database you should click on the **Test Connection** button to ensure that the connection to your database is correct. If there is a problem, it is almost always due to an improper driver being used. If you encounter an error, go back to the screen where you selected the provider and try another database driver.

6. Once your connection is working properly, the wizard will take you to more screens. On the next screen just keep the default settings. The screen after that will ask you to define an SQL statement that will retrieve the initial recordset you wish to connect to. In our case, we will use **Select * From [Contacts]**.

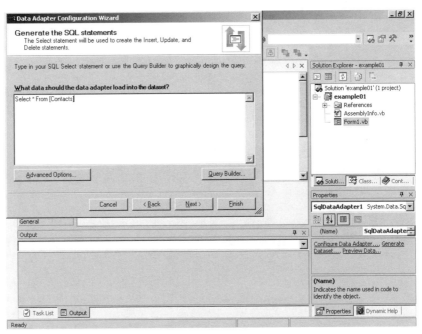

7. Then, click the **Next** button and you will be taken to the final screen of the wizard, which will report to you the status of its various operations.

    Once you have created the connection, you will have to create a dataset to be used by components on your Windows forms. If you highlight the connection you have just created, you will see several options on the lower right portion of the screen, under the Properties window.

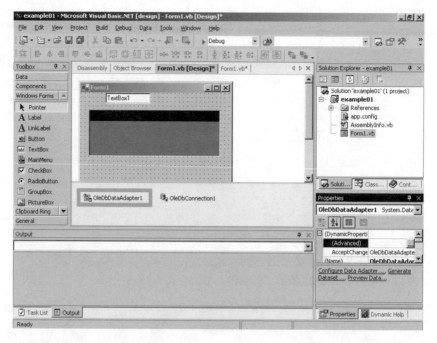

8. Select the **Generate Dataset** option. This will take you to the following screen:

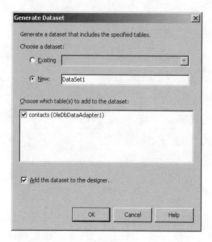

Click the **OK** button.

If you now place a single text box on your form, you can go to its Properties window and select **Data Bindings.** You will be presented with a drop-down list of choices, one of which should be the Dataset you just created. You can then go through its choices to set this text box's Text property equal to a single field in one of that dataset's tables.

This is the essence of data binding. You have just made a connection between your text box and a field in a database table.

9. Connect this text box to the Last Name field in your table. It would also be a good idea to change the text box name to **txtFirstName**. Now create a text box for every field in the database. You will not have to create any more datasets. You can bind each text box to a different field in the dataset you already created. Remember to give each text box a name that indicates what data it holds. Also, place a label next to each text box so that users can see what kind of data is held in that text box. When you are finished, your form should look something like this:

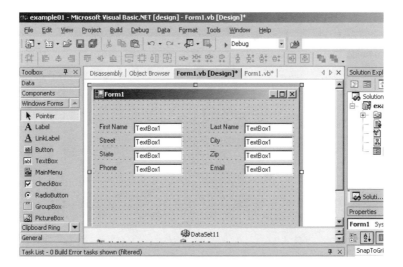

If you run your application now, the default values you placed in the database table will show in all the fields. However, this is still not much of a database program. What about adding new records? Deleting records? Moving around in the database? Well, don't fear; we will cover these topics next.

Chapter 5

You could simply place buttons on your form and use those for your various database operations. However, most professional programs utilize some sort of toolbar. For this reason, before I show you the database code to put in the toolbar, I am going to show you how to create your own toolbar.

1. First, you will need to add an image list and a toolbar. You will find both of these in the toolbox. The image list will appear outside the actual form in the same area your dataset appeared. The toolbar will go to the top of your form and stretch from one end to the other by default. Now click on the **Images** property of the image list to be presented with the Image Collection Editor for the image list.

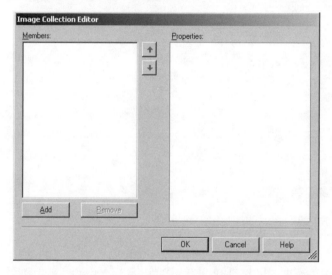

2. From this screen, using the Add button, you can add any images on your system to the image list. For our purposes you will want to add five icons. The graphics files were installed when you installed Visual Studio.NET. In the folder where you installed Visual Studio there is a subfolder named Common and it will, in turn, have a subfolder named Graphics.

3. Once you have added your images, your image collection screen will look like the following image. Simply press the **OK** button when you are done.

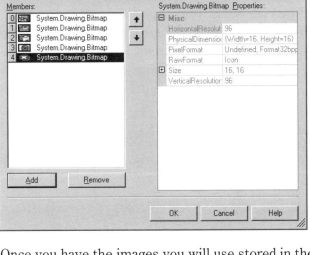

4.   Once you have the images you will use stored in the image list compo-
     nent, it is time to concentrate on the toolbar itself. The first property of
     the toolbar you will need to set is the Image List property. If you click on
     that property, a drop-down box will show you all the image lists associated
     with this form. There should be only one at this point. After you have
     selected the image list, click the **Buttons Collection** property of the
     toolbar. You will then be shown a screen much like the Images collection
     of the image list.

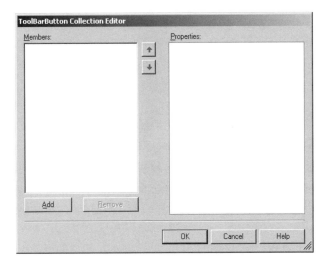

5.   When you add a button, you must set the following properties. First, set
     the image index to match one of the images in your image list. Then, set

the ToolTipText properties. You are going to add five buttons. The first will have the tag tip Add New Record. The second will be Delete Current Record. The third will be Save Current Record. The fourth will be Move Previous. The fifth will be Move Next. With the first three buttons you will set the Text property to be **empty**. The last two will have "<<" and ">>" respectively. Each button must also have its Tag property set. This will be used later to process code in the toolbar. Set the tags to **Add**, **Delete**, **Save**, **Previous**, and **Next**. Once you have added these five buttons, simply click **OK**. At this point your form should look very much like the image you see here. Of course, the images you place on your buttons are likely to be very different.

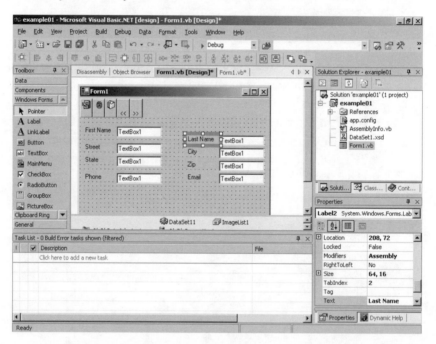

6. Now we are ready to place code in the toolbar's Click event in order to handle our database functions. Double-click on the toolbar and you will be presented with the code window for the Click event. You will then place the following code there.

```
Select Case e.Button.Tag
    Case "add" 'add
        Try
            'Clear out the current edits
            Me.BindingContext(Dataset11, "contacts").EndCurrentEdit()
            Me.BindingContext(Dataset11, "contacts").AddNew()
```

```
          Catch eEndEdit as System.Exception
            System.Windows.Forms.MessageBox.Show(eEndEdit.Message)
              End Try
        Case "delete" 'delete
          If (Me.BindingContext(Dataset11, "contacts").Count > 0) Then
          Me.BindingContext(Dataset11, "contacts").RemoveAt
            (Me.BindingContext(Dataset11, "contacts").Position)
          End If
        Case "save" 'save
          Me.BindingContext(Dataset11, "contacts").CancelCurrentEdit()
        Case "previous" 'move previous
          Me.BindingContext(Dataset11, "contacts").Position =
            (Me.BindingContext(Dataset11, "contacts").Position - 1)
        Case "next" 'move next
          Me.BindingContext(Dataset11, "contacts").Position =
            (Me.BindingContext(Dataset11, "contacts").Position + 1)
        Case Else 'catch all
    End Select
```

I realize that this code looks very convoluted. To be perfectly honest, I think the new methods of data binding introduced in VB.NET are not an improvement over VB 6.0. Data binding was much easier and quicker in VB 6.0, but don't panic. Next, I will show you how to use a very simple wizard that will generate the form, components, and code you need for a data-bound application.

Example 5-2

1. Start a new Windows application.

2. Select **Project | Add Form**.

3. Select **Data Form Wizard**.

   Now this is where we get to the really easy way to develop data-bound forms. The wizard I will now walk you through does everything you need to have a fully working database application.

4. You should now see the first screen of the Data Form Wizard.

Chapter 5

5. Press the **Next** button to begin the process. That will take you to the second screen of the Data Form Wizard.

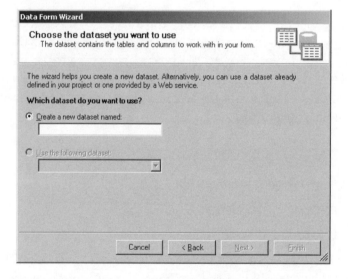

6. You will select the option to create a dataset. For our example, give it the name **MyDataSet**. Then press the **Next** button to continue.

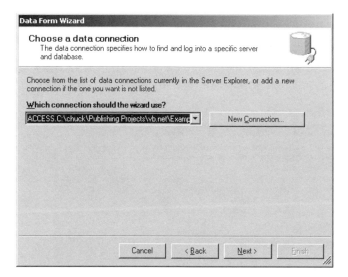

7. You will now be prompted to either use an existing connection (if you did the previous example, that connection will show as one option) or create a new connection. For learning purposes, let's try the new connection. This will take you to the same screens you used in Example 5-1 when you created your dataset. You will start with the Provider tab then move to the Connection tab in order to create your dataset. Since these exact steps are given earlier in this chapter I will not repeat them here. I will instead take you back to the Data Form Wizard and show you what you will need to do after clicking the **Next** button.

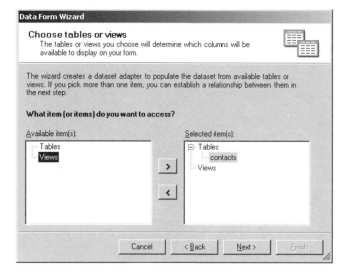

8. You will need to add the **Tables** option to the right side as you saw in the previous image. Then, of course, you will click the **Next** button.

9. On this screen you will simply select which fields from your table you wish to display on your form. For this exercise, you should select all of them.

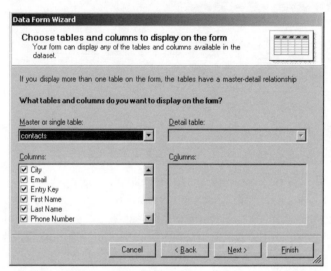

10. After pressing the **Next** button you will be taken to the screen that allows you to choose how you wish to display the records and what buttons (controls) you wish to add. For this example, select **Single record** and all the buttons available.

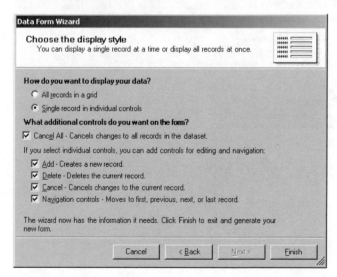

That's it! You now have a fully functioning database application. You can check each of the button's Click events: the code needed for them to operate is already there. Your form should look like this:

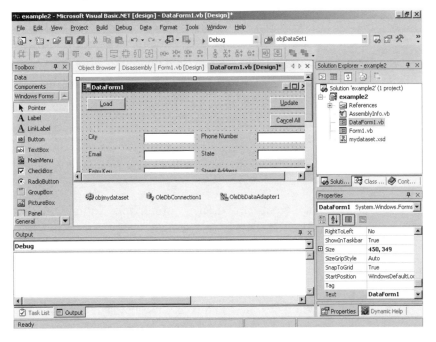

You may need to reread these two examples a few times to ensure that you understand them. The concepts are fairly straightforward:

- The dataset represents a set of records you have retrieved from a database.

- Using either your own code or the wizard you create a connection between your components and this dataset.

- While not the most robust or flexible means of writing database applications, data-bound forms do provide you a quick and easy method for creating simple database applications.

Complex Data Binding

While the previous examples have been very helpful and instructive, they have only shown you one of the two types of data binding. So far you have dealt only with simple-bound components. Now it is time to show you complex-bound components. The term "complex" merely denotes that the component will display more than one field. This does not mean that it will be more complicated to work with. In fact, complex-bound components can be easier to work with.

Example 5-3

1. The first thing we will want to do is to start a new Windows forms application.

2. We will then create an OLEDBConnection. Remember that when you place an OLEDBAdapter on the form it will automatically launch the wizard that will guide you through the process. Also recall that when you have finished creating your connection, you will then go to the Properties window and click **Generate Dataset**.

3. Now we will go to the toolbox and place a DataGrid component on the form. Set its Data Source property to the dataset object you created. Your form should now look like the image you see here.

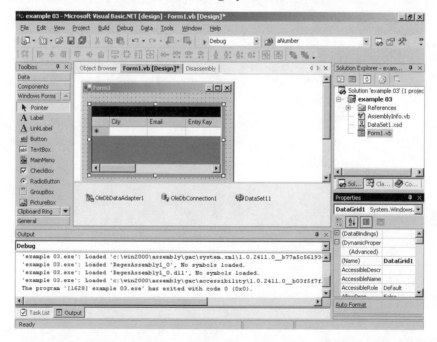

When you run the application, the entire table that your connection object represents will be displayed in the grid.

As you can see, creating data-bound applications is not a very difficult task. Both simple-bound and complex-bound components can be used to display data. Essentially, any component that has a Data Source property can be bound to a dataset. Below is a table summarizing the primary components used in data binding and whether they are simple or complex bound.

Component	Data Binding Behavior
TextBox	Simple bound
Label	Simple bound
PictureBox	Simple bound
DataGrid	Complex bound
ListBox	Simple bound
ComboBox	Simple bound

Each of these components can be bound to either an individual field or an entire recordset. This makes working with databases a much easier task than it would be if you had to manually manage all database connections and activity.

Summary

In this chapter I have shown you the basics of database programming. It is absolutely vital that you fully understand the material in this chapter before proceeding. Virtually all business programming involves database programming. Later chapters will expand upon these concepts and introduce you to more robust and professional methods for creating database applications. Without the foundation provided in this chapter, however, you are unlikely to be able to effectively utilize the later chapters.

Chapter 5

Review Questions

1. What are the two types of data-bound components?

2. What is SQL?

3. List four SQL commands.

4. What is a field?

5. What is a relational database?

6. What is a dataset?

7. What does "simple bound" mean?

8. What does "complex bound" mean?

9. What is a record?

10. What is a table?

More Windows Programming with VB.NET

In this chapter, you learn about:

♦ **Components**

♦ **MDI applications**

♦ **Built-in functions**

Introduction

The previous five chapters have shown you the essentials of Windows programming in VB.NET. This has included object orientation, file manipulation, .NET architecture, and database programming. This chapter will now add a bit of depth to these concepts and show you some other interesting things you can do to enhance your Windows development. One important task we will work with in this chapter is how to use various components available to you in Visual Basic.NET, as well as how to create MDI projects.

Components

In the first chapter of this book, I showed you how to place components onto forms, manipulate their properties, and respond to their events. One of the greatest strengths of Visual Basic has always been the ease with which one can use it to develop the graphical user interface. This is still true with Visual Basic.NET. So far, I have shown you only a few components and discussed only a small number of their properties. It's time now to give you a more thorough look at the most commonly used components.

Common Components

Visual Basic.NET offers numerous components you can use to build your applications. Each of these components has a specific purpose. My goal, in this section, is to acquaint you with these various components, thus allowing you to decide which one to use in a given situation. The following table is a summary of the basic components and their primary functions.

Control	Function
Label	Displays read-only text
LinkLabel	Displays text that is a link to another window or Web address
TextBox	Displays text that can be edited by the user
RichTextBox	Displays text in Rich Text Format (RTF)
ListBox	Displays a list of items
DomainUpDown	Displays a list of text items a user can scroll through with a spin button
NumericUpDown	Displays a list of numeric items a user can scroll through with a spin button
ComboBox	Displays a drop-down list of items, much like a list box
ListView	Displays text in text-only, text with icons, or report view
TreeView	Displays information in a hierarchical display
PictureBox	Displays graphics (*.bmp, *.gif, *.jpg)
CheckBox	Presents options that are not mutually exclusive (as opposed to a radio button, which displays items that are mutually exclusive)
CheckedListBox	Displays a list of items, each with a check mark
RadioButton	Presents mutually exclusive options
TrackBar	Displays a scale on which the user can set a value
DateTimePicker	Displays a graphical calendar from which the user can set a date
Button	A button the user can click
Panel	Holds a scrollable group of controls
GroupBox	Holds a captioned group of controls

Control	Function
TabControl	Provides a tabbed page for organizing and efficiently accessing grouped objects

Some properties are common to many controls. It's important that you be aware of these properties and what they can do for you.

Property	Description
Bindings	This collection holds all the bindings of properties of this control to data sources. You used this in Chapter 5.
Name	Indicates the name used in code to identify the component. This is not necessarily the caption the user will see.
Anchor	The anchor of the control. Anchors define to which edges of the container a certain control is bound. When a control is anchored to an edge, the distance between the component's closest edge and the specified edge will remain constant.
ContextMenu	The shortcut menu to display when the user right-clicks the control.
Dock	The docking location of the component, indicating which borders are docked to the container.
Enabled	Indicates whether the component is enabled.
Location	The position of the upper-left corner of the control with respect to its container.
Locked	Determines if the control can be moved or resized.
Modifiers	Indicates the visibility level of the object.
Size	The size of the control in pixels. There are two parameters: height and width.
Visible	Determines whether the control is visible or hidden.

Label A Label

The Windows Forms Label control allows you to display text in a read-only format. The most common use of the label is to provide descriptive labels for other components such as text boxes. The following table summarizes the most commonly used properties of the Label component.

Chapter

Property	Description
AutoSize	Enables automatic resizing based on font size. Note that this is only valid for labels that don't wrap text. The AutoSize property helps you size a label to fit smaller or larger captions, which is useful if the caption changes at run time.
BackColor	The background color of the label.
BorderStyle	Determines if the label has a visible border, and if so, what type.
Cursor	The cursor that appears when the mouse passes over the label.
Font	The font used in the label.
ForeColor	The foreground color used in the label.
Image	The image that will be displayed on the face of the label. This is new to VB.NET; previous versions of Visual Basic did not have this property.
ImageAlign	The alignment of the image.
ImageIndex	The index of the image in the image list to display in the label.
ImageList	The image list that contains the image you want to display in the label.
TabIndex	Determines the index in the tab order for this label.
Text	The text contained in the label.
TextAlign	Determines the position of the text within the label.
UseMnemonic	If true, the first character preceded by an ampersand (&) will be used as the label's mnemonic key.

Perhaps the most important property of the Label control is the Text property, which contains the label's caption. In previous versions of Visual Basic, the Caption property was used to specify the text displayed in the label. As with most properties of the label, you can set the caption at design time or run time. To set a label's caption at design time, use the Properties window to set the Text property to an appropriate string. To set a label's caption at run time, set the Text property programmatically, as shown here:

```
lbltest.Text = "Cool stuff"
```

LinkLabel

The Windows Forms LinkLabel component allows you to add Web-style links to your Windows Forms applications. The LinkLabel component has all the properties, methods, and events of the Label control. In addition, the LinkLabel component allows you to set its caption as a link to an object or Web page. One good use of LinkLabel would be in the About box of your application to provide a link to your company's Web page. The following table shows the properties of the LinkLabel (not including the properties it has in common with a standard label).

Property	Description
ActiveLinkColor	Determines the color of the hyperlink when the user is clicking the link. Just like the active link property in an HTML document.
DisabledLinkColor	Determines the color of the hyperlink when the link is disabled.
LinkArea	Portion of the text in the label that is a hyperlink.
LinkBehavior	Determines the underline behavior of the hyperlink.
LinkColor	Determines the color of the hyperlink. Just like the link property in an HTML document.

You can set the various link properties using the color constants defined in Visual Basic. These constants are implemented as properties of the Color object.

```
'Set the link color using defined color constants
with lnkWebSite
    .ActiveLinkColor = color.Green
    .DisabledLinkColor = color.Blue
    .LinkColor = color.Blue
    .VisitedLinkColor = color.Purple
end with
```

You can also change the color of a link using decimal values for red, green, and blue. If you wish to mix color values in order to achieve a different shade than the Color object provides, you may use the following decimal method.

Chapter

```
'Set the link color using decimal values for red, green, and blue
with lnkWebSite
    .ActiveLinkColor = Color.FromARGB(255, 0, 0)
    .DisabledLinkColor = Color.FromARGB(100, 0, 255)
    .LinkColor = Color.FromARGB(15, 0, 255)
    .VisitedLinkColor = Color.FromARGB(128, 0, 128)
end with
```

The LinkArea property holds the portion of the LinkLabel's caption that activates the link. The LinkArea.X property determines the start of the link area, and the LinkArea.Y property determines the length of the link area. Here is an example that sets all of a LinkLabel's text to be a link.

```
Mylinklabel.LinkArea.X = 0
Mylinklabel.LinkArea.Y = Len(linklabel1.Text)
```

The Click event of the LinkLabel is an important one, since the Click event determines what happens when the link is selected. The following example shows how to start the default Web browser and link to the Wordware Publishing Web site.

Example 6-1

1. Start a new Windows application project.

2. Place a single LinkLabel on the form.

3. Name that label **lnktopublisher.** Also change the text to **Wordware Publishing**.

4. Place the following code in the Click event.

```
Private Sub lnktopublisher_LinkClicked (ByVal Sender As Object, _
ByVal e As EventArgs)
    'Open the default Web browser and link to the Microsoft Web site
    System.Diagnostics.Process.Start("http://www.wordware.com")
    lnktopublisher.LinkVisited = True
End Sub
```

Now that is pretty easy. The LinkLabel control is new to VB.NET. Previous versions did not include any way to put links in your applications. I think this is a very good addition to Visual Basic and one you will find very useful.

Button   ab] Button

The Windows Forms Button control performs an action when a button is clicked, making it look as if the button is being pushed in and released. When the user clicks the button, the Click event handler is invoked. This is one of the first components I showed you, but I did not show you many of its properties. The following table summarizes the major properties of the Button component.

Property	Description
BackColor	The background color of the button.
BackgroundImage	The background image of the button.
Cursor	The cursor that appears when the mouse passes over the component.
FlatStyle	Determines the display of the button when the user moves the mouse over the button and clicks.
Font	The font used to display text in the button.
ForeColor	The foreground color of the button's text.
Image	The image that will be displayed on the face of the button.
ImageAlign	The alignment of the image that will be displayed on the face of the button.
ImageIndex	The index of the image in the image list to display on the face of the button.
ImageList	The image list to get the image to display on the face of the button.
TabIndex	Determines the index in the tab order that the button will occupy.
Text	The text contained on the button.
TextAlign	The alignment of the text that will be displayed on the button.

In Visual Basic.NET, there are a variety of ways in which a user can click the Button control:

- The user uses a mouse to click the button.
- The user selects the button by pressing the Enter key while the button has focus.
- The user presses the access key (Alt + the underlined letter) for the button.

Chapter 6

TextBox

The text box has been around in Visual Basic since the beginning. Each version of VB simply adds more flexibility to it. In single-line mode a text box can hold up to 2,048 characters, but when displaying multiple lines, a text box can hold up to 32 K of text. Text boxes are most commonly used for editable text, but they can also be made read-only. The following table shows the most commonly used properties of the text box.

Property	Description
AcceptsReturn	Determines if return characters are accepted as input for multiline edit components.
AcceptsTab	Determines if tab characters are accepted as input for multiline edit components.
AutoSize	Enables automatic resizing based on font size for single-line edit controls.
BackColor	The background color for the text box.
BorderStyle	Indicates if there is a border and what type if there is one.
Cursor	The cursor that appears when the mouse passes over the text box.
Font	The font used in the text box.
ForeColor	The foreground color used in the text box.
Lines	The lines of text in a multiline edit control.
MaxLength	Sets the maximum number of characters that can be entered into the edit control. Zero means there is no maximum.
MultiLine	Determines if the text of the edit control can span more than one line.
PasswordChar	Determines the character to display for password input (most people use an asterisk).
ReadOnly	Controls whether the text in the edit control can be changed or not.
ScrollBars	Indicates which scroll bars will be shown for this control. This only works for multiline text boxes.
TabIndex	Determines the index in the tab order for the text box.
Text	The text contained in the text box.
TextAlign	Indicates how the text should be aligned.
WordWrap	Indicates if lines are automatically word-wrapped for multiline text boxes.

You can display multiple lines in a TextBox control by using the MultiLine, WordWrap, and ScrollBars properties. To display multiple lines in a TextBox control:

1. Set the MultiLine property to True.
2. Set the ScrollBars property to None, Horizontal, or Both.
3. Set the WordWrap property to False or True.

CheckBox   ☑ CheckBox

The Windows Forms CheckBox component is a non-exclusive option selection component. This means that you can choose to select more than one check box. You have, undoubtedly, used check boxes in various software packages before. Use the CheckBox control to present a True/False or Yes/No selection to the user. You can group multiple check boxes using a GroupBox control to display multiple choices from which the user may select more than one.

Grouped controls can be moved around together on the form designer. For this reason, and others, it is a good idea to group multiple boxes using the GroupBox component.

Property	Description
Appearance	Controls the appearance of the check box.
AutoCheck	Causes the check box to automatically change state when clicked.
BackColor	The background color for the check box.
BackgroundImage	The background image used for the check box.
CheckAlign	Determines the location of the check box inside the component.
Checked	Indicates whether the check box is checked or unchecked.
Cursor	The cursor that appears when the mouse passes over the check box.
FlatStyle	Determines the display of the check box when users move the mouse over the check box and when it is clicked.
Font	The font used in the check box.
ForeColor	The foreground color used in the check box.
Image	The image that will be displayed on the face of the check box.

Chapter

Property	Description
ImageAlign	The alignment of the image that will be displayed on the face of the check box.
ImageIndex	The index of the image in the image list to display on the face of the check box.
ImageList	The image list to get the image to display on the face of the check box.
TabIndex	Determines the index in the tab order that the check box will occupy.
TabStop	Indicates whether the user can use the Tab key to give focus to the check box.
Text	The text contained in the check box.
TextAlign	The alignment of the text that will be displayed in the face of the check box.
ThreeState	Controls whether or not the user can select the indeterminate state of the check box.

RadioButton   ⊙ RadioButton

The Windows Forms RadioButton component is used to give the user a single choice within a set of two or more mutually exclusive choices. It is a lot like the check box, except that you can choose only a single option. Radio buttons appear as a set of small circles. When an option button choice is set, a dot appears in the middle of the circle.

The radio button and the check box are used for different functions. Use a radio button when you want the user to choose only one option. When you want the user to be able to choose multiple options, use a check box.

Property	Description
Appearance	Controls whether the radio button appears as normal or as a Windows push button.
AutoCheck	Causes the radio button to automatically change state when clicked.
BackColor	The background color used in the radio button.
BackgroundImage	The background image used in the radio button.
CheckAlign	Determines the location of the check box inside the radio button.
Checked	Indicates whether the radio button is checked or not.

Property	Description
Cursor	The cursor that appears when the mouse passes over the radio button.
FlatStyle	Determines the display of the radio button when users move the mouse over the radio button and click the radio button.
Font	The font used in the radio button.
ForeColor	The foreground color used in the radio button.
Image	The image that will be displayed on the face of the radio button.
ImageAlign	The alignment of the image that will be displayed on the face of the radio button.
ImageIndex	The index of the image in the image list to display on the face of the radio button.
ImageList	The image list to get the image to display on the face of the radio button.
TabIndex	Determines the index in the tab order that the radio button will occupy.
Text	The text contained on the radio button.
TextAlign	The alignment of the text that will be displayed on the face of the radio button.

RichTextBox

The RichTextBox is very much like the standard text box with one major exception. It allows you to display all the variations of font you can show in any Rich Text document. This provides a much richer array of display options, similar to what you get when you use WordPad.

Property	Description
AcceptsTab	Indicates if tab characters are accepted as input for the RichTextBox.
AutoSize	Enables automatic resizing based on font size for a single-line RichTextBox.
BackColor	The background color used in the RichTextBox.
BorderStyle	Indicates whether or not the RichTextBox should have a border.
Cursor	The cursor that appears when the mouse passes over the RichTextBox.
DetectURLs	Turns on/off automatic URL highlighting.

Chapter 6

Property	Description
Font	The font used in the RichTextBox.
ForeColor	The foreground color used in the RichTextBox.
Lines	The lines of text in a multiline RichTextBox.
MaxLength	Specifies the maximum number of characters that can be entered into the RichTextBox. Zero implies no maximum.
Multiline	Controls whether the text of the RichTextBox can span more than one line.
ReadOnly	Controls whether the text in the RichTextBox can be changed or not.
RightMargin	Defines the right margin.
ScrollBars	Defines the behavior of the scroll bars of the RichTextBox.
TabIndex	Determines the index in the tab order that the RichTextBox will occupy.
Text	The text contained in the RichTextBox.
WordWrap	Indicates if lines are automatically word-wrapped for multiline RichTextBox.

You can change the font, size, and color of text in the RichTextBox component by using the SelFont, SelFontSize, and SelColor properties. This gives you a much richer set of display options for text than you can get from a standard text box. Because of this flexibility, you can even use a RichTextBox in conjunction with an OpenFileDialog component to open a Rich Text document and load it.

Example 6-2

1. Start a new Windows application.

2. Place one button, one OpenFileDialog component, and one RichTextBox as shown in the following illustration.

3. Give the button the text **Open RTF** and place the following code in its Click event:

```
with OpenFileDialog1
    .Filter = "Rich Text Format|*.rtf"
    .ShowDialog()
end with
Richtextbox1.LoadFile(openfiledialog1.FileName)
```

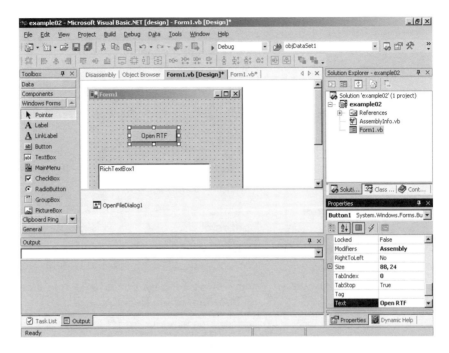

As you can see, you can easily view rich text format (RTF) documents. In the downloadable files available at www.wordware.com/VBNET, the folder Example\Chapter 06 contains an RTF file you can open to illustrate this.

ListBox

A Windows Forms ListBox control displays a list of items. It is commonly used to display longer lists of data. You can also use the Click event of the ListBox to respond to the user clicking an item in the list. This allows you to use the ListBox in a similar fashion to a radio button or check box.

A vertical scroll bar is displayed if the items displayed exceed the height of the box. A ListBox will also display a horizontal scrollbar if the MultiColumn property is set to True. In that case, values are displayed in columns horizontally.

Property	Description
BackColor	The background color used in the list box.
BorderStyle	Determines what type of border is drawn around the list box.
ColumnWidth	Indicates how wide each column should be in a multicolumn list box.

Property	Description
Cursor	The cursor that appears when the mouse passes over the list box.
DataSource	Determines the list that the list box will use to get its items.
DisplayMember	Determines the property to display for the items in the list box.
Font	The font used in the list box.
ForeColor	The foreground color used in the list box.
Items	The items in the list box.
MultiColumn	Determines if values should be displayed in columns horizontally.
ScrollAlwaysVisible	Determines if the list box should always have a scroll bar present, regardless of how many items are in it.
SelectionMode	Determines if the list box is to be single-select, multi-select, or unselectable.
Sorted	Determines whether or not the list is sorted.
TabIndex	Determines the index in the tab order that the list box will occupy.

The SelectionMode property determines how many items in the list can be selected at a time. If the SelectionMode property is set to Selection-Mode.MultiSimple, the user can select more than one item by simply clicking the items in the list. If the SelectionMode property is set to SelectionMode.MultiExtended, the user can select more than one item by holding down the Ctrl key or Shift key and clicking items in the list.

You use the Add or Insert method to place items in a list box. The Add method adds new items at the end of an unsorted list box. The Insert method allows you to specify where to insert the item you are adding. The following code illustrates this:

```
'Add to the end
mylist.Items.Add("VB Is Cool")
'insert at a given position
mylist.Items.Insert(0, "C is cool too")
```

You can use the Remove method to remove an item from a list box. To remove all items from a list box, you use the Clear method of the Items collection.

```
'Remove all names from the Employees list box
mylist.Items.Clear()
```

CheckedListBox   CheckedListBox

The Windows Forms CheckedListBox control, a type of ListBox, gives you all the capability of a list box and also allows you to display a check mark next to the items in the list box.

ListView

The ListView is able to display text in four different ways: text only, text with small icons, text with large icons, or report. It is really a special case of the ListBox.

Property	Description
Alignment	Determines how items are aligned within the list view.
AllowColumnReorder	Determines if the user can reorder columns in the Report view.
AutoArrange	Determines if items are kept arranged automatically.
BackColor	The background color in the list view.
BorderStyle	The border style of the list view.
CheckBoxes	Determines if check boxes are displayed beside items.
Columns	The columns shown in Report view.
Cursor	The cursor that appears when the mouse passes over the list view.
Font	The font used in the list view.
ForeColor	The foreground color used in the list view.
FullRowSelect	Indicates whether all the subitems are highlighted along with the item clicked when selected.
GridLines	Displays grid lines around items and subitems.
HeaderStyle	The style of the column headers in Report view.
HoverSelection	This option allows items to be selected by hovering over them with the mouse.
LabelEdit	Allows item labels to be edited in place by the user.
LabelWrap	Determines whether label text can wrap to a new line.
LargeImageList	The image list used by the list view for images in Large Icon view.
ListItems	The items in the list view.

Chapter **6**

Property	Description
MultiSelect	Allows multiple items to be selected simultaneously.
Scrollable	Determines if the list view will display scroll bars when the data goes beyond the component's dimensions.
SmallImageList	The image list used by the list view for images in all views except for the Large Icon view.
Sorting	Determines the manner in which items are to be sorted.
TabIndex	Determines the index in the tab order that the list view will occupy.
View	Selects one of four different views in which items can be shown.

The View property is perhaps the most important property of the ListView, since it determines which of four different views items will be shown in: text only, text with small icons, text with large icons, or report. The text-only view renders items in much the same manner as a list box. Frankly, if you intend to use the text-only view you might as well just use the Label component. The text with small icons, text with large icons, and report views are similar to the Small Icons, Large Icons, and Detail views you see in Windows Explorer.

The ListItems property holds the items in a list view. If a ListView control has multiple columns, the items have subitems that hold information in the columns beyond the first. For example, a list view with one row and three columns has one item (to hold the information in the first column) and two subitems (to hold the information in the second and third columns).

ComboBox   ComboBox

The Windows Forms ComboBox control displays a list from which the user can select one or more choices. The ComboBox control appears as a text box and an associated list box. Essentially, it is much like the ListBox except the list is displayed as a single text box until you click it. Then, the list drops down for the user to view.

The ComboBox has three different styles you can use: simple, drop-down, and drop-down list. With the simple style, the combo box has an edit box along with a list box. Using the drop-down style, the combo box looks like a text box, but you can click it to see a drop-down list containing its items. The drop-down list style is similar to the drop-down style. The one exception is that, in the drop-down list style, the user can only choose an item in the list. No item can be entered that does not appear in the list.

Property	Description
BackColor	The background color used in the combo box.
Cursor	The cursor that appears when the mouse passes over the combo box.
DataSource	Indicates the list that the combo box will use to get its items.
DisplayMember	Indicates the property to display for the items in the combo box.
Font	The font used in the combo box.
ForeColor	The foreground color used in the combo box.
Items	The items in the combo box.
MaxDropDownItems	The maximum number of entries to display in the drop-down list.
MaxLength	Specifies the maximum number of characters that can be entered into the combo box.
Sorted	Determines if items in the list portion are sorted.
Style	Determines the appearance and functionality of the combo box.
TabIndex	Determines the index in the tab order that the combo box will occupy.
Text	The text contained in the combo box.

You can add items to the combo box at design time the same way you add them to a list box. You also remove items from the combo box the same way you remove them from the list box.

DomainUpDown

The DomainUpDown control displays a list from which the user can select a single choice. This is much like the combo box. However, a DomainUpDown control is used when the items have an inherent order, like days of the week or months of the year.

Chapter 6

NumericUpDown

The NumericUpDown control allows the user to change a numeric value by a chosen increment. The NumericUpDown component is very similar to the DomainUpDown component, except that it is used to display numbers instead of text.

PictureBox

The Windows Forms PictureBox control is used to display images in bitmap, JPEG, icon, or GIF formats. The image can be set at design time or at run time.

Property	Description
BackColor	The background color in the picture box.
BackgroundImage	The background image used for the component.
BorderStyle	Controls what type of border the component should have.
Cursor	The cursor that appears when the mouse passes over the picture box.
Image	The image in the picture box.
SizeMode	Controls how the picture box will handle image placement and component sizing.
TabIndex	Determines the index in the tab order that the picture box will occupy.

You can change the picture displayed at design time or at run time. To set the picture at run time, use the FromFile method of the Image class as shown here:

```
Dim strimagepath As String = "somepic.gif"
```

As you can see, it is relatively easy to change the picture that you display in a picture box.

TrackBar

The Windows Forms TrackBar component is very similar to the scroll bar. The track bar is often used for tasks such as adjusting volume. It consists of a slider with a range of tick marks. The user can adjust the value of the track bar by dragging the slider to the desired value.

Property	Description
AutoSize	Determines if the track bar will resize itself automatically.
BackColor	The background color in the track bar.
Cursor	The cursor that appears when the mouse passes over the track bar.
LargeChange	The number of positions the slider moves in response to the mouse.
Maximum	The maximum value for the slider on the track bar.
Minimum	The minimum value for the slider on the track bar.
Orientation	The orientation of the track bar (i.e., vertical or horizontal).
SmallChange	The number of positions the slider moves in response to keyboard input from the arrow keys.
TabIndex	Determines the index in the tab order that the track bar will occupy.
TickFrequency	The number of positions between tick marks.
TickStyle	Indicates where the ticks appear on the track bar.
Value	The position of the slider.

The track bar's most important property is the Value property. It indicates the position of the slider. You should also be aware of the SmallChange and LargeChange properties. The SmallChange property determines the number of positions the slider will move when the user uses the arrow keys on the keyboard. The LargeChange property determines the number of positions the slider will move in response to mouse clicks or when the Page Up and Page Down keys are pressed.

DateTimePicker

The Windows Forms DateTimePicker control allows you to display dates and times to the user. The DateTimePicker will allow the user to view the days of the week around a particular day selected, or to view different months, just as they would when perusing through a calendar.

The DateTimePicker looks very much like a text box with an accompanying calendar drop-down. The user can input a date in several ways. First, the user can enter a date by just typing it into the text box. Secondly, the user can use the drop-down to navigate to a particular date. Finally, the user can use the drop-down, and simply click on Today's Date to enter the current date, regardless of the month displayed in the drop-down.

Chapter 6

The DateTimePicker can also be used to show time. The DateTimePicker shows time when the Format property is set to Time. In this mode, the DateTimePicker does not show a drop-down calendar, but you can still use it to collect times from the user.

The most important property of the DateTimePicker is the Value property. It holds the currently selected date and time. The Value property is set to the current date by default. If you wish to change the date before displaying the control, use the Value property as follows:

```
dtpmydate.Value = _DateAdd(Microsoft.VisualBasic.DateInterval.Day,
    1, Date.Today)
```

Property	Description
CalendarFont	The font used in the calendar.
CalendarForeColor	The foreground color.
CalendarMonthBackground	The background color.
CalendarTitleBackColor	The background color of the calendar's title.
CalendarTitleForeColor	The color used within the calendar's title.
Cursor	The cursor that appears when the mouse passes over the control.
CustomFormat	The custom format string used to format the date or time displayed in the date-time picker.
DropDownAlign	Controls whether the month drop-down is aligned to the left or right.
Font	The font used in the DateTimePicker.
Format	Determines the format of the display.
MaxDate	The maximum date selectable.
MinDate	The minimum date selectable.
ShowCheckBox	Determines if a check box is displayed in the DateTimePicker. If the check box is unchecked, no value is selected.
ShowUpDown	Determines if an up-down button is used to modify dates instead of a drop-down calendar.
TabIndex	Determines the index in the tab order that this control will occupy.
TabStop	Indicates whether the user can use the Tab key to give focus to the DateTimePicker.

Panel

The Windows Forms Panel control is used to group other components. It is a "container" component. A panel allows you to give the user a logical visual cue of components that belong together. Essentially, you place components that logically belong together on the same panel.

Property	Description
AutoScroll	Determines if scroll bars will automatically appear when controls are placed outside the form's client area.
AutoScrollMargin	The margin around components during autoscrolls.
AutoScrollMinSize	The minimum size for the autoscroll region.
BackColor	The background color in the panel.
BackgroundImage	The background image used in the panel.
BorderStyle	Determines if the panel will have a border, and if so, what type.
Cursor	The cursor that appears when the mouse passes over the panel.
DockPadding	Determines the size of the border for docked controls.
DrawGrid	Determines whether or not to draw the positioning grid.
Font	The font used in the panel.
ForeColor	The foreground color in the panel.
GridSize	Determines the size of the positioning grid.
RightToLeft	Indicates whether the panel should draw right-to-left for RTL languages.
SnapToGrid	Determines if controls should snap to the positioning grid.
TabIndex	Determines the index in the order that the panel will occupy.

Basically you place panels on your form, then place other components on those panels. The panel is used to provide a visual grouping of components that matches their logical function.

GroupBox

The GroupBox control is used to group other controls. However, unlike the Panel control, the GroupBox cannot have scroll bars and only the GroupBox allows you to display a caption with a group of controls. The GroupBox is very similar to the Frame component used in earlier versions of Visual Basic. You can use the Add method to create a group of controls.

Property	Description
BackColor	The background color used in the group box.
BackgroundImage	The background image used for the group box.
DrawGrid	Determines whether or not to draw the positioning grid.
Font	The font used in the group box.
ForeColor	The foreground color used in the group box.
GridSize	Determines the size of the positioning grid.
SnapToGrid	Determines if controls should snap to the positioning grid.
TabIndex	Determines the index in the tab order that this control will occupy.
Text	The text displayed in the group box.

TabControl   TabControl

The Windows Forms TabControl control is used to hold controls separated by tabs. You can place different groups of information on separate tabs of the tab control.

Property	Description
Alignment	Determines whether the tabs appear on the top, bottom, left, or right side of the tab component.
Appearance	Determines if the tabs are painted as buttons or regular tabs.
JustRightCursor	The cursor that appears when the mouse passes over the tab control.
DrawGrid	Determines whether or not to draw the positioning grid.
Font	The font used in the tab component.
GridSize	Determines the size of the positioning grid.
HotTrack	Determines if the tabs visually change when the mouse passes over them.
ImageList	The image list from which the tab control takes its images.
ItemSize	Determines the width of fixed-width or owner-drawn tabs and the height of all tabs.
Locked	Determines if the user can move or resize the component.
MultiLine	Determines if more than one row of tabs is allowed.
ShowToolTips	Determines if tooltips will be shown for tables that have their ToolTips property set.
SizeMode	Determines how tabs are sized.

Property	Description
SnapToGrid	Determines if components will snap to the positioning grid.
TabIndex	Determines the index in the tab order that the tab control will occupy.
TabPages	The number of tab pages in the tab control.

Example 6-3

I would like to show you an example now that uses some of the components you have just seen as well as a variety of simple programming techniques. At this stage in your learning of Visual Basic.NET, this example should be fairly easy for you to follow.

1. Start a new Windows application project.

2. Place eleven numeric buttons and five function buttons on two separate panels; label them as shown below. Your form should look something like this.

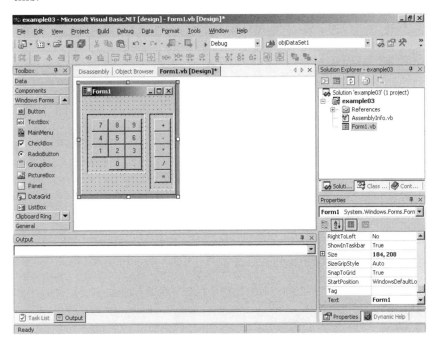

 Note: I changed the panel's border to fixed3d.

3. Change the form text to read **My Calculator.**

4. Add a label at the top with a **white** background, **fixed3d** border, text align to **center right**, and give it a text value of **0**. Change the label's name to **Display.**

5. At the top of the form class's code window (just after Inherits System.Windows.Forms.Form) place the following code:

```
Dim FirstNum as Single
Dim SecondNum as Single
Dim Answer as Double
Dim Operation as Integer


Const PLUS = 0
Const MINUS = 1
Const MULTIPLY = 2
Const DIVIDE = 3
Const DECPOINT = 4
Const EQUALS = 5
```

6. Now in each of the numeric buttons, place code that will set the display label to show its current value plus the value of the button pressed. For example, for the number 9 button you would enter:

```
Display.Text = Display.Text & "9"
```

7. You will now have to place code in each of the function buttons. The code for each button is shown here.

    Add button:

```
FirstNum = Val(Display.Text)
Display.Text = "0"
Operation = PLUS
```

    Subtract button:

```
FirstNum = Val(Display.Text)
Display.Text = "0"
Operation = MINUS
```

    Multiply button:

```
FirstNum = Val(Display.Text)
Display.Text = "0"
Operation = MULTIPLY
```

Divide button:

```
FirstNum = Val(Display.Text)
Display.Text = "0"
Operation = DIVIDE
```

Equals button:

```
SecondNum = Val(Display.Text)
Select Case Operation
Case PLUS
  Answer = FirstNum + SecondNum
  Display.Text = Answer
Case MINUS
  Answer = FirstNum - SecondNum
  Display.Text = Answer
Case MULTIPLY
  Answer = FirstNum * SecondNum
  Display.Text = Answer
Case DIVIDE
  Answer = FirstNum / SecondNum
  Display.Text = Answer
End Select
```

While this simple calculator is unlikely to go down in the annals of computer science, it does illustrate several useful points. The first is that it gives you practice using panels. Secondly, it exposes you to more properties of the label. You are also given additional practice with Select Case statements. An entirely new concept is introduced as well—the constant. A constant is a value that you assign to some word. For example, I used an integer to determine what operation had been selected, and then used constants such as PLUS, MINUS, etc. to represent the integers used. This is a very common practice in programming. It prevents other programmers from having to try and figure out what a particular value references.

MDI Applications

MDI is an acronym for multiple-document interface. It means an application that can have multiple screens open at one time. To illustrate this concept, consider Notepad. This is a single document interface application. You can only view one text document at a time. However, MS Word is a multiple-document interface application that allows you to view multiple Word documents simultaneously.

To create an MDI application, you will require one central form that acts as a container for all the other forms. To do this, simply take a standard form and change its IsMDIContainer property to true. Any children forms of this container will have their property left as false. Only certain components can be placed on an MDI container form, the most common being the picture box and the toolbar. To illustrate the entire MDI concept, follow along with this example.

Example 6-4

1.   Create a new Windows project.

2.   Change the first form to be an MDI container.

3.   Add a new form.

4.   Add a toolbar to the MDI container form. At this point your form should look a bit like this:

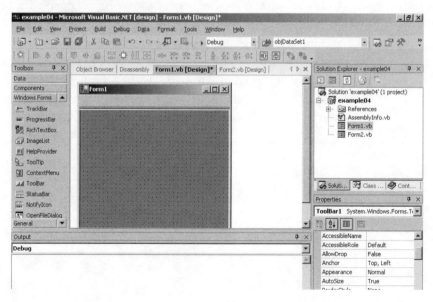

5. Add a single button to the toolbar (remember that Chapter 5 walked you through the process of creating a toolbar in detail).

6. Give that button a text value of **New** and set its tag value to **New** as well.

7. Place the following code in the Click event of the toolbar.

```
Dim X as Form
   Select Case e.Button.Tag
       Case "New"
           X = New Form2()
           X.Show()
       Case Else
   End Select
```

When you run this application and press the New button, an instance of Form2 will be created. A new instance will be created each time you press the button again. This simple example illustrates several points. The first being, of course, how to make an MDI container form. The second thing you should note is that the variable X is of the type Form rather than Single, Integer, etc. You can have a variable that represents any object you wish, including forms. That's how I am able to create new copies of Form2.

Built-in Functions

In addition to interesting components that allow you to create dynamic user interfaces, Visual Basic offers a plethora of built-in functions. There are functions to perform operations on strings, do math, etc. I would like to introduce you to a few of those functions here.

String Functions

There are many functions built into Visual Basic.NET that make manipulation of strings really very easy. Following is a table listing many of those functions and their purpose.

Function	Purpose
Trim(string value)	Takes whatever string is passed to it, removes the leading and trailing spaces, and returns a string.
Len(string value)	Returns the length of a string, including spaces.

Function	Purpose
Ucase(string value)	Returns a string that is the all-uppercase version of the string passed to it.
Lcase(string value)	Returns a string that is the lowercase version of the string passed to it.
Ltrim(string value)	Removes blank spaces from the left side of the string.
Rtrim(string value)	Removes blank spaces from the right side of the string.
mid(string value, starting point, end)	Returns a substring of the string value passed to it, beginning at the first number passed and stopping at the last.

Example 6-5

This example illustrates the use of some of the built-in string functions.

1. Start a new Windows project.

2. Place one text box and four labels on the form. Set the label text to **blank** and border style to **fixed3D**.

3. Place one button on the form, and set its text to **String Func()**.

4. Change your form's text to read **String Stuff**. Now your form should look like this:

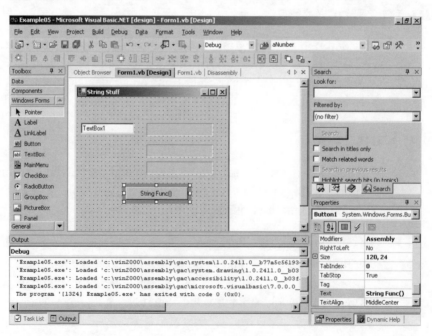

5. In the Click event of the button, place this code:

```
Dim MyString as String
MyString = TextBox1.Text
Label1.Text = Ucase(MyString)
Label2.Text = Lcase(MyString)
Label3.Text = Len(MyString)
```

When you run this application, whatever text you enter into the text box will be displayed in the labels showing it in uppercase and lowercase. Its length will also be shown.

Math Functions

Computers are renowned for their ability to process mathematics very quickly. Visual Basic.NET has a rich set of math functions you can use in your applications. You access each of these functions via the Math class.

Function	Purpose
Sin(number value)	Returns the sine of the angle you pass to it.
Cos(number value)	Returns the cosine of the angle you pass to it.
Tan(number value)	Returns the tangent of the number you pass to it.
Pow(number, power)	Returns a double. That double is the value of the number you pass to the function raised to the power you pass.
Abs(number value)	Returns the absolute value of the number you pass to it.
Sqrt(number value)	Returns the square root of the number you pass to it.

Example 6-6

1. Create a new Windows project with a single form. This form's Text property should read **Math Made easy.**

2. Place one text box on the form and two panels. The first panel's text will be **Trig Functions**, the second **Other Math**. Both panels will have four labels. Those labels will be given a border (**Fixed3D**).

3. You will place two buttons on the form, one with the text **Trig Functions** and the other with the text **Other.** Your form should then look like this:

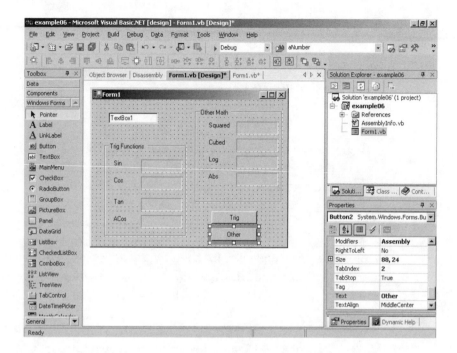

4. In the Click event of the button labeled "Trig," place this code:

```
Dim Num as Single
    Num = Val(TextBox1.Text)
    Label1.Text = Math.Sin(num)
    Label2.Text = Math.Cos(num)
    Label3.Text = Math.Tan(num)
    Label4.Text = Math.Acos(num)
End Sub
```

5. In the Click event of the button labeled "Other," place this code:

```
Dim Num as Single
Num = Val(TextBox1.Text)
Label5.Text = Math.Pow(num, 2)
Label6.Text = Math.Pow(num, 3)
Label7.Text = Math.Log(num)
Label8.Text = Math.Abs(num)
```

This example should show you how easy it is to utilize the Math class to accomplish a variety of mathematical operations.

Summary

In this chapter, I gave you an introduction to the most common components used in VB.NET. You were also given an opportunity for more practice with basic Windows applications. The entire focus of these first six chapters has been to give you the basic tools to be able to produce Windows applications. Before you proceed to the later chapters please be certain that you are very comfortable with the material in these first six chapters. Make sure that you have done the examples and that you have carefully studied the material in the chapters.

Also remember that I did not attempt to cover all of the components a VB.NET programmer has at his or her disposal. I just wanted to ensure that you were familiar with the essential ones.

Review Questions

1. List two container components.
2. What method is used to add items to the end of a list box or combo box?
3. What method is used to add items to some specific position in a list box or combo box?
4. What is the purpose of a link label?
5. What is the primary difference between a check box and a radio button?
6. What types of graphics can a picture box display?
7. What is the purpose of the PasswordChar property of a text box?
8. What does the Value property of a track bar tell you?
9. What is the primary difference between a text box and a label?
10. Name five components.

Chapter 6

ADO.NET

Introduction

ADO, or Active Data Objects, was first introduced with Visual Basic 6.0. It proved to be a more robust and flexible answer to database programming than the previous technologies (DAO—Data Access Objects, RDO—Remote Data Objects). The new .NET architecture takes this same concept and builds upon it. Whatever technology is being used, the idea is the same: connect to a database and get the data you need, or conversely put in the appropriate data.

The ADO.NET architecture uses XML as its native data format. XML, or Extensible Markup Language, is a very popular Web-based technology, similar to HTML (Hypertext Markup Language). This means that ADO.NET is fundamentally different from ADO 2.x. ADO.NET is filled with XML functionality, including XML document objects. In this chapter, I will demonstrate to you how to connect to databases, manipulate data, and disconnect from the data source.

ADO.NET utilizes a connectionless principle that is very useful when working with a distributed architecture. This basically means that you don't need to keep the connection active. Simply connect to the database, get the data you want, and then disconnect. You will reconnect when you are ready to send your data. You are no longer required to maintain an open connection.

Namespace	Description
System.Data	Provides the core ADO objects such as DataTable, DataColumn, DataView, and Constraints. This namespace provides the foundation for all the others.
System.Data.Common	This namespace defines the generic objects shared by various data providers. This includes DataAdapter, DataColumnMapping, and DataTableMapping.
System.Data.OleDb	This namespace defines the objects that we use to connect to and modify data in various data sources. This class is particularly useful if your project connects to many different data sources.
System.Data.SqlClient	This namespace is designed specifically for Microsoft SQL Server versions 7.0 and later. This namespace is able to use the Microsoft SQL Server API directly.
System.Data.SQLTypes	Provides classes for data types specific to Microsoft SQL Server. These classes are designed specifically for SQL.
System.Data.ODBC	This namespace is intended to work with all compliant ODBC drivers. It is available as a separate download from Microsoft.

Connection, Command, DataReader, and DataAdapter are the core objects in ADO.NET. These objects form the basis for all data operations in .NET. They are created from the System.Data.OleDb, System.Data.SqlClient, and System.Data.ODBC namespaces.

XML

A little background on XML is in order before we continue. It is not necessary that you be an XML expert in order to use ADO.NET since the .NET architecture will handle most of the XML details for you. However, at least a passing familiarity with the technology will be helpful to you. XML is a self-describing data format and many tools are already available to automatically create the schemas and documents.

XML stands for Extensible Markup Language. XML is a standard for formatting data that is extensible and self-describing. XML uses a document-based architecture whereby a document contains a few basic elements that are easy to understand and grasp. Moving data using XML is similar to moving data in ASCII. ASCII documents are not processed directly, but are transformed into another format such as HTML.

XML Documents

XML documents are the heart of the XML standard. An XML document
has at least one element that is delimited with one Start tag and one End
tag. XML documents are similar to HTML, except that the tags are made
up by the author. They may have attributes designated by name-value
pairs to further allow for data description:

```
<?xml version="1.0" standalone="yes"?>
<NewXMLDocument>
<MyTable>
  <Column1>Data1</Column1>
  <Column2>Data2</Column2>
</MyData>
</NewXMLDocument>
```

XSL

XSL is an acronym for Extensible Stylesheet Language. XSL documents
are XML documents that, when combined with other XML documents,
transform data into a more useful format. This allows a developer to separate the logic of data presentation and the actual data into two independent
objects. XSL documents use special format objects to control the transfor-
mation of data from one format (XML) to another (HTML).

XPath

XPath describes location paths of data between XML documents and can
be used to query other XML documents. Using a syntax that is similar to
navigating a file system, it allows you to select parts of a document. This
may be useful for developers familiar with creating XPath queries.

ADO.NET Architecture

Now that you have had a brief tour of XML, one of the technologies under-
lying the new ADO.NET, it is time to introduce you to the architecture of
ADO.NET itself. ADO.NET is the latest extension of the Universal Data
Access technology. In the early days of Visual Basic, Microsoft realized
that data access was an important tool. Visual Basic version 3.0 included
DAO (Data Access Objects). This was a very useful tool, but one with

limitations. Visual Basic 6.0 introduced ADO (Active Data Objects). This technology was quite powerful, but still had some limitations. ADO.NET is much simpler, less dependent on the data source, more flexible, and uses a textual data format instead of binary. Textual formatted data is more verbose than binary formatted data, which makes it comparably larger. However, textual data does improve the ease of transportation through disconnected networks, flexibility, and speed. Because ADO.NET is based on XML, it only requires that a managed provider serve up the data in XML. Once you write your data access code, you will only need to change a few parameters to connect to a different data source.

Remoting

Remoting, as the name suggests, is simply the process of accessing data and applications that are remotely located. Under Visual Studio 6.0, this was accomplished using DCOM (Distributed Component Object Model) and MTS (Microsoft Transaction Server). XML is ADO.NET's foundation for remoting. XML and HTML together can be used to create services based on SOAP (Simple Object Access Protocol). Remoting uses the HTTP protocol to communicate.

Maintaining State

ADO.NET uses a connectionless, XML document methodology to handle data access. This means that it connects to the data source, retrieves the information, then disconnects. It does not stay connected between operations. However, this means that maintaining state is not optional when using the DataSet object. When you populate the DataSet, we are retrieving a populated XML document that is a copy of the data stored in the original data source.

You can create a DataSet at application startup and populate it with DataTables that we can use to populate drop-down boxes, list boxes, and other components in our application without having to access the database each time the list needs populating. If you simply add some code to refresh the cache after an update, you will have an in-memory database that we can use to ease the burden on the database server.

Managed Providers

Managed providers are written specifically for a particular database. System.Data.SqlClient is an example of a managed provider that is written specifically for access to Microsoft SQL Server. This provider takes advantage of SQL Server in ways that are unique to Microsoft SQL Server. It is written to use the SQL Server API directly and is thus more efficient than using the more generic providers.

Connection

Connections in ADO.NET are somewhat different than under ADO in Visual Basic 6.0. You simply dimension and instantiate a Connection object, set a connection string and that is all.

Command

The Command objects allow you to execute statements directly against the database. These objects are OleDbCommand and SqlCommand. They provide for a simple and direct route to your data, regardless of where the data resides. If you need to get the return value of a stored procedure, the Command object is the appropriate object to use. Here is an example using a Command object:

```
Dim strSql as String = "SELECT * FROM Orders"
Dim sConn as String = "Provider=SQLOLEDB.1;" & _
        "Password=password;" & _
        "Persist Security Info=True;" & _
        "User ID=sa;" & _
        "Initial Catalog=Northwind;" & _
        "Data Source=localhost"
Dim MyConnection = New OleDbConnection(sConn)
Dim MyCmd as OleDbCommand = New OleDbCommand(strSql,
 myOleDbConnection)
```

Command objects are useful for database operations that do not require records to be returned. They also provide the developer with an object to use for parameterized stored procedures.

Member Name	Description
Input	This parameter is an input parameter. It allows for data to be passed into the command, but not out. You can have more than one.
Output	This parameter is an output parameter. It is used to return variables, but cannot be used to pass data into a command. You can have more than one.
InputOutput	The parameter is capable of both input and output. It is used when we need to pass data into and out of a command in one object. It performs both the input and the output operations. You can have more than one.
ReturnValue	The parameter represents a return value. This is similar to the output parameter, except that you can only have one.

DataReader

The DataReader is a read-only, forward-scrolling Data object that allows you to gain access to rows in a streaming fashion. It is typically used when we need read-only access to data because it is much faster than using a DataSet. A DataSet is populated behind the scenes using a DataReader, so if you do not require the features of a DataSet, you should not create one. A DataReader is created either from the OLE DB libraries or from the SqlClient libraries. Here is a simple example of creating an OleDbData-Reader from a Command object:

```
Dim rReader as OleDbDataReader = myCmd.ExecuteReader()
```

That is all that is required; you now have a populated DataReader object. Here is an example of using that DataReader:

```
While rReader.Read
    '// do some row level data manipulation here
End While
```

The DataReader object allows for much greater speed, especially if you need to access a large amount of data. However, it does not allow us to update information, nor does it allow us to store information as the DataSet object does. This means that for all its speed and ease of use, it has severe limitations.

DataSet

A DataSet is an in-memory copy of a portion of the database. This may be one table or many tables. A good way to envision this is to picture a small relational database stored in a variable. This is a complete copy of the requested data, but it is completely disconnected from the original data.

When you have completed your various operations, the entire DataSet is submitted to the data source for processing. It handles all the standard data processing such as updating, deleting, and inserting records. The DataSet object is an integral part in the ADO.NET object model. A DataSet holds a copy of the data you request.

DataSets are populated from a DataReader implicitly. ADO.NET creates a DataReader and populates the DataSet for you. You are not required to do any manual coding to cause this to happen. The DataSet will temporarily hold data until you pass it along in the form of a DataTable or DataView.

Disconnected Layer

ADO.NET operates in a disconnected mode. This means that it does not maintain a connection to the data source. It will open a connection, retrieve the data, and then close the connection. This allows the data source to free up resources and respond to the next user. This feature is particularly useful for high-traffic database servers.

State of Data

When we change data, ADO.NET maintains the various states and versions of our data as we manipulate it. This allows you to perform a variety of validation operations based on previous values since the last AcceptChanges call. As data is added, updated, or deleted in our application, you can access the versions of the data, display it to the user, and give them undo functionality. It is important to note that this is available until we accept the changes and send them back to the data source.

A table is comprised of DataRow objects. The DataRow objects allow access to the entire row of data. You also have versioning capability built into the row.

Member Name	Description
Default	Default values for a row that was added.
Original	Values in the DataTable are added to the data set.
Proposed	Data that has been added or updated, but has not yet been committed.
Current	Current data in the row as of the last time the row was committed.

In addition to row versions, you also have a RowState property that can give you more information about the condition of a row.

Member Name	Description
Unchanged	No changes since last AcceptChanges call.
New	The row was added to the table, but AcceptChanges has not yet been called.
Modified	A change has been made, but AcceptChanges has not yet been called.
Deleted	The Delete method was used to delete the row from the table.
Detached	The row has either been deleted but AcceptChanges has not been called, or the row has been created but not added to the table. In either case, the row is not currently associated with the table.

In addition to providing the user with the capability to undo changes, this type of versioning allows you to more easily enforce business rules. You can return to a previous state if an attempted operation would violate some business rule that has been established. This versioning capability was not present in previous versions of Visual Basic.

Populating Programmatically

You can create a DataTable object and populate it directly with VB.NET code. You can construct an empty DataTable, and then, using the DataTable methods, populate a DataTable without having to connect to a database. In short, this table is used to hold local data, not data from an external database.

Summary

This chapter took you much deeper into the architecture of ADO.NET and showed you how to work with ADO.NET independently of the data-bound techniques discussed in Chapter 5. I showed you the essential concepts of the underlying architecture supporting ADO.NET and worked through a few examples illustrating how you might use ADO.NET to solve your database access problems. Frankly, hobbyist programmers might choose to ignore the details of the ADO.NET architecture, but professionals cannot.

Review Questions

1. What is a DataSet?

2. Does ADO.NET stay connected to the data source?

3. What is the underlying technology behind ADO.NET?

4. What protocols support remoting in ADO.NET?

5. What is used to populate a DataSet?

6. Is data in ADO.NET stored in binary or text format?

7. Until _____ has been executed, it is possible to return to a previous data state.

8. What is the best object for executing stored procedures?

9. What type of data providers are written explicitly for a particular database?

Web Development with VB.NET

Introduction

In the first seven chapters I've shown you the essentials of developing Windows applications. These applications are designed to run on a single client machine. However, this is not all that Visual Basic.NET is able to do for you. It can also help you develop Web-based applications. This chapter is intended to show you how to use Visual Basic.NET as a development tool for Web applications. The primary way to develop Web pages with Visual Basic.NET is through the use of ASP.NET. ASP (Active Server Pages) was first introduced in Visual Basic 6.0, but the .NET version is much easier to use and offers a great deal of functionality.

Web forms are a part of ASP.NET that make Web development relatively easy. They integrate HTML with server-side and client-side programming logic. Web form applications run equally well in either MS Internet Explorer or Netscape. Web forms will automatically determine the client's browser type and create the appropriate client-side code for that browser.

Web form components are server-side components that provide the user interface as well as programmatic functionality. "Server-side" refers to objects that reside on the Web server and are run on the Web server.

"Client-side" refers to objects that run on the client's machine in their browser. Web form components are different from Windows components in that they are designed to work with ASP.NET. Web form components even have built-in data validation capabilities.

Technological Background

Before I show you how to create Web pages using ASP.NET, it would probably be a good idea to give you an overview of the technologies involved. It will be important for you to understand the problems that ASP.NET is designed to solve, and how it goes about solving them.

The following definitions will be very helpful if you don't have a strong Web development background:

HTTP	Hypertext Transfer Protocol. This is the protocol that is used to transmit Web pages.
HTML	Hypertext Markup Language. This is the language used to write Web pages.
Script	Mini programs, or scripts, can be inserted into HTML to add functionality to otherwise static HTML pages. Popular server-side scripting languages include CGI and Perl. Popular client-side scripting languages include JavaScript and VBScript.
XML	Extensible Markup Language. This is a markup language, quite similar to HTML. It is much more versatile and has become a de facto standard for e-commerce development.
Distributed Applications	These are applications that have components residing in different locations. All the components work together to accomplish the goals of the application.
Firewall	A device that provides a barrier between your network and the outside world.

Web services are a technology that facilitates distributing Web applications across the Internet. Web services are object-based components that use XML and HTTP. This means they are using the standard Internet communication protocols already in place, which means that there will be no need to make any changes to your network in order to implement them. Web services are based on open Internet standards and are able to communicate with components that reside on different operating systems, regardless of what programming languages they are written in.

Another very useful feature of .NET is the ability to use a Windows form as a client-side user interface in a distributed application. This literally means that you can create a rich and dynamic user interface as easily as you create a user interface in a standard Windows Forms project. This is a great advantage: in fact, if I had to list the five best things about .NET this would certainly make my list. If you have used traditional technologies, such as cascading style sheets, to create dynamic Web-based user interfaces, you are aware how tedious this process can be. Web forms make the design of the user interface a simple matter of placing the correct components on the form.

Web Forms

Web forms bring the rapid application development capabilities of Visual Basic to Web applications. Web forms allow you to create Web applications the same way Windows forms are used for Windows applications.

Web forms have their own components, called Web controls. These are very similar to Windows components; however, Web controls are more limited than their Windows counterparts. For example, some of the events found in Windows form controls, such as mouse events, do not exist in Web components.

The integrated development environment (IDE) for Web forms is quite similar to that for Windows forms. However, there are some differences you should take note of. The first item you should note is that the design area does not have a form window. It simply has a blank Web page with a white background and two tabs (labeled Design and HTML) at the bottom. The HTML tab allows you to view and edit the HTML code for the page. Assuming you have some experience with HTML, you will be able to manually edit the HTML code that is generated for you. (Appendix D is a brief introduction to basic HTML.)

On the Design tab you can set two options: absolute positioning (grid layout) and flow layout. Flow layout is the default layout. You can change the layout by using the PageLayout property in the Properties dialog box. The difference between flow layout and grid layout is that in flow layout, the control is dropped where the cursor is currently positioned, whereas in grid layout, the control is placed in the exact x,y position, much like in Windows forms.

With this background, it's time to write a simple Web page using Web forms.

A Simple Web Form

Now that we have discussed the background and the technology behind Web forms, I think it is time we create our first Web form project. Note that for Web projects you will need to have some Web server operating on your PC. You can use the Microsoft Personal Web Server if you wish. Windows 2000 Professional comes with IIS (Internet Information Services), a built-in Web server. In either case, you must have a Web server that supports FrontPage extensions and it must be running when you attempt to create Web form applications.

> **Note:** To use the example included in the downloadable files, it will have to be in the wwwroot directory of your Web server. For IIS, this is in C:\Inetpub\wwwroot.

Example 8-1

1. Start a new project. Choose **ASP.NET Web Application**.

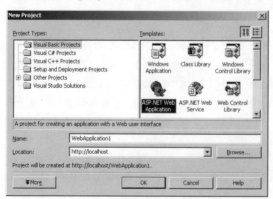

2. Depending on your processor speed and RAM it may take several seconds to create the initial Web application. Once it is created, you will see a screen like this one:

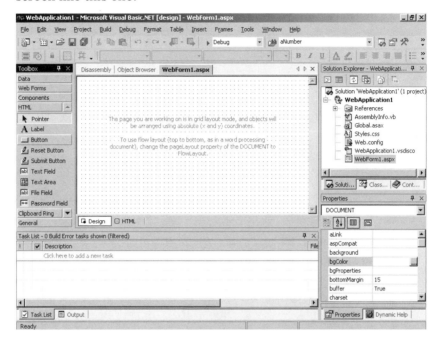

As you can see, you have access to many of the same components you might use in a standard Windows Forms application. If you click on the HTML button in the toolbox, you will be presented with components that are, in actuality, standard HTML objects.

3. For this example we are going to create a project using only HTML elements. Place a label on the form and change some of its style properties. When you click on the Style property in the Properties window you are presented with a plethora of choices as shown in the illustration at the top of the following page.

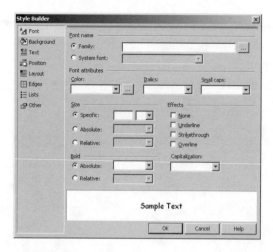

4. Set this label to use a large blue font. Place the text **VB.Net is cool!** in the label.

5. Place a text field and a button on the form and set their properties as follows: Set the text field's max length property to **20**. This limits the number of characters that can be typed in. Set the tab index to **1**. Change its value to **Enter Your Name**. The last thing to do with the text field is to right-click on it and choose **Run as server control**.

    Change the button's Value property to **Click Me** and its tab index to **2**. Right-click on the button and choose the **Run as server control** option.

    This will allow you to write standard Visual Basic code in the button's Click event which will be executed on the server side. The rest of the page will still be HTML code that will run on the client side.

    Next, change one of the form's properties. Set its background to the **wware.jpg** image included with the downloadable files. At this point, your form should look something like the following picture.

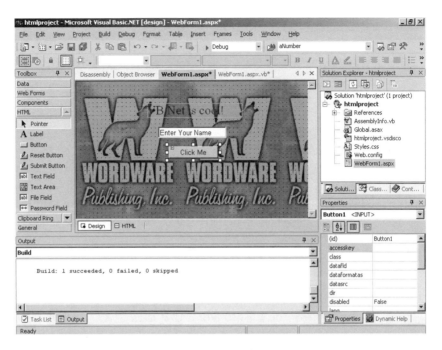

6. Now, put some code into that button's Click event.

```
Dim strName as String
strName = Text1.Value
Text1.Value = "Hello " & strName
```

When you click the button, the text field will change to say hello to you. Visual Basic has actually generated all of the HTML code you need. If you click on the HTML tab, you will see the following code:

```
<% Page Language="vb" AutoEventWireup="false"
Codebehind="WebForm1.aspx.vb" Inherits="htmlproject.WebForm1"%>
<!DOCTYPE HTML PUBLIC "-//W3C//DTD HTML 4.0 Transitional//EN">
<HTML>
  <HEAD>
    <title></title>
    <meta name="GENERATOR" content="Microsoft Visual Studio.NET 7.0">
    <meta name="CODE_LANGUAGE" content="Visual Basic 7.0">
    <meta name=vs_defaultClientScript content="JavaScript">
    <meta name=vs_targetSchema content="http://schemas.microsoft.com/
        intellisense/ie5">
  </HEAD>
  <body MS_POSITIONING="GridLayout" background=file:///C:\Inetpub\
      wwwroot\WebApplication1\wware.jpg>
```

```
        <form id="Form1" method="post" runat="server">
<DIV
style="DISPLAY: inline; FONT-SIZE: large; Z-INDEX: 101; LEFT: 137px;
WIDTH: 185px; COLOR: blue; POSITION: absolute; TOP: 42px; HEIGHT: 21px"
ms_positioning="FlowLayout">VB.Net is cool!</DIV>
<INPUT
style="Z-INDEX: 102; LEFT: 158px; WIDTH: 132px; POSITION: absolute;
TOP: 86px; HEIGHT: 21px"
tabIndex=1 type=text maxLength=20 size=16 value="Enter Your Name" id=Text1
name=Text1 runat="server">
<INPUT id=Button1 style="Z-INDEX: 103; LEFT: 178px; WIDTH: 96px; POSITION:
absolute; TOP: 123px; HEIGHT: 23px" tabIndex=2 type=button value="Click
Me" name=Button1 runat="server">
    </form>
  </body>
</HTML>
```

Now, I will be the first to admit that this is very trivial. However, this simple example illustrates some important points about VB.NET's Web development capabilities. To begin, with you can write HTML code, including server-side components, without knowing much about HTML (for more details on HTML, see Appendix D). Even if you don't understand any of the HTML code this example generated, you can still write Web applications. In my opinion this is one of the most useful features of VB.NET, though I would still recommend you acquire at least a cursory knowledge of HTML. The other point this example should have illustrated to you is that the HTML components can be manipulated via properties in much the same way as standard Windows components. With that in mind, I would like to introduce you to the most commonly used HTML components and explain their properties.

HTML Components

Button

The HTML button is used in much the same way as a standard Windows Forms button. You click it to have some action take place. In HTML, the possible actions are more limited than in a Windows form and the properties you can set are also somewhat limited. The following table summarizes the major properties of the HTML button that you can use in VB.NET.

Property	Description
Datafld	Used to determine what field from the data source will be displayed.
Data format	Used to determine the format of the data displayed.
Datasrc	Used to designate a standard data source for this button.
Disabled	Determines whether or not this button is able to be used.
Name	The name of the button.
Style	This allows you to set a variety of font properties that will be used when displaying the button's Value property.
Tab index	The tab order for this button.
Value	This is the caption displayed on the button. It is the same as the Text property in a standard Windows button.

Note: The Submit and Reset buttons are just special cases of the button.

Text Field

The text field behaves much like the text box in a standard Windows form. It is used to allow the user to input information. It can also be used to allow you to display information to the user. In my Web development experience, the text field and the button have been the two HTML form components that I have used the most. The table below summarizes the major properties of the HTML text field.

Property	Description
Datafld	Used to determine what field from the data source will be displayed.
Data format	Used to determine the format of the data displayed.
Datasrc	Used to designate a standard data source for this text field.
Disabled	Indicates whether or not this text field can be used.
MaxLength	The maximum number of characters that can be entered into the text field. This is very useful in making sure that the user does not enter too much information.
Name	The name of the text field.
Size	The size of the text field.

Property	Description
Style	This allows you to set a variety of font properties that will be used when displaying the text field Value property.
Tab index	The tab order for this text field.
Value	This is the caption displayed in the text field. It is the same as the Text property in a standard Windows text box.

Note: The Password field is merely a special case of the text field. It works just like the text field except that the user will only see some character such as an asterisk appear when they type in text.

Text Area

The text area is much like the text field, except that it is usually used for entering longer blocks of information. The text field is appropriate for having a user enter information such as their name, e-mail address, or any data that uses only a few words. The text area is for lengthy data, even a few paragraphs worth of text. The following table summarizes the primary properties of the text area.

Property	Description
Datafld	Used to determine what field from the data source will be displayed.
Data format	Used to determine the format of the data displayed.
Datasrc	Used to designate a standard data source for this text area.
Disabled	Determines whether or not this text area can be used.
MaxLength	The maximum number of characters that can be entered into the text area. This is very useful in making sure that the user does not enter too much information.
TrightName	The name of the text area.
Read Only	Determines if the text area is editable or not.
Rows	The number of rows that the text area will have.
Style	This allows you to set a variety of font properties that will be used when displaying the text area Value property.
Size	The size of the text field.
Tab index	The tab order for this text area.

Property	Description
Value	The text displayed in the text area.
Wrap	Determines if text will be wrapped to the next line and how it will be wrapped.

Table

Those readers who have done any HTML coding will be intimately familiar with the table. The table works much as it does in any word processing software. It allows you to organize data into clearly defined areas and makes your Web page much more readable. The HTML table is very flexible and has a number of properties you can set. Remember that in any cell in the table you can place any valid HTML code, including an image, button, or even another table. The following table provides you with a brief description of the most important properties of a table.

Property	Description
Background	If you wish to use an image as the background for your table, this property will allow you to set an image.
Bgcolor	This property allows you to set the background color of your table. Note that if you set a background image, it will override the background color you set.
Border color	The color of the border of your table.
Cell padding	Determines how thick the padding on the individual table cells are.
Cell spacing	Determines the spacing between adjacent cells.
Cols	Sets how many columns your table has.
Rules	Determines if there are rule lines and where to place them.
Style	Allows you to set a number of font settings.
Tab index	Determines the tab order of your table.
Title	This is the title that appears at the top of the table.
Width	This property determines how wide the table will be.

Image

I, for one, cannot imagine creating a Web site that does not display images. The HTML image control works very much like the standard picture box. It allows you to display an image on your Web form and to set the parameters of how that image will be displayed. This table summarizes some of the more commonly used properties of the image control.

Property	Description
Align	Determines the alignment of the image.
Alt	Allows you to set some text to display if, for some reason, the image does not.
Border	Allows you to set the border of the image.
Datafld	Used to determine what field from the data source will be displayed.
Data format	Used to determine the format of the data displayed.
Datasrc	Used to designate a standard data source for the image.
Height	Sets the height of the image.
Hspace	Sets a buffer space horizontally on the image.
Ismap	Determines if this image is an image map (i.e., different parts of the image map to different links).
Lowsrc	Allows you to set a smaller image to display for those users who have a slower connection.
Src	Lets you set the standard source for your image.
Tab index	Determines the tab order of your image.
Title	Allows you to set a title to display with your image.
Usemap	Allows you to set a map to use.
Vspace	Allows you to establish a vertical buffer zone around your image.
Width	Allows you to determine the width of your image.

I am certain you will utilize this HTML component frequently if you develop any Web applications at all.

List Box

This component is almost identical in purpose and function to the standard Windows list box. It is used to display a list of items and to respond when the user clicks on one of them. The following table summarizes the most important properties of this component.

Property	Description
Align	Determines the alignment of the list box.
Datafld	Used to determine what field from the data source will be displayed.
Data format	Used to determine the format of the data displayed.
Datasrc	Used to designate a standard data source for this list box.
Disabled	Whether or not this list box can be used.
Multiple	Determines whether or not the user can select multiple items from the list.
Selected index	Tells you what item is currently selected.
Size	Determines the size of the list box.
Tab index	Determines the tab order of the list box.
Title	Allows you to set a title for your list box.

The list box is a very useful HTML component. The combo box is simply a list box that initially appears as a single text field with an arrow on the right side. When the user clicks on that arrow, the other options drop down.

Check Box

The HTML check box is very much like the standard Windows check box. It allows the user to make multiple selections. This component is ideal when you want the user to select one or more options from a list of possible choices. This next table shows you the most commonly used properties of the check box.

Property	Description
Checked	Determines if the check box is checked or not.
Datafld	Used to determine what field from the data source will be displayed.

Property	Description
Data format	Used to determine the format of the data displayed.
Datasrc	Used to designate a standard data source for this check box.
Disabled	Determines whether or not this check box can be used.
Name	Used in code to refer to this particular check box.
Style	Allows you to set the various font properties of the check box.
Tab Index	Allows you to set the tab order of the check box.
Value	Whether or not the user has checked the box.

The radio button is very much like the check box, except that the user can only select one option. This is very useful if you wish the user to make a single, unique selection from several choices.

Form

Just as you can set the properties of the various HTML components, you can also set the properties for the HTML document itself. These properties allow you to alter the form's appearance and behavior. The following table summarizes the most important properties of the form.

Property	Description
Alink	Determines what color active links are displayed in on this page.
Background	Sets a background image for the document.
Bg color	Sets a background color for the document. Note that if you also set a background image, the image will override this color.
Bg properties	Determines if the background is fixed or not.
Charset	Determines what character set to use with this document.
Default client script	Sets what scripting language to use by default with this Web document.
Description	Provides a description of the Web document.
Error Page	Sets an error page to display when errors occur.
Keywords	Allows various search engines to find and list your Web site.
Link	Sets the color of links on the page.

Property	Description
Page Layout	Setting the page layout style to either grid or flow will determine how components are arranged and displayed on the Web page.
Show Grid	Allows you to either show or hide the grid.
Target Schema	Optimizes the HTML code generated for either Internet Explorer or for Netscape.
Title	Sets the title that will appear in the top of the browser when this page is displayed.
VLink	Determines what color visited links will have.

The HTML components I have just covered are by no means all of the components available. They are the most commonly used, and with them you can create some very impressive Web applications. So far, I have concentrated only on HTML components. These are components that you could make and utilize with standard HTML. Personally, I think that if this is all VB.NET has to offer to Web development, it is still quite useful. However, we have just begun to scratch the surface.

You can also utilize Web form components. Web form components, unlike HTML, actually run on the Web server. They do not run on the client's machine. With Web form components you can use standard Visual Basic code. Let's look at an example that uses Web form components and HTML form components in conjunction.

Example 8-2

In this project, I would like to combine some standard HTML form elements with some server-side Web form elements. I believe that this will illustrate to you the true power of ASP.NET.

1. Start a new ASP.NET Web application project.

2. Change the form's bgcolor to **white** and its Title to **Web Form**.

3. Place an HTML table on the form and set its Title to **VB.NET Features**. Also set its bgcolor to **gray**, its Cols property to **2**, and its border color to **blue**. In each of the cells of the table, list one feature of VB.NET (you do this by simply clicking once in the cell then typing.

4. Place a label above the table. Set the label's text to **VB.NET**, its background to **light blue**, its border to **ridge**, and its border color to **blue**.

Also, set its ToolTip property to **VB.NET is pretty cool**. At this point, your form should look like the image you see here.

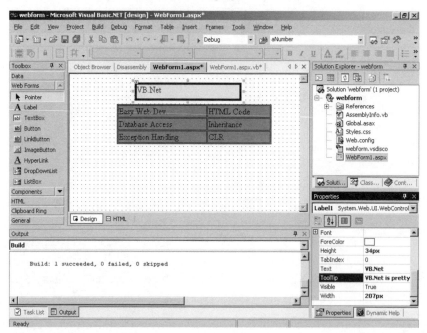

5. Place a hyperlink Web form control on the form. Set its Text property to **My Home Page**, its ToolTip property to **Click here to go to my home page**, and its Navigate URL property to **http://www.chuckeasttom.com**.

This simple example should illustrate several key points about Web forms. First, you can combine standard HTML elements with server-side Web form elements. It is also important, however, to note that what you will be able to accomplish with this depends a great deal on the Web server software you use. Microsoft development tools work best with Microsoft Web servers. I recommend you utilize Microsoft's Internet Information Server with Web form applications.

ASP.NET vs. Windows Forms

Now that you have had an opportunity to experiment a bit with Web forms, it might be a good idea to compare how Web form applications differ from standard Windows applications. There are several areas in which Web form functionality differs from standard Windows forms functionality:

■ Operating Systems — All clients in Windows forms require the .NET framework. Web forms require only a browser, so they can be utilized on any client platform. Of course, the Web server must be running the .NET framework.

■ Resources — Forms are resource-intensive clients, so they rely on the client processor. Web forms are usually thin clients and thus their clients don't have to use high-performance machines since much of the work is concentrated on the server.

■ Speed — Since Web forms run on a server, the client must communicate with that server. That makes response time somewhat slower than with standard Windows applications.

■ Deployment — Since Windows forms run on the client machine, they need to be installed on all user desktops. As the users grow in number, with each new release, the deployment becomes more tedious. Web forms have no client deployment at all. The client requires only a browser to utilize the application. This makes updates very easy.

The primary difference between Web forms and Windows forms is the difference between client/server applications and Web applications. There are arguments to be made for both application development approaches. Fortunately, VB.NET provides you with both technologies.

Web Forms vs. Traditional ASP

Whether you have used VB 6.0 Active Server Pages or not, it may be useful for you to know how traditional ASP compares to ASP.NET. ASP.NET makes it much easier to create Web applications. The basic syntax of traditional ASP is essentially compatible with ASP.NET. However, the underlying architecture has been completely changed to take advantage of the .NET framework. ASP.NET pages are compiled using the Common Language Runtime (CLR). This means that you can use any .NET-compatible language you prefer, including Visual Basic, C#, or JScript.NET.

If you have ever developed applications using traditional ASP, you should be familiar with its limitations. ASP.NET addresses all of these limitations and provides a greatly simplified development environment. The following list summarizes some of the more important differences between ASP.NET and traditional ASP.

- Performance — Since ASP.NET is compiled to CLR, it can take advantage of early binding and JIT (just-in-time) compiling, thus having significant performance gains over traditional ASP's interpreted code.

- Simplicity — ASP.NET makes it easy to perform many common tasks including form submission, client authentication, and site configuration.

- Strong typed language — ASP.NET uses Visual Basic as the programming language rather than VBScript, which supports only the Variant data type. This means that ASP.NET can utilize various data types.

- Event-driven model — ASP.NET supports an event-driven model, just like standard Visual Basic, thus eliminating the need to write extensive segments of code simply to determine which component the user has interacted with.

- State management — ASP.NET provides relatively easy-to-use Application and Session states. In ASP, the Session state resides in the memory of the server. ASP.NET uses a dedicated state server process that runs as a Windows NT service. This state server listens on a port (default port 42424).

- Configuration — ASP.NET uses an XML file to store configuration settings rather than depending on the IIS metabase.

- Web services — ASP.NET allows you to expose your business functions to your business partners over standard Web protocols. This is very important for multi-tiered applications that wish one or more tiers to be accessed via the Internet.

- Security — ASP.NET provides authorization and authentication services in addition to the services provided by IIS. ASP.NET takes the responsibility from you to authenticate and authorize users stored in a database or in a file. Users can be authenticated and authorized using CookieAuthenticationModule and URLAuthorizationModule, which sets a cookie that contains the user authorization and is checked during any subsequent logon attempts.

- Deployment — Deployment of VB.NET Web applications is very simple. You just copy the files to any server supporting .NET. This is because all the configuration settings of the site are in an XML file.

- Compatibility — ASP.NET is backward compatible. This means you can place your ASP.NET solutions on the same server as traditional ASP solutions without any conflict.

Data-bound Web Forms

So far, I have just shown you simple applications you can do with ASP.NET. However, most business applications will, at some level, involve databases. The good news is that you can use database connections and data-bound components in Web forms in much the same way you used them in standard Windows forms. If you need a refresher in how to use the data connection tools available to you, I suggest you reread Chapter 5.

Example 8-3

We are going to create a simple data-bound Web application. For this example, I will be using the small database created in Chapter 5.

1. Start a new application of the type ASP.NET Web Application.

2. Place an OLEDBDataAdapter on the form. This will launch the connection wizard. The steps you follow to connect to the database are the same ones we used in Chapter 5, but I will summarize them here:

    a. On the second screen (immediately after the introduction) choose a connection. If you do not have a previous connection, then use the New Connection button to establish a new one.

    b. Select the **Use SQL Statements** option.

    c. Use the query builder to select all fields from the data source.

3. Select the OLEDBAdapter. This will cause several options to display in the bottom of the Properties window. Click the **Generate DataSet** option. You will then have a dataset you can bind components to.

4. In the toolbox, select **Web Form** so that you can view Web form components. Place a data-bound grid on the form. Set its data source property to the dataset you just created.

That is literally all it takes to create simple database applications on the Web. The ease of displaying data on the Web is a very strong feature of VB.NET—one which I am quite certain you will use frequently.

Web Services

With the advent of the next generation of the Internet, the Internet is no longer used just to display graphical interfaces to user. Now it is also used as a bridge between many applications, such as the business-to-business (B2B) marketplace and e-procurement. Programmable Web site companies can expose their software as a service over the Internet to their business partners and even customers. Such services are called Web services.

A Web service is a component that provides service to a consumer, who uses standard Internet protocols (HTTP, XML) to access these services. These Web services are the custom business components that have no user interface and are meant to be utilized by other applications, rather than directly by users. These are somewhat similar to the ActiveX DLLs that were developed with Visual Basic 6.0. However, Web services, as the name implies, work over the Internet. Any client application that understands HTTP and XML can use Web services. Because Web services use HTTP, they are firewall friendly and have tremendous advantages over the previous distributed technology DCOM (Distributed Component Object Model). One scenario that comes to mind is using Web services to calculate sales tax for an e-commerce application. This application requires maintaining tables for calculating tax and frequently upgrading the data received from the vendor. Instead, if the vendor makes this a Web service accessible over the Internet, it can be accessed easily from anywhere in the world, and any updates can be done in a single location.

How Web Services Work

Web services are programmable components that can be accessed over the Internet using standard Internet protocols. They use XML and Simple Object Access Protocol (SOAP) to communicate with client applications. XML provides a standardized language to exchange data in a format commonly used throughout the IT industry. SOAP is a lightweight protocol based on XML that runs over HTTP. It is used for exchanging information in a distributed environment. In other words, SOAP is a technology based on XML and HTTP working in conjunction.

The basic architecture of Web services is rather simple. The client application sends requests to the Web service over the Internet using the SOAP message format. Once the request arrives, the Web server (usually IIS) that is listening on TCP port 80 routes the request to the ASP.NET handler. ASP.NET, in turn, locates the Web service, creates the business component, and calls the specified method in the object, passing it the data. This business component processes the request and, if necessary, gets data from the database or from other Web services. It then returns results to ASP.NET. The data is then packaged in a SOAP envelope and sent back to the client application. On the client application side, .NET provides a proxy class that converts this SOAP message to a data type. This proxy class also packages the request into a SOAP envelope and sends it to the Web service. SOAP is the default communication protocol for Web services. However, Web services can also be accessed using HTTP-GET and HTTP-POST protocols.

When using Visual Studio.NET to create and utilize Web services, you do not need an in-depth knowledge of the supporting architecture. The .NET framework handles all the underlying processing without your having to directly write code for it. You can create and consume Web services without any in-depth knowledge of XML or SOAP.

Summary

In this chapter, I have shown you how to create basic HTML solutions, and Web form solutions using ASP.NET. I have also shown you how to connect to a database and display data on the Web. The good news is that even all of the material in this chapter is just an introduction to what you can do with ASP.NET. There are a number of books that go into great depth on how to properly and effectively utilize ASP.NET in order to create very innovative Web solutions.

Review Questions

1. Where do Web form components run?

2. Where do HTML form components run?

3. What operating systems can be used with ASP.NET applications?

4. What must the Web server support in order to host ASP.NET applications?

5. What is ASP?

6. What is XML?

7. List five HTML components.

8. Which is faster, a Windows Forms application or a Web Forms application?

9. Which requires more resources from the client?

10. How do you deploy an ASP.NET solution to a Web server?

Creating Custom Windows Controls

In this chapter, you learn about:

- ◆ **Modifying an existing component**

- ◆ **Compound components**

- ◆ **Creating components from scratch**

- ◆ **Components without a user interface**

- ◆ **Web controls**

Introduction

Components, in many ways, are the ultimate realization of the potential of object-oriented programming. Two principles of object-oriented programming that are of paramount importance are encapsulation and code reuse. The component completely encapsulates the code it has, with no external dependencies at all. It also can easily be reused by simply adding it to any project. For this reason, even if you do not wish to create your own components, it is important that you at least have some familiarity with how components are created.

By this point in this book, you have had an opportunity to use several different components. However, you may have found that some don't do everything you would like them to. You may have also wished for some functionality that no component provides. Well, there is an answer to your dilemma. You can create your own components that can then be reused by any VB.NET programmer. There are basically three ways to create a component:

- Extend or modify an existing component
- Create a compound component from two or more existing components
- Create a brand new component from scratch

Modifying an Existing Component

One way to create a new component is to inherit from an existing component and then modify it. For example, let's consider the Button component. You can create your own button to be placed in the Toolbox window. To keep it simple, I will assume that you want to create a custom control that inherits from the Button control but has a different background color and font. This is a small change, but it illustrates all the basic principles of component creation.

Example 9-1

1. Start a new project and select **Windows Control Library** for the project type.

2. Using the Properties window, change the name of your component to **MyNewButton**.

3. Place a button on the component form. Change the button's background color and font to any value you wish.

4. Your new button is basically created now, but you will have to add events and methods to it. In the left drop-down box, choose **base class**. Any events you wish to propagate down to the underlying button or that you wish to write code for will go here.

In our example, we merely want to transmit the call to a few events down to the underlying button so we will add this code:

```
Private Sub MyNewButton_Click(ByVal sender as Object, ByVal e as
        System.EventArgs) Handles MyBase.Click
    Button1_Click(sender, e)
End Sub
Private Sub MyNewButton_Resize(ByVal sender as Object, ByVal e as
    System.EventArgs) Handles MyBase.Resize
    Button1_Resize(sender, e)
End Sub
```

5. Now our task is relatively simple. You compile the new component. Then start a new Windows Forms project and use this component to test it. You can also go to the File menu and add a new project. The new project should be a Windows Forms project. Then go to the Project Explorer window and right-click on the name of the new project and choose **Set as start up project**.

What you have just done is create a project group. This is a group of two or more projects that you have open in the same IDE. This is ideal for testing new components. Whether you use the project group or just start a brand new project, you will still be able to test your new component. In the new Windows Forms project, select **Project** and **Add reference**. You will then select the Projects tab. From here, you can select your component's project. Your new component will then be in the toolbar, and you can use it as you would any other component.

If you will notice in the code you created, the user control framework begins with "Inherits System.Windows.Forms.UserControl." This means that when you create a new component you are inheriting from the system's user control class. You have all the standard methods and properties of the default Windows component. This means that rather than starting from scratch in your component development, you start with a well-established foundation.

Background

It is important, before we proceed, to elaborate somewhat on Windows Forms components, and the creation of new components. The Windows Forms framework offers numerous components that you can use to build applications. You have already worked with many of these components and should be familiar with them. However, there are several instances where you may wish to develop your own components. In advanced applications, these components may not provide the functionality you want. Should this be the case, you can create your own components to provide exactly what you need. Or you may find that you use two or more components in tandem frequently, and decide to simply create a compound component of your own.

All of this begs the question, exactly what is a component? A *component* is a class that is completely self contained and can be used independently. Components provide reusable code in the form of objects. A component may or may not have a user interface. In previous versions of Visual Basic (and Visual C++), the components were either ActiveX controls or ActiveX DLLs. A control is a component with a user interface (such as a button), whereas a DLL is essentially a bag of functions you can utilize as if they were written in your program.

Compound Components

Compound components simply combine the functionality of two or more existing components. To create a compound control you simply take two or more existing controls, combine their features, and perhaps add some new features.

Example 9-2

1.   Open a new Windows Control Library project.

2.   Set the background image to any image you wish.

3.   In the Properties window, change the name to **SliderText**.

4.   In the Project Explorer window, locate UserControl1.vb. Right-click on it and change its name to **SliderText.vb**.

5.   On the User Control window, place a text box and a trackbar control. When you have done this, your screen should look like the image shown here:

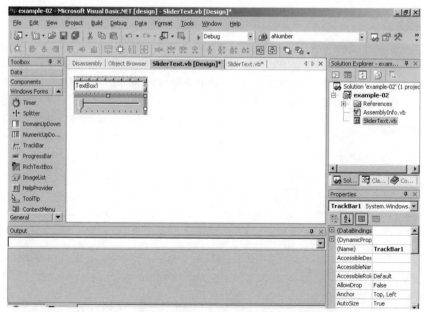

6. Now, let's put some code in a few places. In the section at the beginning of the class, just after the Inherits statement, put this variable declaration:

```
Private bFlagExtreme as Boolean
    Public Property FlagExtreme() as Boolean
        Get
            Return bFlagExtreme
        End Get
        Set(ByVal Value as Boolean)
            bFlagExtreme = Value
        End Set
    End Property
    Public Property Max() as Integer
        Get
            Return TrackBar1.Maximum
        End Get
        Set(ByVal Value as Integer)
            TrackBar1.Maximum = Value
        End Set
    End Property
```

In the trackbar's Scroll event place this code:

```
Private Sub TrackBar1_Scroll(ByVal sender as System.Object, ByVal e as
    System.EventArgs) Handles TrackBar1.Scroll

        TextBox1.Text = TrackBar1.Value
        If bFlagExtreme = True Then
            If ((TrackBar1.Value) >= (0.9 * (TrackBar1.maximum)) Then
                TextBox1.ForeColor = Color.Red
            Else
                TextBox1.ForeColor = Color.Black
            End If
        Else
            TextBox1.ForeColor = Color.Black
        End If
    End Sub
```

In the text box's TextChanged event place the following code:

```
Private Sub TextBox1_TextChanged(ByVal sender as System.Object, ByVal e
    as System.EventArgs) Handles TextBox1.TextChanged
        TrackBar1.Value = Val(TextBox1.Text)
End Sub
Private Sub UserControl_Resize()
```

```
        Text1.Width = UserControl.Width
        Slider1.Width = UserControl.Width
End Sub
```

7. Make sure you set the anchor properties of both the text box and the trackbar. The text box should be anchored to the upper-left corner, and the trackbar to the lower-left corner.

It is now time to test your component. Make a new project that is a standard Windows form application, or you can add a project to this group (as we did in Example 9-1). Once you have a client project to use your component, you only have to add a reference to your component in order to utilize it. Right-click **Reference** in the Project Explorer and add a reference to the component project. You should now see the SliderText in the toolbar.

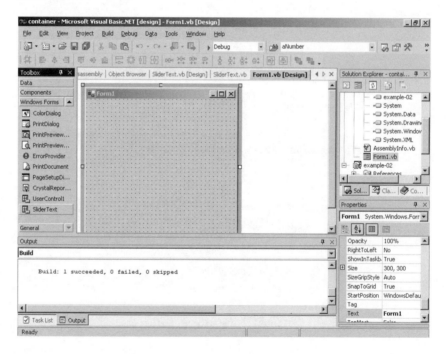

The next step is to use the component we have just created. Place the SliderText on the form.

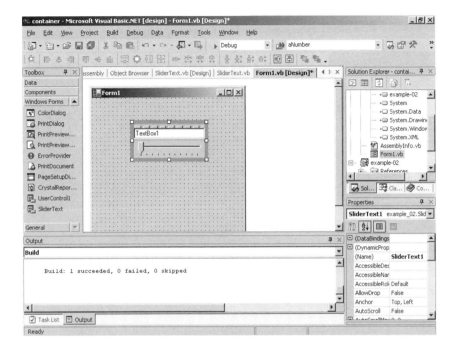

Then in the Form Load event, you need to set a few of the properties of the SliderText.

```
SliderText1.max = 50
SliderText1.flagextreme = True
```

Now you can run the application and see how the component works in action. You should be able to see that whenever you enter a number in the text box, the trackbar moves to match that value. Also, when you move the trackbar, the current value is shown in the text box. Furthermore, since we set the FlagExtreme property to true, if the value you enter is within 10% of the maximum you have set, the text turns red.

As you can see, modifying an existing component and creating a compound component are not particularly difficult and can be quite useful. The next option is to create a component from scratch.

Creating Components from Scratch

This is the most difficult way to create a component. To be honest, it is unlikely that a novice programmer will need to create components from scratch. It is hard to imagine a need for which a component does not already exist or for which an existing one could not be easily modified. However, it is important that I at least show you how this is done, should you ever have the desire.

The only real difference between creating a component from scratch and using existing components as a base is the fact that you start with nothing. By nothing I mean no pre-existing user interface, properties, or methods. However, you will still be inheriting from the System.Windows.Forms.UserControl class so you will have those default methods.

Example 9-3

This component is designed simply to show you how to create your own components, not for any direct practical value in the component itself. We are going to create a component that tells the user everything they might need to know about circles.

1. Start a new Windows Control Library project. Change the component's name to **Circle**. Change the filename to **circle.vb.**

2. We have a new problem. We have to create our own graphic user interface. You can use the Graphics class to create an image if you wish. In our case, that will be perfectly fine. We want our interface to be a circle.

    In the load event of the user control place this code:

    ```
    Dim G as Graphics
    G.DrawEllipse(New Pen(Color.Red), New Rectangle(50, 50, 100, 100))
    ```

3. Immediately after the Inherits statement at the beginning of the class, create some properties and methods for this component. You will need to place the following code at that location.

    ```
    Public Function CircleArea(ByVal Radius as Single)
        Dim Area as Single
        ' I use the math object here to get a more accurate
        ' version of pi.  I then use the math object's 'pow'
        ' method to square the radius.  The formula used here
        ' is A = pi * r^2
        Area = Math.PI * (Math.Pow(radius, 2))
    ```

```
        Return Area
    End Function
    Public Function DrawCircle(ByVal MyColor as Color)
        Dim G as Graphics
        G.DrawEllipse(New Pen(mycolor), New Rectangle(50, 50, 100, 100))
    End Function
```

4. Now, compile your component.

5. Create a new Windows form application (as you did with the first two examples) so that you can test your component.

This component is really quite simple, and probably not of much practical value. But it should illustrate two points to you. The first is that it is possible to start from scratch and to create your own components. The second point is that this is a complex process. In most cases, you will probably simply modify an existing component or you will create a compound component.

Components without a User Interface

It is possible that you will require a given piece of code to be accessible and reusable in many applications. However, you may not require any type of user interface. You may have code that will be used only by the client program. What you are describing is, in essence, a DLL, or dynamic-link library. Visual Basic 6.0 introduced the ActiveX DLL. This was a relatively easy-to-use and easy-to-create DLL. However, it was based on COM and subject to the same limitations as all other DLLs (particularly version compatibility issues). In VB.NET, you simply have a component without a visual interface. This has the same effect as a DLL, but it does not have any compatibility issues.

Example 9-4

For this example, I am going to encapsulate a number of simple conversion functions into a component. That component can then be added to any project that might need to perform any of the conversions provided.

1. Start a new Windows Control Library project.

2. Change the name of the component to **Conversion** and the filename to **convert.vb**.

3. Add the following functions immediately after the Inherits statement.

```
Private Answer as Single
Public Function KGToLB(ByVal KG as Single) as Single
    Answer = KG * 2.2
    Return Answer
End Function
Public Function LbToKG(ByVal LB as Single) as Single
    Answer = LB / 2.2
    Return Answer
End Function
Public Function CmToInch(ByVal CM as Single) as Single
    Answer = CM / 2.54
    Return Answer
End Function
Public Function InchToCM(ByVal Inch as Single) as Single
    Answer = Inch * 2.54
    Return Answer
End Function
```

At this point the component has the necessary functions. However, this is a good opportunity to introduce you to events. You will notice that all the components in your toolbox have events such as Click, Mouse Move, etc. You can create custom events for your components as well. We are going to create an event to notify the client application of any errors.

4. Immediately after the Inherits statement at the beginning of the class, place this event declaration:

```
Public Event ConvertError(Message as String)
```

Now in each of our functions add basic error handling using Try-Catch blocks. However, the Catch block will raise the event we just created. So, for example, the InchToCM function now becomes:

```
Public Function InchToCM(ByVal Inch as Single) as Single
try
    Answer = Inch * 2.54
    Return Answer
Catch
    Raiseevent ConvertError("An error occurred in the InchToCM function")
End try
End Function
```

You can create any events you like at the beginning of your class. Simply use the Public Event EventName(parameters) format. When you are ready to trigger that event simply use the RaiseEvent command. This leaves only one step—testing this component.

5. As you probably guessed, you will need a Windows Forms application to test this component. The big difference is that after you have made a reference to this component, you will not have any way to place it on a form. Instead, inside the Form class you place this code:

```
Dim MyConvert as New Conversion
```

If you want to be able to use the events created inside this component, you need to change it to:

```
Dim WithEvents MyConvert as Conversion
Set MyConvert = New Conversion
```

When you declare an object as WithEvents you will have access to its event procedures just as you have access to the events in a button or text box.

Web Controls

You probably noticed when you created a new project that there is another project option, Web Controls. Web controls are components designed specifically for use with Web applications. Web components are a bit more complex than Windows components. Their creation and function are very similar to Windows controls but with a few differences. The first is the packages that they import:

```
Imports System.ComponentModel
Imports System.Web.UI
```

The second major difference is that this component does not start with any default area for you to create the GUI portion of the component. This must be done manually.

Note: Given that this book is targeted at novice programmers, I will not be illustrating the development of a Web component. These components are more complex, and probably should not be done until you have some more experience with Visual Basic. However, I felt it was important to at least introduce you to the concept so that you would be aware of what they are.

Summary

The ability to create your own reusable components was first introduced to Visual Basic programmers, in a limited fashion, with Visual Basic 5.0. However, with VB.NET you have the ability to create any type of component that a C++ programmer might create—in short, any component you want. The creation and use of components will also give you insight into how Visual Basic works and why object orientation is such an important advance in programming. Even if you have no need to create your own components, it would be a good idea to work through the examples in this chapter, just for the educational value.

Review Questions

1. List three ways to create a new control.

2. Do all components have a user interface?

3. What class do all components inherit from?

4. What two concepts of object-oriented programming do components best illustrate?

5. What COM component are non-GUI VB.NET components most like?

6. How do you declare an instance of an object so that you have access to its events?

7. How do you create a new event for your component or class?

8. How do you raise an event you have created?

9. What two packages do all Web controls import?

Console Applications

Introduction

Most of this book focuses on how to create attractive graphical applications. However, there are times when a console application is more appropriate. A console application runs from the command or DOS prompt. It has no graphical user interface. These types of applications are ideal for any of the following situations:

- The middle tier of a multitiered application
- A service running in the background
- A test application

There are several differences between a console application and a standard Windows form application. To begin with, since there is no graphical user interface, the IDE looks a bit different. You begin with a standard code module that has a Sub Main. That subroutine is the starting point for the console application. You can then create any other standard functions you wish to create.

Input and output with the user is accomplished differently. You cannot display information in labels, message boxes, etc. Instead, you use the System.console.out object's Write and WriteLine methods. To get input back from the user, use the System.console.in object's Read and ReadLine methods.

Before we dive head first into the various nuances of console applications, it might be a good idea to try a simple one.

Example 10-1

I am going to walk you through the process of creating a console application step by step. This simple console application merely converts weight given in pounds to kilograms.

1. Start a new application, and choose **Console Application**.

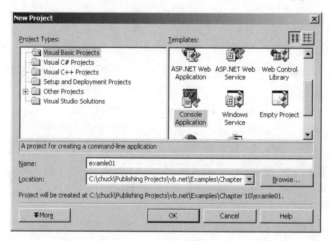

2. Place the following code in the module.

```
Sub Main()
        Dim Weight as String
        Dim LBs as Single
        Dim KG as Single
        System.Console.Out.WriteLine("What is your weight")
        Weight = System.Console.In.ReadLine()
        LBs = CSng(Weight)
        KG = Convert(LBs)
        System.Console.Out.WriteLine("Your weight in kilograms is " & KG)
        System.Console.In.ReadLine()
    End Sub
    Function Convert(ByVal LBs as Single) as Single
        Dim Answer as Single
        Answer = LBs / 2.2
        Return Answer
    End Function
```

This simple program should illustrate for you just how a console application works. If you have ever used Java or C++ to create console applications, then this should be old news to you.

As with everything else in VB.NET, console applications depend on objects and their methods. We have already seen the ReadLine and WriteLine methods used. Before we continue our examination of console applications, I would like to introduce you to the major objects involved and some of their more important methods.

Console Application Objects

Console

This object represents the console window itself. It is through subobjects and methods of this object that you will accomplish virtually everything you wish to do in a console application. This object is, in turn, a subobject of the system object. It has a variety of methods, some of which are summarized in this table.

Property	Description
Out	Encapsulates all the output functions.
In	Encapsulates all of the input functions.
Read	Reads a single character from the prompt.
Write	Writes a single character to the console prompt.
Error	Represents any errors that occur.

Note: The Console object has read and write methods that accomplish the same task as the In and Out objects' Read and Write methods.

In

The In object is used to encapsulate all input. It is very diverse in the methods it gives you for reading in data. It also has methods to assist in creating multithreaded applications.

Property or Method	Description
Close	Closes the input stream and releases any resources.
Peak	Returns the next character without actually reading it out of the input stream.
Read	Reads the next character from the input stream.
ReadLine	Reads an entire line from the input stream.
Readblock	Reads the maximum block available from the input stream.
ReadtoEnd	Reads from the current position to the end of the input stream.
Synchronize	Creates a threadsafe wrapper around the input stream.

Out

Just as the In object encapsulates all the input in your console application, so the Out object encapsulates any output. It is a flexible object that gives you a variety of methods for outputting data to the user. Like the In object, the Out object provides a method to assist in creating multithreaded applications.

Property or Method	Description
Close	Closes the output stream and releases any resources.
NewLine	Moves the cursor to the next line.
Write	Writes the next character to the output stream.
WriteLine	Writes an entire line to the output stream.
Synchronize	Creates a threadsafe wrapper around the output stream.

Error

The Error object provides you with all the information you will need to manage and handle errors that occur in your console applications. This object is flexible and quite easy to use.

Property or Method	Description
Close	Closes streams.
Flush	Flushes input/output streams of errors.
Write	Writes the current error message.

Complex Console Applications

The objects and methods discussed in the previous section are the core parts of the console object that you will need in order to make console applications. With them, you can acquire data from the user, provide output to the user, and manage errors. The code that you use to manipulate the data is the same code you would use in a standard application. You can even use classes inside console applications. Let me illustrate by giving you a more complex console application.

Example 10-2

1. Start a new application of the console type.
2. Add a class module by selecting **Project | Add Class Module**. You will then be presented with the following screen. Click **OK**.

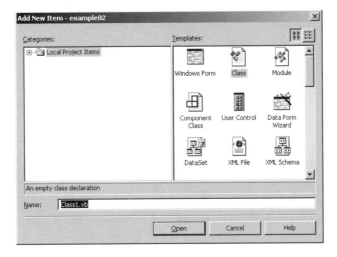

3. We are going to add several methods and properties to our class. Place the following code into your class module.

```
Public Class Class1
    Private Answer as Single
    Public Function KGToLB(ByVal KG as Single) as Single
        Answer = KG * 2.2
        Return Answer
    End Function
    Public Function LBToKG(ByVal LB as Single) as Single
        Answer = LB / 2.2
        Return Answer
    End Function
    Public Function CMToInch(ByVal CM as Single) as Single
        Answer = CM / 2.54
        Return Answer
    End Function
    Public Function InchToCM(ByVal Inch as Single) as Single
        Answer = Inch * 2.54
        Return Answer
    End Function
End Class
```

 Note: You should recognize this class from Chapter 9.

4. We will now place code into the code module.

```
Module Module1
    Private ClsConvert as New Class1()
    Sub Main()
        Make_Menu()
    End Sub
    Sub Make_Menu()
        Dim Menu as String
        Dim iMenu as Integer
        Dim Answer as Single
        Dim nResponse as Single
        Dim Response as String
        System.Console.Out.WriteLine(" ")
        System.Console.Out.WriteLine("*****Converter Menu*****")
        System.Console.Out.WriteLine("1. CM to Inches")
        System.Console.Out.WriteLine("2. Inches to CM")
        System.Console.Out.WriteLine("3. LBS to KG")
```

```vb
System.Console.Out.WriteLine("4. KG to LBS")
System.Console.Out.WriteLine("5. Exit")

Menu = System.Console.In.ReadLine
iMenu = CInt(Menu)
Select Case iMenu
    Case 1
        System.Console.Out.WriteLine("Enter CM")
        Response = System.Console.ReadLine()
        nResponse = CSng(Response)
        Answer = clsConvert.CMToInch(nResponse)
        System.Console.Out.WriteLine(nResponse & " Centimeters
            = " & Answer & " inches")
        Make_Menu()
    Case 2
        System.Console.Out.WriteLine("Enter inches")
        Response = System.Console.ReadLine()
        nResponse = CSng(Response)
        Answer = clsConvert.InchTocm(nResponse)
        System.Console.Out.WriteLine(nResponse & " inches = "
            & answer & " centimeters")
        Make_Menu()

    Case 3
        System.Console.Out.WriteLine("Enter LBs")
        Response = System.Console.ReadLine()
        nResponse = CSng(Response)
        Answer = clsConvert.lbtokg(nResponse)
        System.Console.Out.WriteLine(nResponse & " pounds = "
            & Answer & " kilograms")
        Make_Menu()

    Case 4
        System.Console.Out.WriteLine("Enter KG")
        Response = System.Console.ReadLine()
        nResponse = CSng(Response)
        Answer = clsConvert.kgtolb(nResponse)
        System.Console.Out.WriteLine(nResponse & " Kilograms =
            " & Answer & " pounds")
        Make_Menu()
    Case 5
        Return
```

Chapter 10

```
            Case Else
                System.Console.Out.WriteLine("Invalid Selection")
                Make_Menu()
        End Select
    End Sub
End Module
```

When you run this application you will see a basic menu appear in the Console window.

Viewing this code you should be aware of several issues (besides it being significantly longer than the previous console application example). The first is that we placed all of the conversion code in a class module. This illustrates one very common use for console applications—testing a class. If you have a class you are developing and wish to test its functionality, you can create a quick console application to call the various methods of the class and ensure you get the appropriate results.

The next thing I would like you to be aware of is the use of the menu function. By placing the code to create and handle the menu in a separate subroutine, I can then recall the menu each time an operation is performed. This allows the user to continue to work with the application until they press Exit. Details like this are probably something you have not encountered before when writing standard Windows applications.

Pay particular attention to the menu itself. A command-line menu where the user simply types in their choice is just about the only way to provide any dynamic interaction with the user inside a console application.

Summary

This chapter has introduced you to console applications. These are applications that work in the command prompt or DOS window (depending on the version of Windows you are using). They have a variety of purposes. After reading this chapter and working through the examples, you should be comfortable writing console applications yourself. They are actually significantly less complicated (and hence easier) than Windows applications.

Review Questions

1. What is a console application?

2. What are three uses for a console application?

3. Can you use a button in a console application?

4. Can you use a class in a console application?

5. What is the starting point for a console application?

6. How do you print to the console screen?

7. How do you receive input from the user?

8. How do you provide an interactive user interface in a console application?

Chapter

TCP/IP Programming

Introduction

TCP/IP (Transmission Control Protocol/Internet Protocol) is a suite of protocols that are used for most network and Internet communications. HTTP (Hypertext Transfer Protocol), which is used by browsers to view Web pages, is a part of the TCP/IP suite of protocols, as is FTP (File Transfer Protocol). TCP/IP is the way your computer communicates when you visit a Web page, transfer a file, or log on to the network at your job. The ubiquitous nature of TCP/IP alone makes it an important topic for study.

The way that TCP/IP communication is conducted is that the client machine creates a packet. That packet has a header section that is 20 bytes long and contains information regarding the source IP address of the packet. The header indicates the destination IP and port as well. This packet is then sent to a specific IP address and a specific port on that machine. Assuming there is some type of software listening to that port, the packet is received and the data can be extracted and processed.

Fortunately, you don't have to know many details about TCP/IP in order to write IP clients and servers in Visual Basic.NET. The Winsock component handles all the details; you simply need to access its relevant properties, methods, and events in order to send and receive TCP/IP packets.

The Winsock Control

Creating TCP/IP communications inside of Visual Basic is remarkably easy. The first step is to add the Winsock control to your project. To do this, select Project | References and add in the Winsock control:

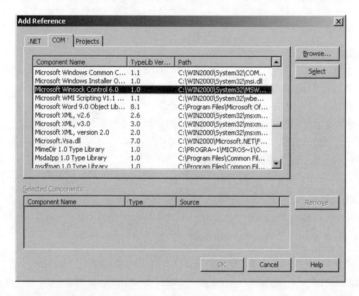

Note: Some versions of Windows did not include the Winsock.ocx. If yours does not, you may be able to obtain a copy from the Microsoft Web site.

In order for TCP/IP communications to work there needs to be a client on one machine and a server on the other. In order to make a server, you place the following code in the Form Load event of the form that has the Winsock component on it.

```
Winsock1.LocalPort = 100
Winsock1.Listen
```

I picked port 100 at random. TCP/IP ports can be anywhere from 1 to a little over 32,000. However, for custom applications, you will want to avoid certain ports, such as 21 (always used for FTP) and 80 (used for HTTP). Now what you have is a Winsock that is listening. But what do you do when someone wants to send it a packet?

In the Winsock_ConnectionRequest event place this code:

```
If Winsock1.State <> sckClosed Then _
Winsock1.Close
' Accept the request with the requestID
' parameter.
Winsock1.Accept requested
```

This allows your Winsock to accept packets from that particular TCP/IP client.

Now how do you get the data? You go to the Winsock_DataArrival event and place this code:

```
Dim strBuffer as String
Winsock1.getdata strBuffer
```

Now the entire data portion of the incoming TCP/IP packet will be placed in the string strBuffer.

> **Note:**   If you open a socket but don't close it, you will have to reboot that machine before you can use that socket again. When you are done, place a statement that closes the socket (Winsock1.close).

Now what about sending data? Well, that's pretty easy:

```
Winsock1.remoteport ' What port do you want to send it too. It has
                    ' to match the port
                    ' that the server is listening in on.
Winsock1.remoteip  ' What IP are you sending it to?
Winsock1.senddata strBuffer ' Just put your data into the string
                            ' and away it goes!
```

Example 11-1

First we will create a TCP client.

1. Start a new Windows application.

2. Add a reference to the Winsock.ocx as indicated at the beginning of this chapter.

3. Add this declaration to the beginning of the Form1 class module:

```
Dim WithEvents MyWinsock as MSWinsockLib.Winsock
```

You will now have a MyWinsock item with events in your Form1 class module.

4. On the form, place three text box components, three labels, and one button. It should look like the following:

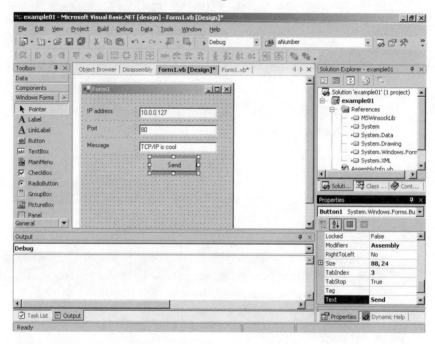

5. In the Click event of the button, place the following code.

```
' set remote ip and port to send to
MyWinsock.RemoteHost = Textbox1.Text
MyWinsock.RemotePort = Val(Textbox2.Text)
' connect
MyWinsock.Connect()
MyWinsock.SendData(Textbox3.Text)
```

To test this code you have to have a server listening. This is best done on multiple PCs. You can place the client on your PC, and the server on another. To create the server, we will have to create a second application.

Example 11-2

1. Start a new Windows application.

2. Create a reference to the Microsoft Winsock component as follows:

    a. Select **Project | Add References**.

    b. Choose the COM tab and find MSWinsock.ocx.

    c. At the beginning of the Form1 class module, place this code:

    ```
    Dim WithEvents WinsockServer as MSWinsockLib.Winsock
    ```

3. Place one text box on the form with its multiline property set to **true**.

4. Place one button on the form with its text set to **Listen**.

5. Place another text box on the form and a label identifying it as **Port** (this will be the port the server listens to).

    Your form should look like this:

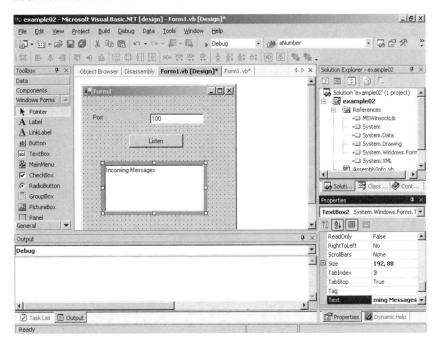

6. In the button, place this code:

    ```
    WinsockServer.LocalPort = Val(Textbox1.Text)
    WinsockServer.Listen()
    ```

7. In the Winsockserver_Connectionrequest event place this code:

```
WinsockServer.Close()
' Accept the request with the requestID
' parameter.
WinsockServer.Accept(requestID)
```

8. Finally, in the Winsockserver_Dataarrival event, place this code:

```
Dim strBuffer as String
WinsockServer.GetData(strBuffer)
Textbox2.Text = strBuffer
```

Some would say that the Winsock component is a COM component and is not, strictly speaking, VB.NET. I include this chapter on using the Winsock component for several reasons. The first is that it illustrates an important point. Even though the entire .NET architecture is moving away from COM and ActiveX, you can still use those technologies inside your VB.NET applications. I also included this section because socket programming has been an important topic in programming since the advent of Windows.

When you have a port and an IP address, and create a connection, you have created a socket. Once a socket is created, the two ends can freely pass TCP packets back and forth. Doing this in C or C++ can be quite tedious. Using the Winsock component, a Visual Basic programmer can easily set up socket communications. I have found socket communications quite useful in my professional career.

More About the Winsock

So far, I have shown you how to use the Winsock object specifically to send TCP packets. However, you can send UDP (User Datagram Protocol) packets with the Winsock. The major difference between the two protocols lies in their connection state:

- The TCP protocol control is a connection-based protocol. That means the reception of one packet is confirmed prior to sending the next packet.

- The UDP protocol is a connectionless protocol. This means that each packet is sent without confirming the receipt of the last packet. Also, the maximum data size of individual packets is determined by the network.

The nature of the application you are creating should determine which protocol you select. The following are a couple of questions that may help you select the appropriate protocol:

■ Will the application require acknowledgment from the server or client when data is sent or received? If so, the TCP protocol requires an explicit connection before sending or receiving data.

■ Is speed of transmission of great concern? Since TCP confirms the reception of each packet, it moves a bit slower.

Applications that use multimedia often use UDP. Since missing a single packet in the transmission is unlikely to even be noticeable by the user, the confirmation of each packet is unnecessary. The time lost confirming each packet would, however, be detrimental to the application's performance.

To set the protocol that your application will use, implement the following code.

```
Winsock1.Protocol = sckTCPProtocol
```

or

```
Winsock1.Protocol = sckUDPProtocol
```

UDP Applications

Creating a UDP application is even simpler than creating a TCP application because the UDP protocol doesn't require an explicit connection. In the TCP application I previously showed you, one Winsock control must explicitly be set to listen for packets, while the other must initiate a connection with the Connect method and send packets. Basically the TCP protocol requires one end to be acting as a server and the other to act as a client. In UDP applications, both sides are equal. To send data between two controls, three steps must be completed:

1. Set the RemoteHost property to the name of the other computer.

2. Set the RemotePort property to the LocalPort property of the second control.

3. Invoke the Bind method specifying the LocalPort to be used.

Because both computers can be considered "equal" in the relationship, it could be called a peer-to-peer application. To demonstrate this, the code

Chapter

11

below creates a "chat" application that allows two people to "talk" to each other in real time:

Example 11-3

1. Create a new Windows Forms application.

2. Change the name of the default form to **frmUDPA**. Change the caption of the form to **UDP Peer A**.

3. Add a reference to the Winsock object (as you did in Example 11-1).

4. Create an instance of the Winsock object:

    ```
    Dim WithEvents UDPPeer as MSWinsockLib.Winsock
    ```

5. In the Form Load event set the UDPPeer protocol to **UDP**.

6. Place two TextBox components on the form. Name the first **txtSend**, and the second **txtOutput**.

7. Add the following code:

    ```
    Private Sub Form_Load()
    ' The control's name is udpPeerA
    With UDPPeer
    ' Note be sure to change the RemoteHost value to the name of your
    computer.
        .RemoteHost= "PeerB"
        .RemotePort = 1001    ' Port to connect to.
        .Bind 1002            ' Bind to the local port.
    End With
    frmPeerB.Show             ' Show the second form.
    End Sub
    Private Sub TxtSend_Change()
    ' Send text as soon as it's typed.
    UDPPeer.SendData TxtSend.Text
    End Sub
    Private Sub UDPPeer_DataArrival (ByVal bytesTotal as Long)
    Dim strData as String
        UDPPeer.GetData strData
          TxtOutput.Text = strData
    End Sub
    ```

Remember that the primary difference between UDP and TCP is the connectionless nature of UDP. You also do not need a separate client and server as you do with TCP.

The Bind Method

In Example 11-3, we utilized the Bind method. You must invoke the Bind method when creating UDP applications. The Bind method "reserves" a local port for use by the Winsock component. For example, when you bind the control to port number 1001, no other application can use that port. This may be useful if you wish to prevent another application from using that port.

The Bind method also has an optional second argument. A machine may have more than one NIC (network interface card). If there is more than one network adapter present on the machine, the LocalIP argument allows you to specify which adapter to use. If you omit the argument, the control uses the first network adapter listed in the Network Control Panel dialog box of the computer's Control Panel Settings.

The UDP protocol allows your Winsock object to freely switch the RemoteHost and RemotePort properties while remaining bound to the same LocalPort. However, with the TCP protocol, you must close the connection before changing the RemoteHost and RemotePort properties.

Note: While it is not necessary to go beyond what I have shown you, it may prove useful for you to have more in-depth knowledge of TCP/IP and Internet communications. Even the ASP.NET that I covered in Chapter 8 depends on this protocol; it simply hides the details from you. If you are not particularly interested in obtaining more depth in your knowledge of Internet communications, feel free to skip the rest of this chapter.

OSI Model

To begin with, all communications, protocols, etc., on the Internet and on local networks take place within the framework of the OSI model. The OSI model is a model for understanding various Internet protocols, networking hardware, and networking communications. OSI stands for Open Systems Interconnection. It is the world-wide standard for networking and the Internet. The following table summarizes the OSI model's seven layers.

Chapter

Layer	Protocols	Description	Hardware
Physical		This is the actual physical connection. This is where the NIC and the cable are located.	NIC (network interface card), repeater, hub
Datalink		Interface between the Physical layer and the Network layer.	Bridge and switch
Network	IP, ARP (Address Resolution Protocol), ICMP (Internet Control Message Protocol	Divides blocks of data into segments called datapackets or datagrams.	Router, BRouter
Transport	TCP, UDP	Error checking	
Session		Responsible for establishing and maintaining a network session.	
Presentation	HTTP, SMTP, POP, IRC	Facilitates communication between Session and Application layer	
Application		Interfacing with application software	

For our purposes, it is not necessary that you become intimately familiar with the entire OSI model, or that you memorize the seven layers. However, you should note that TCP itself operates at the Transport layer while IP operates at the Network layer. Essentially this means that the packets you send and receive via Winsock are predominantly concerned with TCP and the Transport layer, whereas the address you send them to deals with the Network layer.

What is happening when you create and send a packet is that the Winsock component takes the string you pass it and divides it up into segments or packets. The number of packets depends on the size of the string. It may only send a single packet, if the data you pass to it is small enough. Each packet is given a 20-byte header. That header contains many pieces of information. It contains the IP address from which the packet is sent and the port. It also contains the destination IP address and its port. A complete address includes the IP address and the port number. In essence, the IP address tells the packet what machine to go to, and the port tells it where on that machine to connect.

It is common for people to use the same port for a particular protocol. This port is referred to as the default port for that protocol. Below is a list of protocols and their default ports, as well as a description of the protocol.

Protocol	Description	Default Port
FTP	File Transfer Protocol: used to transfer text and binary files over the Internet.	21
NNTP	Network News Transfer Protocol: used to read usenet newsgroups.	119
SMTP	Simple Mail Transfer Protocol: used to send e-mail.	25
POP3	Post Office Protocol (version 3): used to retrieve e-mail from a server.	110
TCP	Transmission Control Protocol	*
HTTP	Hypertext Transfer Protocol: used to view HTML documents.	80
DNS	Domain Name Service: translates domain names into IP addresses.	53

* Varies depending on packet type

While you can use any port you wish, using non-standard ports would make it very difficult for people to communicate with you. For example, if you set up a Web server to listen on port 177, very few people would ever find your Web site. Their browser, by default, will attempt to connect on port 80. On the other hand, you may wish to use a non-standard port to enhance security. Some hackers simply try to get at various standard ports. For example, if your application uses FTP to transfer data, and you do it on port 400, intruders would be trying on port 21.

Network Connectivity

Before you design your Web application you will need to consider the connection speeds of those most likely to visit your Web site. Essentially, if you create a Web site that is too resource intensive and requires lots of download, users with slower connections will not be able to effectively use your applications. Even with intranet applications this can be a serious problem. The primary areas that place demands on connection speed are graphics, multimedia, and database operations.

Chapter

If your application uses very large graphics files, they must each be downloaded to the client's machine before the Web page will finish loading. This will cause users to be very dissatisfied with your application. Multimedia files (music or video) are also very large and take quite some time to load. Finally, if your application is continually going out to retrieve data from a database, this will seriously impact your performance. You may wish to consider the various connection speeds available.

Connection Type	Speed
56.6 K standard modem	56,600 bits per second
DSL	Up to 256,000 bits per second
Cable	Up to 1,544,000 bits per second (1.54 mbps)
T-1	1,544,000 bits per second (1.54 mbps)
T-3	44,700,000 bits per second (44.7 mbps)

While it is highly unlikely that you will be working with clients that have a T-3 or better connection, you will likely have Web site visitors that do use cable modems or T-1 connections. With those speeds, you need not be overly concerned about your application appearing sluggish. However, if you are concerned about users who are accessing the Internet (and hence your Web application) with a 56.6 K modem, then you should take care to make sure your Web site does not unnecessarily use intensive graphics, multimedia, and database access.

Summary

TCP/IP communication can be very easy to implement and an effective way to communicate small pieces of data between remotely located machines. It is not suited to large segments of data, since that data cannot easily be placed in a single packet. A basic knowledge of TCP/IP programming is critical for understanding distributed applications as well as Web-based applications.

Review Questions

1. What is TCP/IP?

2. What two properties must you set before you can send a packet via the Winsock control?

3. What data type does the Winsock control receive data as?

4. What happens if one end of a connection is left open?

5. What event is triggered in the Winsock control when data arrives?

6. What method of the Winsock control is used to send data?

7. What data type is used to send data via the Winsock?

8. What port do Web pages usually operate on?

9. Name two protocols that are part of the TCP/IP suite.

10. What method of the Winsock control is called to accept a request for a TCP/IP connection?

Software Design with VB.NET

Introduction

Proper software design and planning are perhaps the most important skills for a programmer to learn. Unfortunately, they are rarely even mentioned in beginning programming books. Most program "bugs" can be traced to poor planning and poor design. This chapter will not make you an expert in software design, but hopefully it will give you a basic working knowledge of planning, design, and testing.

Types of Errors

Software bugs can be categorized into three distinct types. There are syntax errors, run-time errors, and logic errors. *Syntax errors* are problems with your use of the programming language. Your program will not compile until you correct your syntax errors. This type of error is the easiest to catch and fix, and it will never be in applications you distribute (since you cannot finish compiling until you fix them). Visual Basic is especially helpful with syntax language for two reasons. The first feature is the auto-complete feature. Visual Basic will show you what options you can use in many cases. The second feature VB.NET provides to help you avoid syntax errors is Visual Basic's ongoing syntax checking. Visual Basic will let you know if a line of code is not appropriate syntax as soon as you move off that line.

Run-time errors are caused by attempting to do something that is literally impossible. An attempt to divide by zero or to open a file that does not exist will generate run-time errors. Proper error handling (Try...Catch blocks) and data validation will prevent this. Error handling was introduced earlier in this book and used throughout the book. A good rule of thumb is that you cannot have too much error handling. A second approach that will help you avoid run-time errors is data validation. Data validation is the process of simply making sure data is appropriate before trying to use it. This will be covered in some detail later in this chapter.

Logic errors are the ones that are truly problematic. A logic error occurs when your program compiles and executes, but the data it returns is inaccurate. This inaccuracy may not be immediately obvious. In fact it may not become apparent for quite some time. Not only are these types of errors the hardest to find, they are also potentially the most damaging. If your program computes payroll checks and makes a 10¢ miscalculation on each check, by the time you find the error, you may have cost the company a very large sum of money. This is not likely to enhance your career opportunities.

Fortunately, proper design, planning, and testing can eliminate many if not most logic errors. If you have properly designed your program, checked the logic, and done proper testing, you will catch most logic errors. There are several different approaches to design and planning. I will endeavor to introduce you to a few of them here.

Planning

There are formal planning methodologies we will discuss in this chapter, but first I want to introduce you to some basic concepts. Before you write a single line of code, try planning your project out. There are a number of formal planning strategies available, but at a minimum, you should try the following:

1. Clearly write out the end user needs of your application. Make sure you have clearly defined the goals. Ensure that you have clearly understood what is required of your application. It is also a good idea to make sure you understand the priorities of your application. Some features may be absolutely critical, while others may simply be nice to have.

2. Write out a plan for the major points in the flow of your application. Clearly plan out all the most important facets of your application.

3. Research any new technologies or techniques you may require.

4. Plan out your code in moderate detail. Decide how many forms and what content those forms will have. Decide what code should be in events and what should be in code modules. Decide on the scope of variables. Decide on what methods and algorithms you will use.

5. Now you can start writing code.

Testing

You have to test your code! It does not matter how simple the application is, bugs can and probably will arise. There are a number of sophisticated formal testing strategies available but beginners should just try to follow these steps:

1. First reread your code. Make sure you have proper error handling. Make sure there are no obvious flaws in your logic.

2. Refer back to your user-defined goals and check to see that your application meets them.

3. Now run the program. You should have a written table showing the exact testing conditions (the PC, operating system, etc.) and exactly what items you will test.

4. Try everything. Specifically, try doing things the <u>wrong</u> way—trust me, users will.

Microsoft Solutions Framework

Microsoft defines a relatively straightforward approach to software development that is called the Microsoft Solutions Framework (MSF). This model consists of four stages in the development process:

- Envisioning
- Planning
- Coding
- Stabilizing

Envisioning

It is imperative to have a clear idea of what you are trying to accomplish before you begin writing code. This means having a clear vision of the goals you want your software to reach. This will also often include some brainstorming regarding the possible methods of attaining those goals. During the envisioning process you should create (if you don't already have) a clear list of requirements for the software and establish the parameters of successful development.

Establishing the parameters of successful development is a step often overlooked even by professional developers. It's really fairly simple. What you need to do, before you even begin detailed planning, is decide what criteria you will use for deciding your project is a success. Do you require 99% uptime, or is 95% sufficient? Should your application be able to handle 100 simultaneous users, or perhaps 1,000? All of these criteria should be developed in this initial phase.

This phase is also the time to do some brainstorming regarding the tools and methods you will use to develop this project. First, you will have to decide on what development tools to use, and then what types of development techniques are most appropriate. Do you want to do this project in Visual C++, Visual Basic, Java?

Planning

Once you have a clear idea of what you wish to accomplish and what tools you wish to use, it is then time to develop a specific plan. This plan may be as simple as a few pages of notes, or as complex as hundreds of UML diagrams (UML is discussed later in this chapter). The specific planning methods used and the level of detail will depend on the project and on your team's abilities. A novice programmer should be fairly detailed in his or her planning. This allows you to examine your programming logic before you write the code.

Even an experienced developer will have to do extensive planning if the project in question is in an area that he or she is unfamiliar with. Some projects, by their very nature, require extensive planning. You might not need very detailed planning to write a POS (point-of-sale) program for a mom and pop grocery store, but you had better do some serious planning if you wish to develop an inventory system for a nationwide food chain.

Coding

This should actually be a relatively short portion of the development cycle. If you have properly conducted the first two phases of the development process, the coding is simply a matter of typing it in. You should not have to make any fundamental changes to the program's logic or flow in this phase. If you do, you have not performed the first two phases adequately.

Stabilizing

This is the process of testing and debugging. Rigorous testing is a key element to successful software development. Make sure you test every facet of your program. Try to do everything you can to break the software. It's much better to find a bug now than after you have distributed the program to 200 users!

UML

You will also find that there are specific design strategies for object-oriented programming. One very popular strategy that I personally use is the Unified Modeling Language. UML is essentially a methodology for creating a serious of diagrams to plan out your project. It is a tool for designing object-oriented programs. Each diagram becomes successively more detailed. Following is a brief outline of the various UML diagrams. This is not meant to make you proficient at UML but to give you enough information so that you can decide whether or not you wish to invest the time to learn UML.

Chapter

Unified Modeling Language is a methodology of systematically planning large-scale object-oriented development. With this method you gradually proceed from very general user needs to very specific programming criteria. Each model either concentrates on a different view of the development process or takes the previous model and adds more detail.

The UML process is an iterative design process whereby you begin with user-defined goals and business rules in the Use-Case model and move down to actually programming specifications in class diagrams, activity diagrams, state charts, and deployment diagrams. This approach allows you to begin with general ideas of the desired function of the application and gradually develop specifications based on the desired functionality.

Most UML experts encourage iterative development to proceed concurrently with the latter stages of UML design. For example, by the time you begin making class diagrams, you can actually begin coding the framework of your application. As the design becomes more detailed, so will the code.

Below are the various models used in UML.

Use-Case models: This is a diagram showing the actual functionality of an application from a user's perspective. The elements in this diagram are actors (anything that can act on the application) and the business rules that govern the application.

Interaction diagrams: This is the next stop in UML modeling. This basically shows how the elements of this application, such as the user, database, etc., interact.

Sequence diagrams: This diagram basically takes the interaction diagram and begins to translate that into actual objects that correspond directly to programming objects.

Collaboration diagrams: This diagram concentrates on the actual distribution of the objects involved.

Class diagrams: This is where you take the data from previous diagrams and actually plan the classes you will use in your application.

Activity diagrams: These diagrams show the actual flow and function of the application.

State charts: This is a model of the various states the application's objects may be in.

Component diagrams: These diagrams show the various components of a distributed application.

Deployment diagrams: This model shows the actual physical location of various components.

While each of these diagram types has its purposes, the one I find most often used is the class diagram. A class diagram is simply a box with three sections. The first section contains the name of the class. The second section holds the declarations for all member variables. The third section holds the declarations for the class's methods. Since UML diagrams are not specific to any language, symbols are used to denote the access modifiers. A plus sign (+) denotes public, a pound sign (#) denotes protected, and a minus sign (–) denotes private. If we were to create a class diagram for the class used in Example 3-1, it would look something like this:

Class1
(-) sname as string
(-) ssalary as single
(-) iage as integer
(-) sjobtitle as string
(+) computesalary() as single

This is merely a cursory introduction to the topic of the Unified Modeling Language, but it is important that you at least have some familiarity with the subject. Of course, a hobbyist or amateur programmer can feel free to ignore this topic altogether. But for a professional programmer, or one aspiring to be such, a knowledge of UML is vital. I strongly suggest you delve deeper into this topic. One excellent book on the subject is *Iterative UML Development Using Visual Basic 6.0* by Patrick W. Sheridan and Jean M. Sekula, published by Wordware Publishing. Though it is designed with an earlier version of Visual Basic in mind, the UML is applicable to any object-oriented programming language.

Chapter 12

Three-Step Plan

This is my own development plan that I have slowly put together over the past two years. I find it to be relatively easy to follow and easy to remember, and it meshes well with other design methodologies like UML. This plan consists of three phases, each of which has three steps.

1. Planning
   - Notes and requirements
   - Diagrams
   - Testing plan
2. Coding
   - Framework
   - Complete coding
   - Desk check
3. Testing
   - Valid data
   - Invalid data
   - Extreme data

I have been teaching this methodology to programming students for over a year now with some success. I will illustrate and explain each of the phases to you in the following pages.

Planning

Planning is the most important phase, just as it is in the MSF model. I further divide planning into three steps. The first step, notes and requirements, sets the foundation for the rest of the development process. The very first thing to do is to clearly define the requirements for your software. You might get these from a client or from a supervisor. When they give you these requirements, you will need to ask lots of questions. Make certain you are crystal clear on exactly what is required of your application. During this questioning, you should begin taking notes to clarify the requirements.

After you have defined and clarified the requirements, you should then develop some brief notes regarding your design strategy. This is quite similar to the envisioning process in the MSF model. You will need to decide on what development tools to use, how to store data (MS Access, SQL, Oracle), how to communicate with other components, and any other details about your development approach.

Once you have completed the notes and requirements you are ready to do your diagramming. This can be any type of diagram you prefer. I personally like to use UML diagrams, but some people stick to an old-fashioned flowchart. It really does not matter what diagrams you use. What is important is that the diagrams are clear enough and detailed enough to guide your coding.

Coding

Obviously, you will need to actually write the code. I find it helpful to divide this into three distinct steps as well. I find it helpful to first write out a simple framework. Then I declare variables, and write functions with just the declaration and the error handling. Next, I create the GUI and write calls to the functions I have written. Essentially, I build a skeleton for the program. This is exactly how buildings are built—first a framework, then the details. After you have the framework, go back and fill in the coding details. I would recommend that you do this one function at a time and make sure that function is correct. This is where the third step, desk check, comes in. After you have completed coding any function, give it a quick read through. Make sure you have not made any simple mistakes. Make certain the logic of the function works. If you follow this coding procedure, you are unlikely to find many errors in your testing phase.

Testing

Testing is really a matter of running your program and entering data to ensure that it works properly. If you have properly executed the preceding two phases, this phase will go quickly. How you test is really the key. This will be determined, in large part, by the criteria you established during the planning phase. You will have to test all the criteria you established. However, there are three things you must always test:

- Valid data
- Invalid data
- Extreme data

Chapter

Valid data is simply data that you are expecting to receive. If your program does not work with valid data, you have a serious problem. For example, if your program requires people to enter an age, a number such as 27 or 44 should be processed without any problem.

Invalid data is simply data that is completely improper. If you ask the person to enter their age and the user enters "fred", what will your program do? Will it crash? Or will it gracefully inform the user of their error, and give them another chance to enter the data?

Extreme data is a problem that too many programmers forget to account for. It is data of a value that simply does not make sense. If you ask the user to enter their age, and instead of typing 33, they type in 333, what will your program do? Will it inform the user of the problem, or will it simply process the age of over three hundred years? It is vital that your program have some "common sense."

Debugging

Let's face it, you will get bugs in your programs. It is that simple. A *bug* is any error in your program. Any point at which your program fails to function properly is a bug. The real question is not whether you will get them, but what you will do about them. There are a variety of techniques you can use to find and correct bugs in your applications.

Setting Project Debugging Options

Select Tools | Options. This will display the following screen.

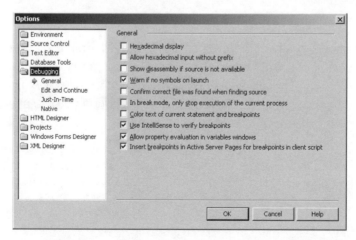

If you select Debugging, you will see several items to choose from. The first section, General, gives you some general items you might wish to select. The first three options are somewhat advanced and would probably not be of much use to you at this point in your Visual Basic learning. You can probably leave the default values for this screen.

In the Edit and Continue section are options that will affect how you utilize debugging when your program is stopped at a breakpoint.

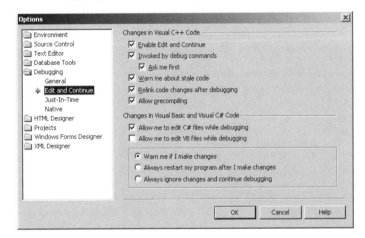

Two options you would want to select on this screen are Allow me to edit VB files while debugging and Warn me if I make changes. The first option will allow you to directly change your code when it is stopped at a breakpoint. The second will warn you if you have changed anything. That will keep you from inadvertently saving changes you did not intend to make.

Appropriate utilization of these options will make your development and debugging process a bit simpler.

The Build Window

As you must have noticed by now, when you compile a program, a window at the bottom shows you the steps in the compilation process. If you have ever used Visual C++ then this window will be very familiar to you. If not, let me introduce it to you. When you select Build for your project, either all will go well or you will get errors. If all goes well you will see a Build window like the following at the bottom of your IDE.

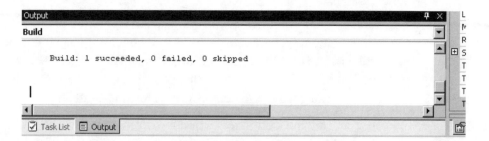

However, if you receive any errors you will see a Build window like this:

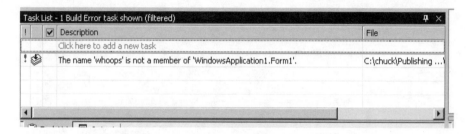

What you are looking at is a list of all the errors detected in your program. Remember that during compilation, only syntax errors can be checked. If you click on a given error, the code window where that error was generated will open, allowing you to see the problem. This is a vast improvement over previous versions of Visual Basic and gives you a very useful tool for debugging syntax errors.

Breakpoints

If you have an error in a subroutine you can "step through" your program. The way you do this is to go to the last line of code that you are sure works and highlight it. Then you go to the drop-down menu and select Debug | Toggle Breakpoint. Now when you run the program it will stop at this line of code. You can then go through the code line by line simply by selecting Debug and Step Into. The program will execute one line at a time. At each line you can highlight any variable and select Debug | Instant Watch. This will tell you what is currently in this variable.

These simple debugging techniques allow you to more thoroughly check out your program before you make an executable and distribute it. One of the biggest problems in software development today is software that has not been thoroughly tested.

Don't forget a few other concepts:

Structure: Too often beginning programmers just slap together some forms and code modules in a goo they call code. You must have some structure and design to your program. Lack of structure is one of the most common causes of bugs. Take the time to sit down and think out a program before you start to develop, and maybe even draw out a chart of the major routines and how they connect to each other and to the data. Think about how you want the program to flow.

If you carefully follow the concepts outlined in this chapter on software planning and design, you will have far fewer bugs to track down, and it will be much simpler for you to locate and fix those bugs.

Spaghetti code: This is a term for code that is so convoluted that it is nearly impossible for someone to follow its flow. An example of spaghetti code would be a routine that calls another routine, which, in turn, calls another routine...you get the idea. You would be better off having each routine called from the main event that triggers them (like the Click event of a command button).

Summary

This is by no means an exhaustive look at planning, designing, and testing. I am merely trying to get you acquainted with the concept. I do hope that you will include at least some level of planning and testing in your development. I must confess that earlier in my programming career I gave too little importance to planning. I merely did a small amount of cursory planning that was simply not adequate. I was able to get away with that for several years, until I started developing telecommunications software. After a couple of major faux pas I decided that planning was very vital.

Chapter

Review Questions

1. What is UML?

2. What are the three sections in a class diagram?

3. What is MSF?

4. What are the phases in MSF?

5. What three things must be covered in the testing phase of the three-step plan?

6. What are the three main phases of the three-step plan?

7. What are the three types of errors?

8. List four types of UML diagrams.

9. What is the most difficult type of error to fix?

10. What is a syntax error?

Computer Science with VB.NET

Introduction

Hopefully, you have seen that Visual Basic is an easy-to-use software development tool. It allows you to create powerful business applications with relative ease. If you have ever programmed in other languages like C++ this difference becomes abundantly clear. This is one reason Visual Basic is the language of choice for so many business applications. However, this leads to a problem. Many Visual Basic programmers lack any background in computer science. Concepts and techniques familiar to any college sophomore majoring in computer science may be unknown to some professional Visual Basic programmers with several years of experience.

This gap in knowledge for many (but certainly not all) Visual Basic programmers has led to two serious issues. The first is that there are situations in which this knowledge would be quite helpful in developing more stable and efficient applications. The other is the lack of respect other developers (such as C++ and Java programmers) sometimes show to Visual Basic programmers. Go to any online programming discussion board and you will see at least some Visual Basic bashing.

This chapter strives to ameliorate that situation. My goal in this chapter is not to make you a computer science guru. Even an entire book could not achieve such a lofty goal. What I do hope to accomplish is to give you a basic familiarity with some essential computer science concepts as they apply to Visual Basic. I would further hope that the material in this chapter, coupled with the chapter on software design, would allow you to begin taking your programming skills beyond simply putting together business solutions. Hopefully, you will begin to understand how software engineering is meant to work. Obviously, if you have a strong computer science background, you should feel free to skip this chapter.

Data Structures

Data has to be stored in some format. This should not be a great revelation to you at this point. You have already seen data stored in variables, arrays, and even in relational databases. However, what you have not seen is the underlying format of the data storage. There are specific structures used to hold data. Some data is simply not appropriate to store in a simple variable or in a simple array. Data structures also define the way in which data will be processed into and out of the structure.

Technically, an array is a data structure. However, we will be working with more complex data structures. I am going to start with two data structures that you have already worked with (even if you did not realize it).

Queue

A *queue* is a data structure that stores items sequentially, much like an array. In fact, the only real difference between a queue and an array is the way data is moved into and out of storage. In a queue, data is placed into the queue in the order it is received. Data is then processed from the queue in a first-in/last-out process (referred to as FILO). Usually an array of some type is used to store the data that is in the queue. Then two variables (usually an Integer or a Long) are used as placeholders. The first variable, called the "head," will show the position on the array where the last entry was added. The second variable, called the "tail," will show the position in the array where the last entry was processed.

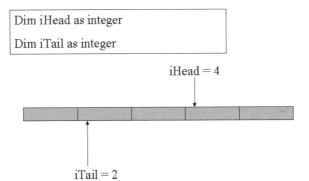

```
Dim iHead as integer
Dim iTail as integer
```

iHead = 4

iTail = 2

When you print to a network printer, a print queue is used. Documents are added to the print queue sequentially, and then removed and processed in a FILO order. When the head reaches the end of the queue it starts over at the beginning. This is referred to as a circular queue. If your head should catch up to the tail, you will have a problem. Essentially, if you are putting in data faster than it can be processed, eventually the head will circle back to the beginning and catch up to the tail. If you have ever gotten the "print queue full" error message, this is the cause.

A queue is very easy to set up in Visual Basic. Simply create an array of whatever data type you need to store, and then create two integers to track where in the queue you are currently processing. Let's look at an example.

Assume that your application receives TCP/IP packets and the data in those packets is a string that you need to add to a database. A TCP socket can receive a large number of packets in a single second. However, your data processing is likely to be significantly slower. It would, therefore, be a good idea to store that data in a queue and process it as you can.

Declare these variables in the general declarations section of the form that has your Winsock control on it:

```
Dim MyQueue as String(100)  ' create an array that can hold up to
                            ' 100 strings.

Dim iTail as Integer
Dim iHead as Integer
```

Now in the Winsock's data arrival event we place this code:

```
If iHead < 100 then
    IHead = iHead + 1
Else
    IHead = 0
End If
Winsock1.getdata myqueue(iHead)
```

In the function you build to actually process the data from the queue into the database, you simply increment the tail:

```
If iTail < 100 then
    ITail = iTail +1
Else
    ITail = 0
End If
```

Then, you process MyQueue(iTail).

This is a fairly straightforward and easy-to-comprehend data structure arrangement. It is a good place to begin your study of data structures. The queue is a commonly used data structure that clearly defines how the data is to be stored and in what order it will be processed (thus fulfilling our definition of a data structure). I have found many instances as a professional programmer where a queue was an ideal data structure to use in my programs.

Stacks

Another common data structure is the *stack*. The registers in your computer's CPU use stacks to store data. A stack is so named because it stores data like a stack of plates. The first item you process from the stack is the last item you put on. This is referred to as a last-in/first-out, or LIFO, arrangement. This would, again, be implemented with an array, but you would only need one pointer, since it would point to the last item you placed on the stack and hence the first item you processed. If you wished to rewrite the previous code as a stack, use the following code:

```
Dim MyQueue as String(100)   ' create an array that can hold up to
                             ' 100 strings.

Dim iHead as Integer
```

Now in the Winsock's data arrival event we place this code:

```
If iHead < 100 then
    IHead = iHead + 1
Else
    IHead = 0
End If
Winsock1.getdata MyQueue(iHead)
```

In the function you build to actually process the data from the queue into the database, you simply process the current item pointed to by the head:

```
MyQueue(iHead)
```

Personally, I very much prefer the queue to the stack. However, both are very important data structures and provide a foundation for your continued study of this topic.

Other Structures

There are many other data structures you can use in your programs, including lists, linked lists, binary trees, double linked lists, and hash tables. While the scope of this book prevents me from giving in-depth coverage of all the commonly used data structures, I would like to provide you with a brief definition of a few of the most popular.

Tree	A data structure accessed beginning at the root node. Each node is either a leaf or an interior node. An interior node has one or more child nodes and is called the parent of its child nodes. Unlike a physical tree, the root is usually shown at the top of the structure, and the leaves are represented at the bottom.
Binary tree	A tree with at most two children for each node.
List	A set of items accessible one after another beginning at the head and ending at the tail.
Linked list	A list implemented by each item having a link to the next item.
Double linked list	A variant of a linked list in which each item has a link to the previous item as well as the next. This allows easy access to list items backwards as well as forwards.

Hash table   A dictionary in which keys are mapped to array positions by a hash function. Having more than one key map to the same position is called a collision. There are many ways to resolve collisions, but they may be divided into open addressing, in which all elements are kept within the table, and chaining, in which external data structures are used.

Recursion

Another important concept in computer science is *recursion*. Recursion is essentially the process of a function calling itself. Several of the sorting algorithms you will see later in this chapter use recursion to sort lists. There are many examples used to teach recursion, and most come from mathematics.

A good example of recursion is the use of the mathematical Factorial function. If you are not familiar with this, it refers to multiplying a number by all the integers between 1 and that number. It is denoted by the number followed by an exclamation point such as N!. For example, 6! is 6 * 5 * 4 * 3 * 2 * 1, or 720. You can write a Visual Basic program to accomplish this quite easily.

1. Create a new Windows application project.

2. Place a single text box and a single command button on your form.

3. In the Click event of the command button place this code:

```
Dim Num as Long
Dim Answer as Long
Dim Temp as Long
Dim Counter as Integer
Dim FactorialNumber as Long
Num = Val(Text1.Text)
 For Counter = (Num -1 ) to 1 Step -1
  Temp = Num * Counter
    Answer = Answer + Temp
 Next Counter
Msgbox (Num & " factorial  is " & Answer)
```

This simple program will give you the factorial of any integer you enter into the text box. It also shows you a slightly different approach to recursion. In this case you use a loop to continually execute the same line of code until the answer is reached.

Now that example simply used a loop to calculate the answer, but the same thing can be accomplished with a recursive function. Let's look at an example of this.

Example 13-1

1. Start a new Windows Forms project.

2. On the form, place two text boxes and one command button, labeled as you see here.

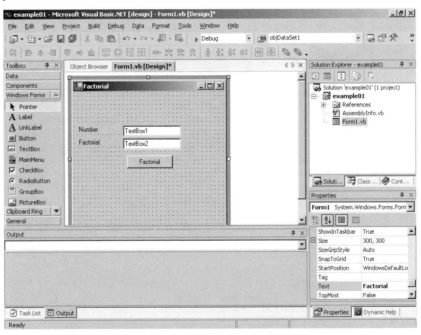

3. Place the following code in the button's Click event.

```
Dim Number as Double
Dim dFactorial as Double
Dim Status as Integer
If Not IsNumeric(Textbox1.Text) Then
    Beep()
    Exit Sub
End If
```

```
Number = CInt(Textbox1.Text)
dFactorial = Factorial(Number)
Textbox2.Text = CStr(dFactorial)
```

4. Place the following function at the beginning of the Form class.

```
Public Function Factorial(ByVal Num as Integer) as Double
    Dim Value as Double
    Value = 1
    Do While Num > 1
        Value = Value * Num
        Num = Num - 1
    Loop
    Return Value
End Function
```

When you run this application you will be able to enter any integer into the first text box, and see its factorial value in the second text box.

Algorithms

The American Heritage Dictionary defines an algorithm as "A step-by-step problem-solving procedure, especially an established, recursive computational procedure for solving a problem in a finite number of steps." I usually tell beginning students that an algorithm is a systematic method for solving a problem. In either case, an algorithm is a problem solving tool. Given that the entire reason for having computers and computer programs is to solve problems, the study of algorithms is a very important topic for computer science.

Sorting Algorithms

One of the most common types of algorithms for computer scientists to study are sorting algorithms. A sorting algorithm is used to sort a set of data. This may sound like a trivial thing, but it can be quite demanding. If the list of items you wish to sort is only 10 or 20 items long, it really does not matter what type of sorting algorithm you use. However, if it is 100,000 items long, the sorting algorithm you choose will be crucial to your application's performance.

Before I introduce you to specific algorithms, I want to introduce you to the concept of algorithm analysis. There is a very definite way to evaluate the efficacy of an algorithm. You can evaluate it based on the amount of memory it uses and/or the amount of time it takes to complete. For our purposes, we will concentrate on speed.

If an algorithm can completely sort a list by passing through it one time, that algorithm is a 1N algorithm (where N is the number of items in the list). If the algorithm requires two passes through the list to sort it, that algorithm is said to be a 2N algorithm. You can have a variety of algorithm speeds. An algorithm can require a number of passes equal to the number of elements in the list squared. This would be considered an N^2 algorithm. This type of notation of algorithms is called *Big O notation*.

With Big O notation, we are only concerned with the most time-consuming part of an algorithm. For example, if an algorithm takes 2N + 1 passes to sort, it would still be considered a 2N algorithm. The reason for this is that as the list grows, the constant factor (+ 1) is really not affecting the speed of the algorithm. If, for example, you had 100 items in your list, a 2N + 1 algorithm would take 201 passes to sort. The one extra pass hardly makes any difference. Even when the list grows to 1,000 elements, the difference between 2,000 and 2,001 passes is hardly measurable.

Bubble Sort

Regardless of what programming language you use to implement a bubble sort, the mechanism is the same. The sorting is accomplished by comparing each adjacent pair of items in the list in turn, swapping the items if necessary. It continues, repeating the pass through the list until no swaps are left. Its name comes from the fact that it "bubbles" through the list, swapping entries as needed.

Example 13-2

1. Start a new Windows project.

2. Place a text box, two list boxes, and two buttons on the form.

3. Label the first list box as **Unsorted** and the second as **Sorted**.

4. Set one button's Text property to **Add To List** and the other's to **Bubble Sort**. Your form should look like this:

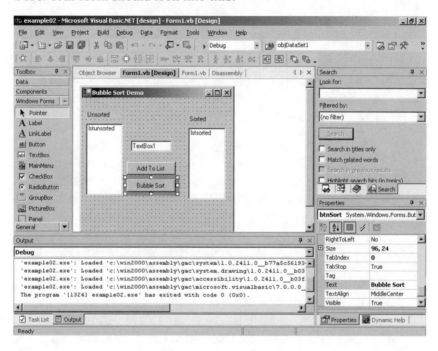

5. Place the following code at the beginning of the Form class module:

```
Private Sub bubblesort(ByVal min as Long, ByVal max as Long)
        Dim LastSwap as Long
        Dim I as Long
        Dim J as Long
        Dim lTemp as Long
        ' Bubble up
        Do While Min < Max
            LastSwap = Min - 1
            I = Min + 1
            Do While I <= Max
                If aNumbers(I - 1) > aNumbers(I) Then
                    lTemp = aNumbers(I - 1)
                    J = I
```

```
                Do While aNumbers(J) < lTemp
                    aNumbers(J - 1) = aNumbers(J)
                    J = J + 1
                    If J > Max Then
                        Exit Do
                    End If
                Loop
                aNumbers(J - 1) = lTemp
                LastSwap = J - 1
                I = J + 1
            Else
                I = I + 1
            End If
        Loop
        Max = LastSwap - 1
        ' Bubble down
        LastSwap = Max + 1
        I = Max - 1
        Do While I >= Min
            If aNumbers(I + 1) < aNumbers(I) Then
                lTemp = aNumbers(I + 1)
                J = I
                Do While aNumbers(J) > lTemp
                    aNumbers(J + 1) = aNumbers(J)
                    J = J - 1
                    If J < Min Then
                        Exit Do
                    End If
                Loop
                aNumbers(J + 1) = lTemp
                LastSwap = J + 1
                I = J - 1
            Else
                I = I - 1
            End If
        Loop
        Min = LastSwap + 1
    Loop
```

6. In the first button (labeled Add To List) place this code:

```
LstUnsorted.Items.Add(Textbox1.Text)
```

7. In the second button (labeled Bubble Sort) add this code:

```
Dim I as Integer
' redim the array to equal the number of
' items in the unsorted list.
ReDim aNumbers(LstUnsorted.Items.Count)
' now retrieve all the numbers in the unsorted
' list and place them in the array.
For I = 0 to (LstUnsorted.Items.Count - 1)
    aNumbers(I) = LstUnsorted.Items(I)
Next I
' Pass that array to the bubblesort function
bubblesort(1, 5)
For I = 0 to (LstUnsorted.Items.Count - 1)
    LstSorted.Items.Add(aNumbers(I))
Next I
```

Note that the second number passed to bubble sort is the total number of items in the list.

This algorithm is an easy-to-implement sorting algorithm that you may find quite helpful. But most importantly for us, this algorithm illustrates the basic concepts of algorithms. It takes a systematic approach to sorting an array or list of items. That same procedure can be applied to any array or list of items and get the same results.

The basic principle behind the bubble sort is quite simple. It just compares two items in the list and if they are not in proper order, it switches them. It continues this process until there are no more swaps to be made. This algorithm usually works at a speed of $O(n^2)$, but if the list is already somewhat sorted, it may approach $O(n)$.

Quicksort

Another popular sorting algorithm is the quicksort. This is a recursive algorithm. It basically uses a divide and conquer approach. It divides the list into smaller sublists, and tackles them each separately.

```
Public Sub Quicksort(lArray () as Long, Min as Long, Max as Long)
dim MedianValue as Long
Dim Hi as Long
Dim Lo as Long
   if Min >= Max then
   Exit Sub
   MedianValue = lArray (Min)
```

```
        Lo = Min
        Hi = Max
        Do
            Do While lArray (hi) >= MedianValue
                    Hi = Hi - 1
                    If Hi <= Lo Then Exit Do
            Loop
            If Hi<= Lo Then
                lArray (Lo) = MedianValue
                Exit Do
            End If
            lArray (Lo) = lArray (hi)
            Lo = Lo + 1
            Do While lArray (lo) < MedianValue
                    Lo = Lo + 1
                    If Lo >= Hi Then Exit Do
             Loop
            If Lo >= Hi Then
                    Lo = Hi
                    lArray (hi) = MedianValue
                    Exit Do
            End If
            List (hi) = List(Lo)
        Quicksort( List(),Min,Lo -1)
        Quicksort( List(),Lo + 1, Max)
     End Sub
```

The quicksort picks an element from the array (the pivot point), partitions the remaining elements into those greater than and less than this pivot, and then recursively sorts the partitions. There are many variants of this basic approach. The quicksort has a worst-case run time of $O(n^2)$, but it will usually work at $O(n \log n)$. This means that it usually executes faster than the bubble sort.

Other Algorithms

It is beyond the scope of this book to go into depth on all the sorting algorithms that are commonly used, but I would like to give you a brief introduction to and definition of some of the more commonly encountered sorting algorithms.

Merge sort	A sort algorithm that splits the items to be sorted into two groups, then recursively sorts each group, and merges them into a final, sorted sequence
Selection sort	An algorithm that orders items by repeatedly looking through remaining items to find the least one and moving it to a final location.
Bingo sort	A variation of the selection sort that orders items by repeatedly looking through remaining items to find the greatest value and moving all items with that value to their final location.

Optimizing for Speed

At times, you will need to improve the speed of execution for your application. There are a number of techniques you may find useful. The first and most important technique is to use integers whenever possible. Visual Basic considers all variables to be of the default Variant type. Unless you specify otherwise, everything, text and numeric, will be a Variant.

The following code illustrates the variations in speed you will have with different data types. It does this by implementing a very long loop and showing the time it takes to complete the loop depending on what data type is used as a loop counter.

```
A 50-Million-Loop Time Test
Dim I as Long
Dim B as Byte
Dim Start as Double
Dim Elapse as Double
Start = Timer
For I = 1 To 200000
    For B = 1 To 254
    Next B
Next I
Elapse = Timer - Start
MsgBox( "The time elapsed was " & Elapse)
End Sub
```

When this form loads, the inner loop counter B is defined as a Byte variable type for the first test. The starting and ending times are held in the variables Start and Elapse. We make them so they will permit great precision. Then we begin with Start = Timer to get the current time. We use the Timer function in VB (unrelated to Timer controls). It calculates elapsed time since midnight each day and then resets. Then, we start running the nested loop. When the loop finishes, we subtract the starting time from the current (Timer) time and print the results on the form.

To test each variable type, all we have to do is change the type of J in the first line of the program: Dim J as Integer, Dim J as Long, and so forth. Below you can see which variable is fastest. (Actual times will vary on different machines.)

Data Type	Time
Integer	1
Long	2
Byte	3
Currency	4
Variant	5
Single	6
Double	7

As you can see, the type of variable you use can make a difference in application performance. The Integer variable type runs quite a bit faster than the floating-point types.

Obviously, you can't use integers everywhere in all your programs. Calculations requiring greater precision (such as a result including a fraction) must be made with floating-point variable types (Single or Double). Calculations requiring a large range cannot be made with integers (which can manipulate only the numbers between −32,768 and 32,767). In that case, you have to resort to "long integers" (Long), floating-point (Single or Double), or Currency data types.

There are a number of ways to increase the user's perception of the application's speed. One method is to load all forms at the outset of the program. For example, if your application has five forms in it, rather than simply loading only the main form and loading each additional form when you need it, load them all. Just set the Visible property of all forms to false. Then, when you need the form, set its Visible property to true. This will make it appear to load instantly.

The AutoRedraw property is available only for a form or a picture box. AutoRedraw is false by default. Set it to true, and VB will create everything in the form or picture box. Nothing will be redrawn on the fly. VB will keep a copy, a bitmap picture, of the entire form or picture box in memory. This will increase the speed of the application, but remember that, like the method of loading the forms all at once, this does tax the memory of the machine. Fortunately, most modern machines have plenty of RAM!

Remember that an image box displays faster than a picture box. Also, do not use subroutines for code that is not being called from multiple places. If code will only be used in one event, put that code in that event. It is faster for an event to execute code that is in the event than to call out to an external (external to the control, that is) subroutine.

Summary

In this chapter you have been introduced to data structures, recursion, algorithm analysis, specific algorithms, and optimizing for speed. It is my hope that this knowledge will allow you to become a more effective programmer. Yes, it is true that you can make a career out of simply putting some Visual Basic forms together and making interesting user interfaces; however, without at least a cursory familiarity with the material in this chapter you are unlikely to progress far. For a typical bachelor's degree in computer science, students take an entire course in data structures and an entire course in algorithm analysis. Obviously, this chapter cannot make up for two semesters of college work, but it should at least give you a foundation from which to start.

Review Questions

1. What is a data structure?

2. How does a queue process data?

3. What is Big O notation?

4. Is there a difference in the Big O notation for an algorithm that requires 2N passes and one that requires 2N + 1 passes?

5. How does a stack process data?

6. How does a quicksort work?

7. Is an array a type of data structure?

8. List four different data structures.

9. What happens if the head pointer on a queue reaches the same value as the tail pointer?

10. Which variable is usually the fastest in any speed test?

Object Models

Object-oriented programming has been one of the hottest buzzwords in programming for the past four or five years. Unfortunately, most programmers are not sure why it's such a cool thing, they just want it on their resume. Perhaps the best example of why object orientation is such a powerful technology can be seen by examining object models. An object model is simply a hierarchical representation of the objects that are exposed by a given application. All Microsoft Office products, Internet Explorer, many BackOffice products, and Visual Basic all have an object model that you can utilize to manipulate that application in any way you wish.

Object models provide structure to an object-oriented program. By defining the relationships between the objects you use in your program, an object model organizes your objects in a hierarchical fashion. This facilitates programming with the objects in the model.

Typically, an object model illustrates the fact that some objects in the model are more important than others. These objects can be viewed as containing other objects, or as being made up of other objects.

For example, you might create a business object as the core of your program. You might want the business object to have other types of objects associated with it. You might have a product object, an employee object, etc. Each of these objects is subordinate, too, and dependent on the business object.

A root object is at the base of an object model. It is the object that contains all the other objects in the object model. Root objects are usually externally creatable. This means that clients can create instances of the root class. The creation of a root object is accomplished by using the New operator or the CreateObject function.

Most programs use objects that are private to that program. You can create objects from any class the program defines. However, client applications cannot create any objects from your application. Externally creatable objects are those that a client application can create. You create an instance of such an object by using the New operator with the Set statement (by declaring a variable As New) or by calling the CreateObject function.

The externally created object actually simply gives a reference to the client. When a client uses one of these mechanisms to request an externally creatable object, the component returns a reference the client can use to manipulate the object. The life cycle of the object the client is using is clearly defined. When the client sets the last variable containing this reference to Nothing, the component destroys the object. The object is also destroyed if it goes out of scope. You can make a public object externally creatable by setting the Instancing property of the class module to any value other than Private or PublicNotCreatable.

When an object is contained within another object, it is referred to as a dependent object. Client applications can manipulate dependent objects, just as they can manipulate externally creatable objects, but they cannot create dependent objects using CreateObject or New. Usually, the externally creatable objects also have methods to create their dependent objects.

If you want to make an object dependent on another, set the Instancing property of a class module to PublicNotCreatable. You then create a method in the externally creatable object that your class is dependent on; that method will allow for the creation of the dependent object. Dependent objects are sometimes referred to as nested objects.

For example purposes, we will examine the Outlook object model.

Outlook's Object Model

An extensive discussion of the Outlook object model is beyond the scope of this book. However, we are going to address some of the most important objects and a few of the things you can do with them.

Application	This object represents Outlook itself. With this object you can access and gain control of a currently running instance of Outlook, or you can launch an instance of Outlook.
Namespace	This object represents the current MAPI session. It allows you to manipulate, start, or end a MAPI session.
Explorer	This object represents the current window.
Folders	This object represents all of the folders in Outlook.
Folder	This object represents the currently selected folder.
Items	This object represents all the items in a folder.
Item	This object represents a specific item in a folder.

Example 14-1

This example utilizes the Outlook object model. The code is simply to give you an idea of what you can do with this particular object model. Obviously, it is dependent on having MS Outlook installed on your machine.

1. Start a new Windows application.

2. Select **Project | Add Reference**.

3. On the COM tab, select **Microsoft Outlook 9.0 Object Library** and click **OK**.

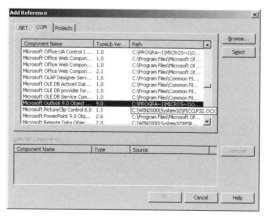

4. Just after the class declaration for the Form1 class, place the following code:

```
Dim WithEvents ObjApp as Outlook.Application
Private Sub Outlook_Object_Model_Demo()
Dim ObjNameSpace as Outlook.NameSpace
Dim ObjFolders as Outlook.Folders
Dim ObjExplorer as Outlook.Explorer
Dim ObjItem as Outlook.MailItem
Dim MyItem(10) as Outlook.MailItem
Dim ObjItems as Outlook.Items
Dim ObjFolder as Outlook.MAPIFolder
Dim iCount as Integer
' Set your application object equal to the current instance of
' Outlook.
Set ObjApp = GetObject("", "Outlook.Application")

' Set your namespace object equal to the mapi session
Set ObjNameSpace = ObjApp.GetNamespace("MAPI")

' Set the explorer object to the active view
Set ObjExplorer = ObjApp.ActiveExplorer
' Get the collection of all folders
Set ObjFolders = ObjNameSpace.Folders
' Set your folder object to the current folder
Set ObjFolder = ObjApp.ActiveExplorer
' set your items object equal to the collection of items in the current
' folder
Set ObjItems = ObjFolder.Items
For iCount = 1 to ObjItems.count
   Set MyItem(iCount) = ObjItems.Item(iCount)
   iCount = iCount + 1
Next iCount
  ' Now the array MyItem contains all the mail items in your inbox.
End Sub
```

Following are examples of some of the ways you can access MS Outlook via your code. To make things easier, in this table I use the same variable names that were created in Example 14-1.

Item Object	Description
objItem.Attachments	View any attachments
objItem.BCC	Find out who was BCC'd on the message
objItem.CC	Find out who was CC'd on the message
objItem.CreationTime	Get the item's creation time
objItem.MessageClass	Find out what kind of message it was
objItem.Subject	Get the subject line
objItem.Size	Find out how big the message is
objItem.Move (destinationfolder)	Move the message to another folder
Folder Object	
objFolder.MoveTo (someotherfolder)	Move an item to another folder
objFolder.Items	Get a collection of all the items in a folder
Explorer Object	
objExplorer.Caption	The current caption being displayed
objExplorer.CurrentFolder	The Current folder being displayed
objExplorer.CommandBars	The command bars currently being displayed
Namespace Object	
objNameSpace.AddressLists	Retrieve address lists
objNameSpace.CreateRecipient	Create a new recipient
objNameSpace.GetDefaultFolder	Retrieve the default folder
objNameSpace.Logoff	Logout
Application Object	
objApp.CreateObject (objectsname)	Create an instance of the Outlook object
objApp.CreateItem (typeofitem)	Create any item

All the Office applications have objects representing their various items and functions. The coding can be a little bit tricky, and it's important to use the object hierarchy in the proper fashion. I will use the Outlook model as an example, but the same principles can be extrapolated to the rest of Office. To do any of this, however, you must manually set a reference to the Office object's DLL.

Chapter

14

At the top level of the hierarchy we have the Application object. This represents the Outlook application. You can create a new instance of Outlook using the CreateObject method:

```
Set OutApp = CreateObject(Outlook.Application")
```

You can access a currently running instance of Outlook with:

```
Set outApp = GetObject("", "Outlook.Application")
```

Once you have the Application object set, you then set the Namespace object. That object represents the actual folders contained in Outlook. It has default properties for accessing any default folders. However, you need to do a little more to access custom folders.

```
Set OutNamespace = OutApp.GetNamespace("MAPI")
```

The next object in the hierarchy is the Explorer object. This represents the window that is currently open:

```
Set OutExplorer = OutApp.ActiveExplorer
```

The current folder is represented by:

```
Set OutView = OutApp.ActiveExplorer.CurrentFolder
```

You have a fairly large array of other objects you can use, which are in the following table.

Object	Purpose
Application object	Represents the actual Outlook application
Namespace object	Represents the application's working area
Explorer object	Represents the currently active window
Folder object	Represents any folder
Item object	Can represent any item
Command bar object	Represents the Outlook toolbar
Exception object	Represents errors

The objects in this model are arranged in a hierarchical fashion.

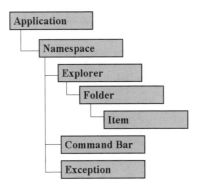

These are just a few of the objects you have access to. Each object has a host of methods and properties. Essentially, if you familiarize yourself with Outlook's object model, you can do anything in your code that Outlook might do. You can take complete control of Outlook.

The important thing to realize is that each of the products in the Microsoft Office suite has an object model you can access in similar fashion, as does Internet Explorer. In each case you simply create a reference to that application and begin creating items in the object hierarchy.

Internet Information Server

Internet Information Server (IIS) is Microsoft's Web server. When you read the chapter on Web forms and ASP.NET you were introduced to this application. As you might expect, IIS has an object model that you can manipulate in your programs.

> **Note:** With VB.NET much of this is handled behind the scenes by ASP.NET. With previous versions of Visual Basic you had to directly interact with this entire object model in order to create Web applications.

This section is provided for two purposes. The first is to give you a second example of object models. The second is to give you a more thorough understanding of how IIS works. Fortunately, with ASP.NET much of what is described in this section is handled for you, but it is useful for you to understand what is happening in the background.

IIS applications are hosted by an ASP (Active Server Pages) file and make use of several of the objects in the Active Server Pages object model. In previous versions of Visual Basic, you had to create Web classes that would work with these objects. ASP objects that a Web class can use include:

- Request — Receives requests from end users in the browser.
- Response — Sends information to the browser in order to display it to the user.
- Session — Maintains information about the current user session and stores and retrieves state information.
- Application — Manages state that is shared across multiple Web class instances.
- Server — Creates other objects and determines server-specific properties that might influence the Web class's processing.
- BrowserType — Determines the capabilities of the user's browser and makes processing decisions based on that information.

The ASP Request Object

The Request object is used to retrieve information from or about the current user. The Request object provides you with access to all of the information passed in any request. HTTP requests contain information about the current user and any data they entered.

The most frequent use of the Request object is to retrieve information from an HTML form. This would include retrieving all of the form elements passed in a Submit event.

You can also use the Request object's associated collections to access information. These collections include:

- QueryString — This will retrieve the values of additional arguments in a URL when a request is passed using the Get method. Get is used by the Web server to retrieve objects from an HTML form.
- Cookies — This will retrieve any data contained in cookies sent with the form request. Cookies are small parcels of information used to store data about the current user.

- Form — Retrieves the value of form elements passed in an HTTP request when the request is passed using the Post method. Post is a method used by the Web browser to send the information from an HTML form. Post is the most commonly used method for sending form information.
- ServerVariables — Retrieves information such as header values, logon name, or server protocols in use.
- ClientCertificate — Retrieves information stored in certificate fields when the browser sending the request supports client certificates. Certificates identify a user to the Web server.

The ASP Response Object

The Response object is used to return information to the browser. For example, you might use the object's Respond event to write HTML to the browser. There are several methods you can use with the Response object:

- Use the Write or BinaryWrite method to send information directly to a browser.
- Use the Redirect method to direct the user to a different URL than the one the user requested.
- Use the Cookies collection to set cookie values to return to the browser and store these values for future use.
- Use the Buffer property to postpone a response while the entire page is processed.

The ASP Session and Application Objects

The Session and Application objects both store state information about the end users. The Session object is used with a single user in the current session and the Application object is used with multiple users.

You use the Session object to maintain information about the current user session and to store and retrieve state information. You can even use the Session object to retain information about where the user has already been.

The Application object is used to store information about multiple users. For example, suppose you want to keep track of the number of users who access a Web site. You can do this by storing a count in the Application object and incrementing it each time a user accesses a part of the Web site.

The ASP Server Object

The Server object is used to create objects and determine server-specific properties that might influence processing. It is the central, or root, object for this object model.

The ASP BrowserType Object

The BrowserType object provides you with information about the specific browser the user has. It can be used to determine the capabilities of the user's browser and make processing decisions based on that information. For example, suppose you have an application that contains a button called ChkInventory which allows the user to check available inventory. You provide two versions of the event procedure for this button in your code. You might use the two versions to handle code specific to a given browser. With this scenario, you could use the BrowserType object to determine which procedure to use by determining the browser's capabilities.

Summary

This chapter showed you, briefly, how to access and utilize the inherent object models in various applications in order to write your own integrated applications. Writing Visual Basic applications that integrate with MS Office is a common task. After you have a solid mastery of the basic elements of Visual Basic.NET you will probably want to work on expanding your knowledge of the various Office product object models.

Review Questions

1. What is the purpose of the Application object in the Outlook model?

2. How do you create a reference to the Outlook object model?

3. What is the code to create an instance of the object model that references a currently running instance of the application?

4. What object represents the current window?

5. What object represents the toolbar?

6. What is the code to create an instance of the object model that starts the application running?

7. List three properties of the Item object.

Chapter 14

Encryption in VB.NET

Encryption is an exciting word in programming, but also a daunting one. It probably brings up visions of complex mathematics and machine-level programming. Encryption and cryptography have long been important topics, especially in this day of increasing computer security concerns.

History of Encryption

As far back as the Roman Caesars, history records people attempting to obfuscate the meanings of their written communications. This can be for many reasons, including military and political. Frequently, people have found it advantageous to have others not be able to read their writings.

During World War II, mathematician Alan Turing developed a method to decrypt Nazi military messages. He employed the aid of dozens of women in the Women's Royal Naval Service to each perform a very simple task, repeated many times on each shift around the clock. Each day these women were given a template that contained a word or phrase that was likely to be embedded within a German message. These women basically worked assembly line style to decrypt messages.

Computer programs that perform encryption and decryption have supplanted this kind of assembly line work. But Alan Turing's work with mathematical concepts has earned him a valued place in the history of encryption.

VB Simple Substitution Encryption

A number of methods have been developed through the years to encrypt a message. We will look at a practical method to do this in Visual Basic.

Let's say we have some message we wish to encrypt. We have placed this message in a variable we will call sMessage.

Example 15-1

1.   Start a new Windows application.

2.   Place two text boxes on the form, one named **txtinput** and the other **txtoutput**. Make sure you change their Text properties to be blank.

3.   Place one button on the form and change its text property to **Encrypt**.

Your form should look like this:

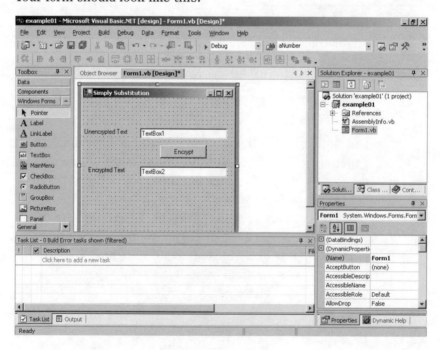

4. In the button's Click event place this code:

```
Dim I as Integer  'counter
Dim X as Integer  'used in encryption
Dim sMessage as String
Dim Z as Char
Dim Y as Integer
sMessage = Txtinput.text
For I = 1 to Len(sMessage)
    Z = Mid(sMessage,I,1)
    Y = Asc (Z)
    y = y +1
    Txtoutput.Text =  Txtoutput.Text & Chr(Y)
Next I
```

When you run this code, whatever text you enter into the first text box will be altered.

This subroutine takes your message, grabs one character of it, changes it to ASCII format (with the Asc() function), adds one to that ASCII code, and then changes it back to a character and displays the new message.

To decrypt messages, you would simply reverse this process. This is basically an elementary substitution code. It will work fine for most basic encryption needs, but don't think that this kind of encryption will foil the CIA for more than a few milliseconds! This just gives you an idea of how computer encryption works. You create an encryption key, which you provide to those people you want to be able to decrypt your encoded messages. You could easily write a simple program with a form that allows a person to input a message and then click on either an Encryption or Decryption button.

This simple substitution algorithm is referred to as a Caesar cipher. It is alleged that the Roman Caesars used this algorithm. However, it would not do much to keep a modern cryptographer from unraveling the message's secrets.

You could complicate your encryption in many ways. You could change the increment step (Z + 1) to something more complex. You could make your output backward (last character first). There are a vast number of methods you could use to make your own message encryption far more effective.

Advanced Encryption Concepts

Encryption is basically a form of substitution. For example, if I use the number 1 in place of A and 2 in place of B and 3 in place of C, etc., I am using the simplest form of encryption. A more complex sequence might be to take the number corresponding to the place in the alphabet (such as A = 1) and perform some mathematical operation on it. I might add 2 and divide by 3 or take the arc cosine of the number. No matter what the process, the idea is to have some new symbol for the letter. The problem with basic encryption such as this is that it still leaves a back door to crack the code. That back door is frequency. Basically, certain letters appear in the English language with a certain frequency. For example, if I use the basic encryption (a = 1, b = 2, etc.) with the phrase "a dog eats the bone," I get 1- 4 - 15 - 7 - 5 - 1 - 20 - 19 - 20 - 8 - 5 - 2 - 15 - 14 - 5. The vowels "a" and "e" are most likely giving my code away due to their frequency. How can we prevent this from happening? The answer is multiple encryption alphabets. For example:

A	B	C	D	E	F
1	2	3	4	5	6
4	5	7	R	T	y
Z	X	4	3	2	W

Now if I attempt to encrypt the phrase "A Cab" using just a simple substitution I get:

1 - 3 - 1 - 2

What multiple alphabet substitution says is that I will use the first substitution alphabet for the first letter, the second alphabet for the second letter, and so forth. Thus "A Cab" becomes:

1 - 7 - Z - 2

Now there is no frequency for any decoder to pick up on. You can utilize this with as many substitution alphabets as you like, but I think five would be sufficient to stop most snoopers.

My Cryptography Algorithm for More Serious Cryptographers

My encryption algorithm is actually simply a variation on traditional multiple alphabet encryption. I simply use the following steps:

1. Convert the character to its ASCII equivalent.
2. Adjust that value according to the first substitution alphabet.
3. Convert that value to hexadecimal.
4. Adjust that value according to the first substitution alphabet.
5. Repeat the process for each character.

I also encrypt the key and place a value inside the encrypted message denoting what key will match it. This last part makes having an exact key essential to decoding the message.

More Encryption

The techniques I have shown you are ideal for putting simple encryption algorithms into your Visual Basic.NET programs. However, this is not how secure messages are usually encrypted. What normally happens is that the message is converted into ASCII codes, and those codes are then converted into binary numbers. Each character becomes an 8-bit binary number. Those numbers are then encrypted with an encryption key. That key is also in binary format. The way the message is encrypted is using what is called an exclusive OR operation. Let me explain to you what OR, AND, and XOR (exclusive OR) operations are. Let's assume we have two binary numbers 01110 and 11101. Now let's examine each of the aforementioned operations on this pair.

AND

$$01110$$
$$11101$$
$$\overline{}$$
$$01100$$

Any place that has a 1 in both numbers becomes a 1, otherwise it becomes a 0.

OR

$$01110$$
$$11101$$
$$\overline{}$$
$$11111$$

Any place where there is a 1 in the top or bottom number (or even in both) becomes a 1.

XOR

$$01110$$
$$11101$$
$$\overline{}$$
$$10011$$

Any place where there is a 1 in either number but <u>not</u> in both becomes a 1.

Now imagine that your message, when converted from characters to ASCII codes and then to binary is 110101010. It would actually be quite a bit longer since it takes eight binary digits to represent any character, but this will allow us to illustrate the point. Now assuming your encryption key is 1101, here is how you encrypt the message:

```
       110101010
XOR    110111011
       ─────────
       000010001
```

To decrypt it you simply apply the key again:

```
       000010001
XOR    110111011
       ─────────
       110101010
```

As you can see, you get back your original message!

Note that the key is only four digits, so it must be repeated to encrypt the whole message.

Now here is the really tricky part. The size of the key used to encrypt the message is the entire secret. A computer can simply try various combinations of 1s and 0s until something breaks it. The longer the key, the more attempts it will take to break it. Let me illustrate it with this table.

Digits	Number of Possibilities	2^n
1	2 (0, 1)	2^1
2	4 (00, 01, 10, 11)	2^2
3	8 (000, 001, 010, 011, 100, 101, 110, 111)	2^3
4	16	2^4
5	32	2^5

There is an obvious pattern here. Essentially the number of possibilities for any given key is the 2 raised to the power equal to the number of digits in the key. If you have any, even passing, familiarity with encryption, you will have heard of 128-bit encryption. This is encryption that uses a 128-bit key—2^{128} possibilities, or $3.024 * 10^{28}$ possible combinations. Even a supercomputer will have a difficult time with this.

A very popular encryption algorithm is the PGP, or Pretty Good Privacy, algorithm. You can download software on the Internet, for free, that implements PGP encryption on your messages. Following are a few Web sites that will allow you to download a free copy of software that implements PGP. You can also learn more about PGP at these sites:

- http://web.mit.edu/network/pgp.html
- http://www.mccune.cc/PGP.htm
- http://www.pgp.net/pgpnet/

Creating Secure Applications

It is a fact that there will be intruders that will attempt to gain access to a company's network. It does not matter whether they are attempting to send a virus, steal data, or are just curious, it will happen. You might be thinking that this is the responsibility of the network administrator, not you, a programmer. If so, you couldn't be more wrong.

The way in which intruders usually gain access to a system is via "holes," or flaws in software products. Web server software is often the target of hackers attempting to exploit flaws. Another good example is Microsoft Outlook. This particular product has vulnerabilities that have been exploited by several virus attacks. The real question is what can you do to make your applications secure.

The first step you can take is to implement some type of encryption. If an intruder does gain access to the system, the data should not be easily read. It should require some decrypting. If you have sensitive data, then store it in an encrypted fashion. This includes passwords. I have actually seen applications that go to the trouble of having a logon and password, but then they store that information in a simple flat file (initialization or .ini file) that can be easily opened and read in Notepad. It does take additional work to encrypt and decrypt such information, but it is well worth the effort.

Also, consider the transmissions we talked about in Chapter 11. We put simple text data into a packet and sent it across a network or perhaps the Internet. Anyone using a "packet sniffer" can get a copy of that packet, open it up, and read it. If you are sending any sensitive data, including passwords, that data is vulnerable to intruders. If you combine the encryption techniques we have discussed in this chapter with the socket programming discussed in Chapter 11, you will have reasonably secure Internet communications.

Another area of application security involves the use of object models. In Chapter 14, I introduced you to the subject of object models. These useful items are also useful to hackers. When you are exposing the functionality of your application you must ensure that what you are exposing is either not sensitive data or cannot be exploited. Most viruses that target Microsoft Outlook do so by manipulating its object model. Outlook exposes all of its functionality via objects, and it is a relatively simple matter to write a script that will utilize and exploit this object model.

When you create applications that have an object model that is exposed for others to utilize, make certain that you have not exposed features that might be exploited by a hacker. You do not want your application, or its data, to be the door through which an intruder walks.

Summary

This topic is a very complex one, and a single chapter will hardly make you a master of cryptography. However, this chapter should give you the skills required to understand encryption and even to implement simple encryption methods in your own programs. If you wish to delve deeper into the subject, particularly from a Visual Basic perspective, check out Appendix B for some recommendations for further reading.

Review Questions

1. How many possible combinations are there for a 4-bit key?

2. What do you call an encryption algorithm that simply replaces each character with a different character?

3. What do you call an encryption algorithm that uses several different substitution schemes?

4. What is another term for encrypting a message?

5. What is another term for decrypting a message?

6. What is so special about 128-bit encryption?

7. What is PGP?

Deploying Your Application

Introduction

After you have successfully developed and tested your application, there is still another step left in the development process. The final stage in developing an application is preparing it for deployment. Your application will not be of much use if you do not deploy it to users. The first impression a user gets from your application is the installation. If problems arise during installation, the user already has a negative perception of your application. Luckily for you, deploying your application in Visual Basic.NET is relatively simple. To begin with, .NET applications will not have conflicts with other applications or components. This is a major improvement over previous versions of Visual Studio. Windows applications can get complicated with many DLLs needed and so many different versions available. The .NET framework will allow different versions of a component on the same computer without any conflict.

Packaging your application can be as simple as copying all of the files into a common directory. Your application is comprised of one or more assemblies. Because assemblies are self-describing, you are not required to provide any information to the operating system about your application. You do not need to register your application or the components with the Windows Registry.

If you want your application to set up the Start menu or to create an icon in the Quick Launch toolbar, you may want to package your application to be installed by the Windows Installer. This way the Windows Installer can create the Start menu item or the icon for your user.

As I stated, for simple applications, installation is as easy as simply copying your files over to the destination drive. Much of this book was written using the Beta 2 and the release candidates of Visual Basic.NET. Neither of those came with any deployment wizard. So far, every version of VB has had a deployment wizard, so it is a fairly safe bet that the final release of VB.NET will have a fairly easy-to-use deployment wizard as well. The bulk of this chapter is concerned with preparing deployments of your applications manually, using a variety of command-line utilities. No matter what the final release of Visual Basic.NET has or does not have, you will be ready to deploy your applications.

You can also write a simple batch file that copies all the required files from a source (such as a CD) to a destination. You can write batch files in any text editor; I use Notepad. You then save them with a .bat extension. A sample install.bat is included in the downloadable file in \Examples\Chapter 16\. It copies the files for Example 2-1 onto the C drive.

The complexity of configuring your application will vary depending on how you develop the application. If you use private assemblies, then all you have to do is copy all the files to the same directory. If you want to use public assemblies or use different directories for some assemblies, you will need to create a configuration file. This is just an XML file that contains configuration information. The applications we have done in this book simply used a single private assembly, so they should present no complications when installing. Remember, however, that the client machine must support .NET or your .NET application will not run.

Deploying your application can be as simple as copying the files from a CD-ROM or across the network to a directory on the user's computer. Because the assemblies in your application are self-describing and contain all necessary references internally, the application executes, and it will search for these references itself. However, this simple installation may not always be suitable for your needs. In this chapter, I will show you how to install your Visual Basic.NET applications using the Windows Installer and creating Web downloads. When deploying controls, you need to take some additional factors into account.

Packaging Code

The first step in getting your VB.NET application deployed is getting it packaged. Depending on the complexity of your application, it will consist of one or more DLL and/or EXE (executable) files. You have to package them into one or more assemblies. An assembly consists of two to four parts:

- Assembly manifest — This is mandatory because it contains the metadata that the CLR needs to execute the code.

- Type metadata — This describes the types (class and methods) that are contained in the assembly.

- Executables — The .exe you compiled (mandatory).

- Resources — This can be any type of non-executable file that needs to be used by code in the assembly.

The first thing we will need to examine is the manifest. This part is vital since it provides all the information about your application. By using the Intermediate Language Disassembler (ildasm.exe), you can see what is contained in an assembly.

Creating Cabinet Files

The installation utility uses Cabinet (Cab) files to store everything your application needs to run. You will need to create these cab files. You can do this with the utility Makecab.exe. Cab files also compress the files they contain, thus reducing the amount of data you have to distribute. Cabinet files are often used to download controls over the Internet using a Web browser.

You can also use Visual Studio.NET to create MSI files for the deployment of your application. An MSI file is a Microsoft Installation file. It is what Microsoft needs to run its built-in installation program. If your user double-clicks on an .MSI file the Microsoft Installer will automatically launch.

Version numbers have always been important. Have you ever seen a dialog box that told you that you needed a DLL with version 1.2.3456 or higher? You may have originally had the correct version of the DLL, but some other application you subsequently installed overwrote that DLL with a different version. This was often referred to as "DLL Hell." This has changed with the .NET framework because you can have as many different versions of an assembly on your system as you like. Each is self contained and does not conflict with any other. You can even have different applications that use an assembly with the same name, but with a different version. This means that the version number has become more of a "compatibility number" and controls the way the CLR locates the appropriate assembly.

A version number must have the following structure:

```
Major.Minor[.Build[.Revision]]
```

This means that the Major and Minor are mandatory, and that Build and Revision are optional. However, if you want to use Revision, you must have Build. The value of all the four parts can range from 0 to 65,534. This will be enough, especially with the speed at which Microsoft changes technologies. However, you will not usually see numbers go this high. The Major version number is usually used to denote a major change and release of a product. The Minor version number is usually used when some improvement or bug fix has been done to a Major revision. The Build number is simply a record of how many times you have compiled a product and which compilation this is. The Build number is often omitted in commercial products but can be very useful for beta testers. Revision numbers are often used when a quick bug fix is implemented. It should not be used if any significant change has been made in the program.

Remember, the version number can also be thought of as a compatibility number, so a change in version number can reflect the following compatibility phases:

Compatible   Only the Revision number changes. Change of revision is seen as a quick fix engineering (QFE) update and the assemblies are assumed to still be compatible.

Possibly compatible   The Build number has changed. There is no guarantee for backward compatibility. It will be up to you, as the programmer, to decide if different Build numbers will be compatible.

Incompatible   Minor and/or Major changes.

The versioning is essential for the CLR to find a compatible assembly. Consider this process step by step:

1. The CLR reads the application configuration file, the machine configuration file, and the publisher policy configuration file to determine what the correct version number is for the assembly that is referenced, and thus needs to be loaded.

2. The CLR checks to determine if this assembly has already been requested in the application domain. If that is the case, the already loaded assembly is used. Note that this check is based on the assembly's full name: name, version, etc.

   You can get in trouble if you have two assemblies with the same name, although one has the .dll extension and the other .exe. After the .exe version is loaded and another assembly makes a reference to the .dll version, the CLR will conclude that that assembly is already loaded because the CLR makes the distinction based on the full name, which does not include a file extension.

3. If the assembly is not loaded, the CLR checks the Global Assembly Cache (GAC). If the assembly is not located in the GAC, the CLR checks the configuration file if a <codeBase> is provided. If so, this directory is checked for the presence of the assembly. In case the assembly is not located in the <codeBase> directory, the lookup fails. If no <codeBase> is provided, the application base is checked. If no match can be found, it checks the privatePath directories.

Configuring the .NET Framework

It is vital when deploying an application to make sure that the installation process on a computer goes smoothly and that the application executes as you intended it to. You should also remember how and where the CLR finds the right assemblies, how it chooses which assembly version to use, and how it sets security. The list goes on and on. Before .NET, you mainly needed the Registry to accomplish this. Now, you create the same information in XML-coded configuration files. These configuration files contain all the information needed. There are three types of configuration files—machine, application, and security.

Chapter 16

Creating Configuration Files

Obviously, if configuration files are required for you to install your application, you will need to understand how to create them. The configuration files, like nearly all other setting files within the .NET framework, are XML-coded, adhering to a well-formed XML schema. In general, a configuration file consists of the following sections:

- Startup — Holds settings that are related to the CLR to use.
- Runtime — Holds settings that are related to the CLR working, especially how and where the CLR can find the proper assemblies.
- Remoting — Holds settings related to the remoting system.
- Security — Holds the settings of the security policy.
- Class API — Holds the settings related to the use of Windows API.
- Configuration — Holds the settings that are used by the application.

Technically speaking, you could find or put any of these sections in any configuration file. However, if a section does not apply to the use of the configuration file, it will be ignored. Therefore, it is recommended that you only place configuration data in the configuration file designed for that purpose.

It is important to realize that configuration files have an impact on the workings of all applications that make use of the .NET framework. This is especially true for the machine and security configuration files. For this reason, you must be very careful with making changes to these files before assessing the impact they will have. A good rule of thumb is to only alter the files you absolutely must alter, and then only as much as you need to, no more.

Application Configuration Files

The application configuration file should be located in the installation directory of the application and named after the application's program executable name with .config added after the extension. An example would be myprogram.exe.config. The CLR checks the application directory for this file. Because an application does not need its own configuration file, it can completely depend on the machine configuration file. Application configuration files are not required. They are only necessary if you want your application to use something other than the default values. However, the CLR will only look in the program's installation directory for the file. If you place it somewhere else or use a different suffix, the CLR will not find it, which may mean that the CLR will not be able to load the application. In the case of a browser-based application, the HTML page should use a link element to give the location of the configuration file, which resides in a directory on the Web server.

The application configuration file can be useful for assembly binding settings that relate to specific assembly versions an application needs and the places the CLR has to look for the application's private assemblies. This is referred to as probing.

Machine/Administrator Configuration Files

When the .NET run-time system is installed on a machine, the machine.config file is also installed. You will find this file in the Config subdirectory of the .NET installation directory. For example, on my machine, this config file is located at C:\WIN2000\Microsoft.NET\Framework\v1.0.2914\CONFIG\. This file is important since it contains the correct assembly binding policy of that machine. The file also contains the settings for remoting channels. The settings in the machine configuration file take precedence over those in any other configuration file and cannot be overridden by any other file. The machine.config file is expected to reflect the entire machine; any change to it may result in the disruption of the functionality of the CLR. You are unlikely to need to alter these configuration files, but it is useful for you to know what they are.

The following is an excerpt from a machine.config file so that you will be familiar with the content.

```xml
<?xml version="1.0" encoding="UTF-8" ?>
<configuration>
   <configSections>
      <!-- tell .NET Framework to ignore CLR sections -->
      <section name="runtime"  type="System.Configuration.
         IgnoreSectionHandler, System, Version=1.0.2411.0,
         Culture=neutral, PublicKeyToken=b77a5c561934e089"
         allowLocation="false" />
      <section name="mscorlib" type="System.Configuration.
         IgnoreSectionHandler, System, Version=1.0.2411.0,
         Culture=neutral, PublicKeyToken=b77a5c561934e089"
         allowLocation="false" />
```

```
<section name="startup"  type="System.Configuration.
   IgnoreSectionHandler, System, Version=1.0.2411.0,
   Culture=neutral, PublicKeyToken=b77a5c561934e089"
   allowLocation="false" />
<section name="system.runtime.remoting" type="System.
   Configuration.IgnoreSectionHandler, System,
   Version=1.0.2411.0, Culture=neutral,
   PublicKeyToken=b77a5c561934e089" allowLocation="false" />
<section name="system.diagnostics" type="System.Diagnostics.
   DiagnosticsConfigurationHandler, System, Version=1.0.2411.0,
   Culture=neutral, PublicKeyToken=b77a5c561934e089" />
<section name="appSettings" type="System.Configuration.
   NameValueFileSectionHandler, System, Version=1.0.2411.0,
   Culture=neutral, PublicKeyToken=b77a5c561934e089" />
<sectionGroup name="system.net">
<section name="authenticationModules" type="System.Net.
   Configuration.NetAuthenticationModuleHandler, System,
   Version=1.0.2411.0, Culture=neutral,
   PublicKeyToken=b77a5c561934e089" />
```

Let me point out a few vital items you should take note of. The foremost is that what you see here is only a fragment of a machine.config file. This file is somewhat large and quite complex. I would encourage you not to make any changes to this file unless you are absolutely certain of what you are doing. It might also be a good idea to make a backup copy of your machine.config file. Then I would further suggest that you keep a log of any changes you make to your main machine.config. In a worst-case scenario, this information will be helpful should you need to call technical support due to inappropriate changes you may have made to the config file.

Security Configuration Files

Security configuration files describe the security policy settings. There are at least three applicable security configuration files:

- Enterprise — This file resides in the same location as the machine.config and is called Enterprise.config.

- User — Resides in the directory %USERPROFILE%\Application Data\Microsoft\CLR and is called Security.config.

- Machine — Resides in the same directory as the machine.config and is called Security.config.

These files determine the security settings for your entire .NET framework. I strongly caution you against altering them unless you know exactly what you are doing and why. I also recommend that you make backup copies of these files.

Summary

This chapter introduced you to the various nuances of application deployment. The most critical piece to remember is that most simple applications can be deployed by simply copying the required files to the destination machine. You can write a batch file to accomplish this for you. However, if your application does require more complex configuration, you can manually create or edit configuration files to accomplish what you need. As a beginning VB.NET programmer, it is very unlikely that you will need to do this, but I would be remiss if I did not even mention the subject.

Review Questions

1. Where is machine.config located?
2. When should you reconfigure the security config files?
3. Must all applications have an application config file to be distributed?
4. If I use only private assemblies, what must I do to install my application?
5. How do I account for DLL version conflicts when installing my .NET application?
6. Where does the CLR check for application config files?
7. How many security config files are there?

Chapter 16

Converting Existing Applications

Introduction

This book has focused on giving you the basic skills to develop VB.NET applications. However, just as no person is an island, neither is any technology. VB.NET does not exist in a programming vacuum. Visual Basic has been around for ten years, and VB 6.0 has been around since 1998. That means that a lot of code done in previous versions of VB is still out there. If you are an experienced VB programmer making the transition to VB.NET then you undoubtedly have some old code you will be considering upgrading. If you are new to Visual Basic, you are likely to encounter older code written by other programmers that you may choose to upgrade. In either case, you should be aware of the various factors that are involved in upgrading an existing application to VB.NET. However, I am certain that this chapter will be of greatest interest to those readers who have experience with previous versions of Visual Basic.

The .NET architecture is quite a departure from previous versions of Visual Basic and many applications will require significant changes if you choose to upgrade them. Visual

271

Basic.NET has transitioned to making everything an object, prompting significant programming changes. You will have to modify data types to match the new Common Type System (CTS), which will impact applications using the Variant data type. There are other considerations. Some keywords have been changed or even removed, and your Visual Basic forms will need to be upgraded to Windows forms. Error handling will be completely different as well, and you will have to convert all existing error handling to the new exception-based format.

As you have seen, data access has changed drastically and is based on XML. This is a fundamental paradigm shift, and addressing these issues can take considerable effort. Interfaces and events have changed from previous versions of Visual Basic. Fortunately, Microsoft has provided Visual Studio.NET with an upgrade tool. If you open a VB 6.0 project with VB.NET, the upgrade tool will attempt to upgrade your application from Visual Basic 6.0 to Visual Basic.NET. Unfortunately, not all aspects of your application can be automatically upgraded. The sections of your application that the upgrade utility cannot upgrade will be commented out. You will then have to manually convert them. Some applications will still require a large development effort in order to upgrade.

Upgrade Considerations

As I already mentioned, some applications will be very difficult for you to upgrade. There are some key points to examine when deciding whether or not upgrading the application is even feasible, and if so, how much effort will be required. The following are considerations you should carefully look at before deciding on upgrading. Each of these issues will be explained in detail.

- Early binding of variables
- ADO Data Access
- Using the Date data type to store dates
- Using constants instead of actual values

Early Binding

Like Visual Basic 6.0, Visual Basic.NET supports either early-bound or late-bound objects. Early binding refers to the technique of declaring a variable a specific data type. Late binding an object is the practice of declaring a variable to be of the generic data type Object, and waiting until run time to assign it to an instance of a specific class. The advantage of early binding is that the compiler can catch a variety of errors. This includes errors involving using incorrect properties or calling nonexistent methods. This is because the compiler knows what type of object it is and knows what methods and properties it has. This is made possible by using a type library.

Using late binding objects has some disadvantages. The primary disadvantage is that the compiler does not know what type of object it is, and cannot check for property or methods. So, essentially, if your VB 6.0 application uses late binding, you will have some problems upgrading.

Another issue to consider is that some properties don't have the same name they used to have. For example, labels used to have a Caption property. That is now the Text property. It is also important to remember that the Default property feature has been removed from the controls. In Visual Basic 6.0, each component had a Default property. You did not have to write Textbox1.Text = "Hi"; you could just write Text1 = "Hi".

The upgrade tool will convert all references to the Caption property to Text property. However, if you use a late-bound object with the Caption property, it will not get converted. In such cases, you will have to change the code yourself.

ADO Data Access

VB.NET is backward compatible with regards to data access. This means that Visual Basic.NET still supports DAO, RDO, and ADO code, but with some slight modifications. However, Visual Basic.NET does not support data binding with DAO and RDO. So, if a data access application has DAO or RDO data binding, it is better to upgrade it to ADO before migrating to Visual Basic.NET.

It is even possible to run existing data access applications that utilize VB 6.0-style ADO using Visual Basic.NET with only minor modifications. In order to accomplish this, right-click the Reference node in the Solution Explorer and choose Add Reference. In the References window, choose ADO library from the supplied list of registered COM components.

The Date Data Type

In Visual Basic 6.0, you could use the Double data type to store and manipulate dates. This is no longer supported in Visual Basic.NET; therefore, the following code is invalid in Visual Basic.NET:

```
Dim dblVal as Double
Dim dtVal as Date
dtVal = now
dblVal = dtVal     'This is invalid in Visual Basic.NET
```

However, VB.NET provides two methods that do the conversion between Dates and Doubles. The functions are FromOADate and ToOADate. The ToOADate function converts a Date type value to a Double and FromOADate converts a Double value to Date.

Variants

A Variant is a special data type. What makes the Variant data type so unique is that it can be assigned to any primitive data type such as Empty, Nothing, Integer, String, Boolean, etc. The only limitation with the Variant data type is that it cannot be assigned to fixed-length strings. However, the Variant data type is no longer supported in VB.NET.

Visual Basic.NET uses the Object data type, which effectively replaces the Visual Basic 6.0 Variant data type. The Object data type can also be assigned to any primitive data type, Empty, Nothing, Error, Null, and as a pointer to an object. The default data type in Visual Basic.NET is Object. When a project is migrated to Visual Basic.NET, all variables of type Variant are converted to Object.

Integers

In Visual Basic 6.0, the Long data type was used to represent signed 32-bit numbers, while the Integer data type was used to store 16-bit numbers. This has been changed in Visual Basic.NET. In Visual Basic.NET, the Long data type is used to store signed 64-bit numbers, Integer to store 32-bit numbers, and Short to store 16-bit numbers.

Fixed-Length Strings

In Visual Basic 6.0, variables can be declared with fixed-length strings except for public variables in class modules. Fixed-length strings are not supported in Visual Basic.NET. If the application contains fixed-length strings, the Upgrade Wizard uses a wrapper function to implement the functionality. This is shown in the following Visual Basic 6.0 code, where:

```
Dim MyString as String * 20
```

becomes:

```
Dim MyString as New VB6.FixedLengthString(50)
```

Arrays

In Visual Basic 6.0, it was possible to declare arrays with any lower or upper boundary numbers you liked. The Option Base statement was used to determine the lower boundary number if a range was not specified in the declaration. In VB.NET all arrays start with zero. This makes VB.NET compatible with all other programming languages. However, it means that the Option Base statement is obsolete.

During the upgrade process, all Option Base statements are removed. All arrays that have their lower boundary as zero are left as is while those that are non-zero based are upgraded to an array wrapper class.

Chapter 17

Internet Information Server (IIS) Applications

The WebClass is the building block of all IIS applications in VB 6.0. It is a Visual Basic component that resides on a Web server, responding to input from the browser. WebClasses no longer exist in Visual Basic.NET. The migration tool upgrades all WebClass applications to Web forms instead. As a result, migrated applications have to undergo some modifications before they are ready to run.

Converting Forms

Visual Basic forms have been replaced with Windows forms in Visual Basic.NET. The object model of Windows forms is different from Visual Basic 6.0 forms. However, the object models are compatible. The Upgrade Wizard converts Visual Basic forms to Windows forms during the upgrade operation. User controls are then upgraded to Windows controls. However, custom property tags and accelerator key settings are not upgraded.

Windows API

A majority of the Windows API functions can be used as they are in Visual Basic.NET. The only modification you will have to make is to change the data types accordingly.

AND/OR/NOT

In Visual Basic 6.0, the AND, OR, XOR, and NOT operators perform both logical and bitwise operations depending on the expressions. In Visual Basic.NET, AND, OR, XOR, and NOT operators only apply to the Boolean type. Visual Basic.NET uses new bitwise operators for bitwise operations. They are BitOr, BitAnd, and BitXor.

The Upgrade Wizard upgrades an AND/OR statement which is non-Boolean or contains functions, methods, or properties that use a compatibility function with the same behavior as that in Visual Basic 6.0. Boolean statements are upgraded to use the native Visual Basic.NET statement.

Error Handling

In Visual Basic 6.0 the On Error statement was used to handle errors. The Err object was provided to give diagnostic information about the error. The Number and Description properties provided the error code and a description of the error. The main drawback of this kind of error handling is the inability to trap errors raised by Windows DLLs. System errors that arise during calls to Windows DLLs do not raise exceptions and cannot be trapped by this style of error handling.

Visual Basic.NET uses structured exception handling to handle errors and exceptions. Most programming languages (C, C++, Java, etc.) use this technique to handle errors. This handling is accomplished via the Try...Catch blocks you have already seen in this book. The Common Language Runtime (CLR) uses structured exception handling based on exception objects and protected blocks of code. When an exception or an error occurs, an object is created to represent the exception. The exception objects created are objects of Exception classes derived from System.Exception. It is also possible to create custom exception classes.

It is possible to code multiple Catch blocks for a Try block. A Catch block that contains a filter for a specific exception type is invoked when that exception is thrown. You can then have separate Catch blocks to handle different types of errors. The Catch block that contains no parameters, also called a general exception handler, is invoked for all other exceptions. The Finally block follows the Catch block and contains the cleanup code.

It is important to note the order of the Catch statements if you are coding a general exception handler as well as specific exception handlers. The general handler should be the last if you are coding Catch blocks to handle specific exceptions. If the general handler is coded first followed by other specific handlers, the runtime invokes the general handler by default since the general handler handles all exceptions. The rule of thumb is to go from specific exception handlers to general exception handlers.

Chapter

Using Constants

It is a good programming practice to use constants rather than the actual values that represent the constants or variables that store these values. In Visual Basic.NET, the value of True has been changed from –1 to 1. The usage of constants ensures that the correct values are replaced when your project is upgraded. However, even if an actual value is used, it is quite possible your project will be upgraded properly.

The Upgrade Wizard

As soon as you attempt to open a Visual Basic 6.0 project in Visual Basic.NET, the Upgrade Wizard will launch.

The first step in the wizard summarizes the actions that will be done throughout the Upgrade Wizard. It then creates a new Visual Basic.NET project in a separate folder that you specify. This means you will still have the original unchanged project you can return to if need be. This is a very important feature.

After the initial screen is displayed, the next step in the upgrade process is to choose what kind of project the existing project should be upgraded to. The Upgrade Wizard will determine the project type of the existing Visual Basic 6.0 project and selects the appropriate option.

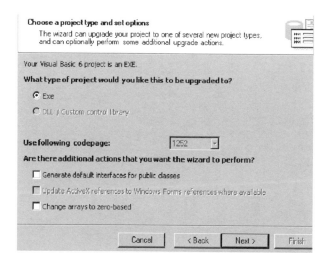

Next, you will specify where the new upgraded project should be created. Note that your existing project will be left unchanged.

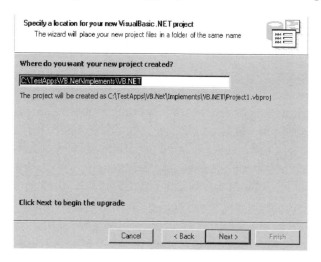

Next you will see the screen informing you that the project is ready to be upgraded. If you are set to proceed, click Next.

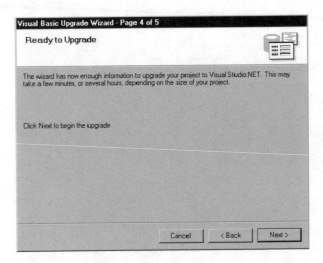

When the project is upgraded, the language is modified for any syntax changes and Visual Basic forms are converted to Windows forms. More often than not, you will have to make changes to the code after it is upgraded. This is necessary because certain objects either have no equivalents, or the properties of some objects have been erased or renamed.

The last screen will display the current status of the upgrade process. After the project is upgraded, the Upgrade Wizard creates an upgrade report that itemizes problems and inserts comments in the code, informing the programmer of what changes should be made. It is not difficult to find the parts of the code that need updating, because the Upgrade wizard marks the code that needs changing, even including comments with the designation. The comments begin with the text TODO, and the IDE picks up these statements and lists them in the TaskList window. (Notice that the TODO is borrowed from Visual C++ wizards. They have been doing this for quite some time.) Navigating to the appropriate line is as easy as double-clicking the item in the TaskList window. Each item in the upgrade report is even associated with a related online help topic, which not only explains the need to change the code, but how to do it.

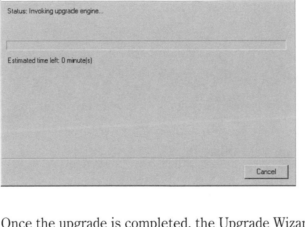

Once the upgrade is completed, the Upgrade Wizard will attach various comments to the upgraded code. These can be categorized into the following four types, based on their severity:

- UPGRADE_ISSUE — These errors will generate build errors and prevent the application from compiling. As a result, they are marked as compiler errors. It is absolutely necessary to correct them before running the project.

- UPGRADE_TODO — These errors will not hinder the compilation process, but may result in run-time errors.

- UPGRADE_WARNING — These are errors that will not result in compiler errors but that might still cause an error when referencing the item during run time. It is not absolutely necessary to rectify them, but it is highly recommended that you at least review them.

- UPGRADE_NOTE — This indicates serious changes in the code. Upgrade notes are added when there is a major structural change in the code. You will have to look closely at these to make sure that the conversion went smoothly.

After the Visual Basic 6.0 project has been upgraded to Visual Basic.NET, an upgrade report is added to the project. This report contains the following details and is named _Upgradereport.htm:

- Project name
- Time of upgrade

- Upgrade settings: Upgrade settings consist of the following key-value pairs:

    A Boolean value indicating whether ADO+ was used

    A Boolean value indicating whether the user requested the Upgrade Wizard to generate public interfaces for classes

    The name of the logfile

    The kind of project this project migrated from

    A Boolean value to indicate if the user preferred to change the arrays to zero-based

    The path to the output directory

    The name of the project that was created

    The actual path to the project that was created

- A list of project files with information regarding the new filename, the old filename, file type, status, errors, warnings, as well as other issues.

Summary

Clearly, upgrading from Visual Basic 6.0 to VB.NET can be a difficult task. It is recommended that you seriously consider the difficulties involved before you embark on this process. In some cases you may determine that a project should simply be left in VB 6.0. I should also point out that you should not attempt to upgrade earlier versions of VB to VB.NET.

Keywords

This list is by no means exhaustive. It is simply a quick reference of those keywords covered in this book. These are the keywords that I have found beginners are most likely to use.

Abs	This method of the Math class returns the absolute value of the number passed to it.
Acos	This method of the Math class returns the arc cosine of the number passed to it.
App.Activate	This statement allows you to activate a program that is already running. You can activate a program either by using its name as it appears in the toolbar or by using the Windows handle returned to lShell.

```
App.Activate lShell
```

or

```
App.Activate "MS Word"
```

Cbyte	This converts a variable of one type into a byte. If the expression you are converting lies outside the acceptable range for a byte, you will get an error. The syntax is:

```
Cbyte(MyVariable)
```

Cdate	Much like Cbyte, this expression converts a variable to the Data type. Its syntax is:

```
Cdate (MyVariable)
```

There are also statements like Clong, Cint, etc., to convert a variable to an Integer or a Long value.

Chr

This returns the actual character denoted by an ASCII character number. For example, chr(65) returns "A".

Clear

This keyword can be applied to the Clipboard object, a combo box, or a list box. It causes all items stored therein to be cleared. Example:

```
List1.Clear
```

Cos

This will return the cosine of a number. For example, you can use Cos(15) to get the cosine of 15.

Date

This simply returns the current system date. Example:

```
Let TxtDate.Text = Date
```

Extends

This very important keyword allows the class on the left to inherit the class on the right. Example:

```
childclass Extends parentclass
```

FileCopy

This command causes a file to be copied from its source to a destination file. Example:

```
FileCopy "sourcefile.txt" ,"destinationfile.txt"
```

FileLen

This function returns the length of a file in bytes. Syntax:

```
FileLen("myfile.txt")
```

Format

This allows you to change the format of any variable, text box, or label. Let's look at some examples.

If I want the date to be yymmdd, I use the Format command like this:

```
Let TxtDate.Text = Format(date,"yymmdd")
```

I place an open parenthesis after the Format command and then tell it what I wish to format. In this case, that is "date." The letters in quotation marks tell it how to format it. We can also format numbers. For example, if you want a number to appear as a dollar amount:

```
Let TxtMyNumber.Text =
Format(TxtMyNumber.Text,"$###,###.##")
```

	Your number will show a dollar sign, six digits, a decimal point, and two additional digits.
Hide	This makes whatever you are referring to invisible. Example:

```
FrmOrders.Hide
```

The form is still loaded, but it's not visible.

Import	This keyword allows you to import other namespaces. Once you have imported a namespace, you can instantiate classes that are defined in that namespace, or you can inherit from them and create your own classes.
IsDate	This function will return a Boolean value (True/False) indicating whether or not a variable can be converted to a date. Example:

```
IsDate(MyVariable)
```

IsNull	This function is used to see if another variable is null. Example:

```
IsNull(MyVariable)
```

IsNumeric	This function is used to see if a variable is numeric. It returns a Boolean.
Left	This command allows you to get the left portion of a string. For example, if you want to get the left three characters in a text box you can use this code:

```
Private sMyString as String
Let sMyString = Left(TxtMyText.Test,3)
```

This will place the left three characters of TxtMyText into the string sMyString. If the text box TxtMyText had the word "Hello" in it, sMyString would now have "Hel" in it.

Len	If you want to get the length of some variable or text, you can use the Len command to get that value. Here are two examples:

```
Let iLength = Len(TxtName.Text) 'this will take the length
                                'of the text in txtname
                                'and place it in the
                                'variable iLength
```

```
Let iLength = Len(iAccount) 'This will take the length of
                            'the variable iAccount
                            'and place it in the variable
                            'iLength
```

Load

This will load a form. If you have a main form and you wish to load other forms, you can use this command. For example, if you have a form called frmOrders and you have a command button you wish to use to load it in, place the following code in that command button's Click event:

```
Load frmOrders
```

Ltrim

This command will remove all trailing spaces from the left side of a string.

Mid

This command will return the substring of a string passed to it. Example:

```
MyString = Mid(somestring, 3,5)
```

Returns the substring of "somestring" beginning at the third character and going to the fifth character.

Msgbox

This keyword simply tells the computer that you want to display a message box.

Pow

This method of the Math class returns a Double that is the number passed to it, raised to the power passed to it; Pow(5,2) returns 5 squared, or 25.

Right

This is very similar to the Left command, except that it returns the right side of the string requested. For example:

```
Private sMyString as String
Let sMyString = Right(TxtMyText.Text,2)
```

If the text box TxtMyText had the word "Hello" in it, sMyString would now have "lo" in it.

Sendkeys

After using App.Activate, you can send keystrokes to a program. For example, if you have activated Notepad.exe you can then use the code:

```
Sendkeys "My Dog Has Fleas"
```

And the phrase in quotes will appear in Notepad.

SetFocus	This tells the program to change focus to another control. You might place something in your cmdAddNew button that sets focus to the first text box on your form. Example:

```
btnAddnew_Click()
        TxtFirst.SetFocus
End Sub
```

Shell	This is a very useful keyword. By using the Shell command, you can start other programs. Example:

```
Private lShell as Long
lShell = Shell("c:\path\name.exe",1)
```

This tells the computer to take the pathname and start the program Name.exe in standard mode (1) and return its Windows handle to the variable entitled lShell.

Show	This shows something that is hidden. If you use it in conjunction with a form that is not loaded, it will first load the form then show it. Example:

```
FrmOrders.Show
```

Sin	This will return the sine of a variable such as Sin(45) returns the sine of 45.
Time	This returns the current system time. You can display this to the user with some code like:

```
Let LblTime.Text = Time
```

Tan	This method of the Math class returns the tangent of the angle passed to it.
Trim	This command will remove all blank spaces from a string.
Ucase	If you wish to compare two values but you don't care if their cases match (lower- or uppercase), you can compare the uppercase values of both. Example:

```
If Ucase(sSearchValue) = Ucase(TxtLastName.Text) then…
```

You can also compare the lowercase values using the same technique with the keyword Lcase.

Other Resources

This book is simply meant to get you started with Visual Basic.NET. There is a lot more you can learn. Below is a list of some of my favorite resources. This list is not exhaustive, but most of the Web pages listed have links to other Web pages.

Web Pages

Comp.lang.basic.visual.misc: This is a usenet newsgroup where you can ask questions and usually get answers.

Chuck Easttom's Visual Basic Page (http://www.geocities/~chuckeasttom/vb/Vb.htm): This is my own page for Visual Basic beginners.

Carl and Gary's VB Page (http://www.cgvb.com): This is the mother of all Visual Basic pages.

Ed's VB Page (http://www.tiac.net/users/efields/vbhp.htm): This is a pretty good page with lots of resources.

Microsoft Certification Page (http://www.microsoft.com/mcp/ie30.htm): If you are interested in getting certified from Microsoft, this is the page for you.

Zarr's VB Site (www.zarr.net): An excellent Visual Basic Web site with lots of content and links.

Visual Basic Web Magazine (www.vbwm.com): This is an online magazine.

Visual Basic Developers Corner (http://www.mvps.org/vbnet/): A really top-notch site.

Other Books

I think my book is a good start for you. However, that is all it is—a start. It is not meant to make you an expert in all things Visual Basic or all things programming. Let me recommend a few books you might consider reading in the future to expand your knowledge a bit.

Iterative UML Development Using Visual Basic 6.0 by Patrick Sheridan and Jean M. Sekula from Wordware Publishing. While this book was designed with VB 6.0 in mind, UML is not language specific. It is a design methodology and can be applied to any programming language.

Learn MS Access 2000 Programming by Example by Julitta Korol from Wordware Publishing. As I've mentioned, it is vital that you have a good grounding in MS Access in order to be a professional VB programmer. You should also consider learning about SQL Server or Oracle.

Learn SQL in Three Days by José Ramalho from Wordware Publishing. A thorough knowledge of Structured Query Language is a critical thing for professional business programming.

Learn Encryption Techniques with Visual Basic and C++ by Gilbert Held from Wordware Publishing. This book will give you a pretty good grounding in encryption and show you applications in both Visual Basic and C++.

The Practical SQL Handbook by Judith S. Bowman, Sandra L. Emerson, and Marcy Darnovsky from Addison-Wesley Developers Press. This book gives a very thorough coverage of SQL.

Ready to Run Visual Basic Algorithms by Rod Stephens from Wiley Computer Publishing. Rod Stephens' book is the most thorough coverage of data structures and algorithms for VB programmers that I have ever seen. I highly recommend this book.

Magazines/Journals

The premier Visual Basic developers magazine is *Visual Basic Programmers Journal*. You may wish to seriously consider getting a subscription to it, which you can do at http://www.windx.com/.

Answers to Review Questions

Chapter 1

1. What is a GUI?

   Graphical User Interface; it is the part of your application that a user sees and interacts with.

2. List two ways to run an application inside the IDE.

   a. Use the F5 key.

   b. Press the Play button on the toolbar.

   c. Use the drop-down menu.

3. Write a line of code that will display the length of a string called "MyString" in a text box named "Textbox1."

   ```
   Textbox1.Text = len(MyString)
   ```

4. What is a variable?

   A place in memory set aside to hold data of a particular type.

5. What is a statement?

A line of code that performs an action.

6. What does the F7 key do?

It shows the Code window for the currently selected object.

7. List four components.

Button, label, list box, picture box, combo box, text box, command button, group box

8. What is an event?

An event is a function that is called automatically in response to either a user or a system action.

9. What does the F4 key do for you in the IDE?

It displays the Properties window for the currently selected component.

10. What is an IDE?

Integrated development environment

Chapter 2

1. What does the Val() function do?

It takes a string argument and returns its numeric value.

2. What does the Ucase function do?

It returns the uppercase equivalent of a string.

3. What is the purpose of the Format function?

To display a string in a specific format.

4. List four VB.NET data types.

Integer, Long, Single, Double, String, Boolean, Byte, Short, Char, Date, Object

5. List four VB.NET operators

+, −, *, /, =, %, &

6. What is the purpose of the modulus operator?

It divides the number on the left by the number on the right, and returns the remainder.

7. What is a parameter?

    It is a variable that is passed to a function when that function is called. Sometimes parameters are also referred to as arguments.

8. What are the three parts to the message box function called?

    Message, buttons, and title

9. What is a function?

    It is a group of related statements that work together to perform some task.

10. What is the purpose of a Select Case statement?

    It works much like an If-Then statement, except that it is more useful when there are multiple options. It literally selects the path of code execution based on the status of the variable upon which the Select Case is based.

Chapter 3

1. What does the term "encapsulation" mean?

    It refers to the data and the functions that work on that data being wrapped together into a class.

2. What is a term for a class that is being inherited from?

    It can be called a base class or a parent class. Some developers even call it a superclass.

3. Can you inherit private functions?

    No, you can only inherit public and protected functions.

4. What is a method?

    It is a function that is inside a class.

5. What is an access modifier?

    A keyword that determines if a variable or function can be accessed from outside the module it is in.

6. What is the purpose of the protected modifier?

    It causes a variable or a function to behave just like a private one, but it allows it to be inherited.

7. What is the purpose of a Set property?

    To change the value of a class's property.

8. What does the WithEvents keyword do?

    It causes the events associated with a class to also be generated.

9. What is the code to raise an event?

    ```
    RaiseEvent Event_Name(Event Parameters)
    ```

10. What is the code to create a new event?

    ```
    Public Event Event_Name(Event Parameters)
    ```

Note: This should be declared in the general declarations section of the class module.

Chapter 4

1. What is generational garbage collection?

    This is a garbage collection algorithm based on looking at how old an object is. The newer the object, the more likely it is to be eligible for garbage collection.

2. What class do VB.NET primitive data types inherit from?

    Value

3. List three methods of the Graphics class.

    DrawEllipse, DrawRectangle, DrawLine, DrawArc, DrawIcon, DrawBeziers, DrawCurve, DrawClosedCurve, DrawPolygon, DrawString

4. What is an assembly?

    Reusable, self-describing packages that are self contained. Everything you need to run a particular application is contained or described in the assembly.

5. What is typecasting?

    Changing a variable from one data type into another data type.

6. What is metadata?

    Metadata is simply binary information that describes just about every aspect of your code. It contains information about every type defined and referenced within your assembly.

7. What package must you import in order to utilize the File and FileStream classes?

    Imports System.IO

8. What is the purpose of the Common Type System?

    It has many purposes but the one most discussed in this chapter was the ability to have data types that are consistent throughout all the .NET languages.

9. What method of a class do you utilize if you wish to destroy that class?

    Dispose

10. What method of a class do you use if you wish to finalize the class, but still have it eligible for reuse?

    Close

Chapter 5

1. What are the two types of data-bound components?

    Simple and complex

2. What is SQL?

    Structured Query Language. It is the language of databases.

3. List four SQL commands.

    INNER JOIN, DISTINCT, SELECT, FROM, ORDER BY

4. What is a field?

    A single piece of data in a database (such as a first name).

5. What is a relational database?

    This is a method of storing data where various records and tables can be related to each other based on the values held in certain fields.

6. What is a dataset?

    It is a Visual Basic object that represents a set of records.

7. What does "simple bound" mean?

A single Windows component is bound to a single field in the database.

8. What does "complex bound" mean?

A single Windows component is bound to a group of records in a database.

9. What is a record?

A set of fields that represent one item in a database.

10. What is a table?

A set of related records.

Chapter 6

1. List two container components.

Panel and Groupbox

2. What method is used to add items to the end of a list box or combo box?

Add

3. What method is used to add items to some specific position in a list box or combo box?

Insert

4. What is the purpose of a link label?

To provide a link to a Web site.

5. What is the primary difference between a check box and a radio button?

A checkbox is non-exclusive. A radio button is exclusive.

6. What types of graphics can a picture box display?

Bitmap (bmp), Graphics Interchange Format (gif), and Joint Photographic Experts Group (jpg).

7. What it the purpose of the PasswordChar property of a text box?

If you wish to create a password screen where the user's password is hidden from anyone looking over their shoulder, this property provides an easy means to do that.

8. What does the Value property of a track bar tell you?

The current value of the slider.

9. What is the primary difference between a text box and a label?

   A label displays text as read-only. A text box can display either read-only or read and write.

10. Name five components.

    Button, TextBox, Label, LinkLabel, PictureBox, ComboBox, ListBox, DateTimePicker, TrackBar, TabControl

Chapter 7

1. What is a DataSet?

   The data returned from a request to a data source.

2. Does ADO.NET stay connected to the data source?

   No, ADO.NET does not stay connected.

3. What is the underlying technology behind ADO.NET?

   XML

4. What protocols support remoting in ADO.NET?

   SOAP and HTTP

5. What is used to populate a DataSet?

   A data reader

6. Is data in ADO.NET stored in Binary or Text format?

   Text

7. Until _____ has been executed it is possible to return to a previous data state.

   AcceptChanges

8. What is the best object for executing stored procedures?

   The Command object.

9. What type of data providers are written explicitly for a particular database?

   Managed providers

Chapter 8

1. Where do Web form components run?

   On the server.

2. Where do HTML form components run?

   On the client in the browser.

3. What operating systems can be used with ASP.NET applications?

   Any

4. What must the Web server support in order to host ASP.NET applications?

   .NET

5. What is ASP?

   Active Server Pages

6. What is XML?

   Extensible Markup Language

7. List five HTML components.

   Button, text field, text area, submit button, reset button, table

8. Which is faster, a Windows Forms application or a Web Forms application?

   The Windows Forms application will run faster.

9. Which requires more resources from the client?

   The Windows Forms application requires more resources from the client.

10. How do you deploy an ASP.NET solution to a Web server?

    Simply copy all the files over.

Chapter 9

1. List three ways to create a new control.

   a. Modify an existing component.

   b. Create a compound component from two or more existing components.

   c. Create a component from scratch.

2. Do all components have a user interface?

   No

3. What class do all components inherit from?

   System.Windows.Forms.UserControl

4. What two concepts of object-oriented programming do components best illustrate?

   Encapsulation and code reuse

5. What COM components are non-GUI VB.NET components most like?

   ActiveX DLLs

6. How do you declare an instance of an object so that you have access to its events?

   ```
   Dim WithEvents MyObject as Someclass
   ```

7. How do you create a new event for your component or class?

   ```
   Public Event MyEvent(parameters)
   ```

8. How do you raise an event you have created?

   ```
   RaiseEvent MyEvent(parameters)
   ```

9. What two packages do all Web controls import?

   Imports System.ComponentModel and Imports System.Web.UI

Chapter 10

1. What is a console application?

   An application that runs in the command or DOS prompt and has no graphical user interface.

2. What are three uses for a console application?

   NT Services, testing a class, or simple applications.

3. Can you use a button in a console application?

   No

4. Can you use a class in a console application?

   Yes

5. What is the starting point for a console application?

   `Sub Main()`

6. How do you print to the console screen?

   System.console.out.writeline and system.console.out.write

7. How do you receive input from the user?

   System.console.in.readline and system.console.in.read

8. How do you provide an interactive user interface inside a console application?

   By creating a menu.

Chapter 11

1. What is TCP/IP?

   A suite of protocols used on networks and the Internet.

2. What two properties must you set before you can send a packet via the Winsock control?

   RemoteIP and Port

3. What data type does the Winsock control receive data as?

   String

4. What happens if one end of a connection is left open?

   That port will become "hung" and unusable.

5. What event is triggered in the Winsock control when data arrives?

   Winsock_DataArrival

6. What method of the Winsock control is used to send data?

   SendData

7. What data type is used to send data via the Winsock?

   String

8. What port do Web pages usually operate on?

   80

9. Name two protocols that are part of the TCP/IP suite.

   HTTP and FTP

10. What method of the Winsock control is called to accept a request for a TCP/IP connection?

Winsock1.Accept requested

Chapter 12

1. What is UML?

Unified Modeling Language — it is a tool for designing object-oriented programs.

2. What are the three sections in a class diagram?

Name, member variables, and member functions

3. What is MSF?

Microsoft Solutions Framework

4. What are the phases in MSF?

Envisioning, planning, coding, stabilizing

5. What three things must be covered in the testing phase of the three-step plan?

Valid data, invalid data, and extreme data

6. What are the three main phases of the three-step plan?

Planning, coding, and testing

7. What are the three types of errors?

Syntax, run-time, logic

8. List four types of UML diagrams.

Class, use-case, activity, component, deployment, interaction, sequence, collaboration, state

9. What is the most difficult type of error to fix?

Logic error

10. What is a syntax error?

An error in the use of the language itself.

Chapter 13

1. What is a data structure?

    A structured way of storing and processing data.

2. How does a queue process data?

    Data that is first in is also the first to be processed (FIFO).

3. What is Big O notation?

    A methodology for noting the speed of an algorithm.

4. Is there a difference in the Big O notation for an algorithm that requires 2N passes and one that requires 2N + 1 passes?

    No, since the constant value +1 will not significantly alter the algorithm's speed, both algorithms would be considered 2N.

5. How does a stack process data?

    The last data put into the stack will be the first to be processed (LIFO).

6. How does a quicksort work?

    By dividing a list in half and recursively working through each half.

7. Is an array a type of data structure?

    Yes

8. List four different data structures.

    Stack, queue, list, linked list, double linked list, list tree, binary tree, hash table

9. What happens if the head pointer on a queue reaches the same value as the tail pointer?

    If there is proper error handling and validation, the user will get a message indicating that the queue is full. If not, the queue will begin to overwrite unprocessed data with new data.

10. Which variable is usually the fastest in any speed test?

    Integer

Chapter 14

1. What is the purpose of the Application object in the Outlook model?

    It represents the Outlook application.

2. How do you create a reference to the Outlook object model?

    Select Project | Add Reference

3. What is the code to create an instance of the object model that references a currently running instance of the application?

    ```
    Set OutApp = GetObject("", "Outlook.Application")
    ```

4. What object represents the current window?

    Explorer

5. What object represents the toolbar?

    Command bar

6. What is the code to create an instance of the object model that starts the application running?

    ```
    Set OutApp = CreateObject("Outlook.Application")
    ```

7. List three properties of the Item object.

    CC, BCC, CreationTime, MessageClass, Subject, Size

Chapter 15

1. How many possible combinations are there for a 4-bit key?

    16

2. What do you call an encryption algorithm that simply replaces each character with a different character?

    Caesar cipher

3. What do you call an encryption algorithm that uses several different substitution schemes?

    Multiple alphabet encryption

4. What is another term for encrypting a message?

    Enciphering

Appendix

5. What is another term for decrypting a message?

    Deciphering

6. What is so special about 128-bit encryption?

    The longer the key, the more difficult it will be to break.

7. What is PGP?

    Pretty Good Privacy; it is a 128-bit encryption algorithm.

Chapter 16

1. Where is machine.config located?

    In the operating system's Microsoft.NET\config directory.

2. When should you reconfigure the security config files?

    Never, unless you are absolutely certain of what you are doing.

3. Must all applications have an application config file to be distributed?

    No, they only need an application config file if they require some non-standard configuration.

4. If I use only private assemblies, what must I do to install my application?

    Simply copy the files to the destination directory.

5. How do I account for DLL version conflicts when installing my .NET application?

    You don't; in .NET there are no DLL conflicts.

6. Where does the CLR check for application config files?

    In the application's directory.

7. How many security config files are there?

    Three

HTML Primer

It is certainly not necessary for you to know HTML in order to do Visual Basic programming. However, Web applications are a major focus of the .NET architecture. Thus, it seems prudent to give you a brief introduction to HTML, the language of the Web, so that you have a better understanding of what is being done. The Web Forms application will generate HTML code for you, but if you should need to "tweak" that code, a knowledge of HTML will be most helpful.

HTML, or Hypertext Markup Language, is a relatively simple markup language that Web browsers can use to display Web pages. You can write HTML code in any text editor; I personally use Windows Notepad. When you save the file, remember to save it as an .htm or .html file. The browser recognizes files with the .htm and .html extensions and will look in them for valid HTML code. HTML has had a long history and has gone through a number of revisions. Each successive revision adds more functionality to HTML and with the current version (as of this writing Version 4.0), HTML is a very powerful language that can take some time to learn. Fortunately, most work on Web pages can be done with just the essentials of HTML, and that is what this appendix will teach you.

> **Note:** Many tags in HTML <u>must</u> be closed. The <B> tag must be closed with </B>. However, some tags such as <TD> and <TR> do not have to be closed. Some HTML programmers prefer to close them anyway. I do not. This is simply a style difference, but one you will see throughout this book.

The first question is how to get the Web browser to know that the document has HTML codes for it to read. HTML code is composed of tags that let the browser know what is to be done with certain text. At the beginning of your document, place the command <HTML> and at the end put </HTML>, and the Web browser will know that the codes in between are supposed to be HTML.

```
<HTML>
    put HTML code here
</HTML>
```

You have to admit that this is pretty simple, but this Web page won't do much of anything at all. So let's do the obligatory "Hello, World" sample that every programming book starts off with. It will show you how to do text and some basic HTML.

```
<HTML>
<HEAD>
    <TITLE>My First HTML Page</TITLE>
</HEAD>
<BODY>
<P><CENTER>
<B><FONT SIZE="+2">Hello World</FONT></B>
</CENTER>
</BODY>
</HTML>
```

Believe it or not, this little snippet shows you most of what you need to know about HTML. To begin with, note that everything is contained between the <HTML> and </HTML> tags. These two commands define the beginning and the end of the HTML document. The Web browser will ignore any items outside these commands. Next, we have a section that is contained between the <HEAD> and </HEAD> commands. This is the header portion of your HTML document. The <TITLE> and </TITLE> commands contain the title that will actually appear in the title bar of your browser. Much more can be done in the HEAD section, but that will be addressed later.

Then, we have the <BODY> </BODY> commands. As you might have guessed, this is the body of your HTML document. This is where most of your Web page's code goes. Inside the BODY section, we have some text and some additional information that will define how the text will appear in the browser. The <P> command defines the beginning and the end of a paragraph. The <B> and </B> commands tell the browser to make whatever text is between them bold. The <FONT SIZE="+2"> tells the browser how big the text should be (there are a variety of methods for doing this, as we shall see). The </FONT> command ends the Font section of the HTML code.

By now, I trust you have noticed a pattern. All the commands have an opening command and a closing command. Well, this is true for all but a very few HTML commands. Just remember this rule: you close the commands in opposite order of how you opened them. Notice that in the sample code I opened the commands before the text like this: <P><CENTER> <B><FONT SIZE="+2">, and then closed them like this: </FONT></B></CENTER>. (<P> does not need to be closed.) This is important to remember. You can think of this as "backing out" of your commands.

Images and Hyperlinks

The code we have written so far gives you a very simple Web page that displays one phrase in bold text. Admittedly, this is not very impressive, but if you understand the concepts involved with using these HTML commands, you conceptually understand HTML. Now let's expand your knowledge of HTML. Usually Web pages contain more than simply a title and some text. Other items you might put in a Web page would include images and links to other Web pages. Placing an image on an HTML document is rather simple.

```
<IMG SRC="imagepath\imagename" WIDTH=52 HEIGHT=88 ALIGN=bottom>
```

You simply provide the path to the image and the name of the image, including its file extension (such as .gif, .bmp, .jpg, etc.). The other properties in this command allow you to alter the placement and size of the image. You can alter its width and height as well as its alignment.

You will also note that when you first place an image on an HTML page it has a border around it. You can get rid of this by adding "border = 0" into the tag, as in this example:

```
<IMG SRC="somepic.gif" BORDER =0>
```

Putting a hyperlink to another Web site or to an e-mail address is just as simple:

```
<A HREF="http://www.wordware.com">
```

This link will connect to the URL (Uniform Resource Locator) contained inside the quotation marks. In order to use this methodology to create an e-mail link, simply use this:

```
<A HREF="mailto:sombody@somemail.com">
```

You simply have to change the "http://" portion to "mailto:". Notice that all three of the preceding methods have one thing in common: they do not close the command in the typical manner that other HTML commands are closed. Now let's examine the source code for a simple but complete HTML document:

```
<HTML>
<HEAD>
    <TITLE>Test HTML Page</TITLE>
</HEAD>
<BODY BGCOLOR="blue">
<P>
<CENTER><B><FONT SIZE="+2">My First Web Page </FONT></B></CENTER>
<P>I am learning HTML !. I <B><I>LOVE</I></B> HTML!
<P><CENTER><IMG SRC="java.gif" ></CENTER>
<P>
<P><CENTER>You can email me  at</CENTER>
<P>
<CENTER><A HREF="mailto:myemail@someemail.com">Email ME</A>
</CENTER><
<P><CENTER>Or go to this publisher's Web Site </CENTER>
<P><CENTER><A HREF="http://www.wordware.com">Wordware
    Publishing</A></CENTER>
</BODY>
</HTML>
```

First, let me make a few clarifications. You should note a new command at the beginning:

```
<BODY BGCOLOR="blue">
```

You can change the background color of your page using this command and any standard color. You can also set a background image for your HTML document with a similar command:

```
<BODY background="mypicture.gif">
```

Now, I will be the first to admit that this sample Web page is very trivial. But it does contain the basics of HTML. With the material we have covered so far, you can display images, text, links, e-mail links, background colors, and background images—not too bad for just a few short pages. You may also want to look at the Sample HTML folder in the downloadable files to see several sample HTML documents for various purposes. These can be used as templates for your own Web pages. Examining these can give you a deeper understanding of basic HTML.

Colors and Backgrounds

Let's examine a few other simple items we can add to our HTML documents. The first is altering text color. You can set the default text color for the entire document, and you can alter the color of specific text. You alter the default text color for the entire document using a technique very similar to the one used to alter the background color of the document:

```
<BODY TEXT="blue">
```

This text simply tells the browser that unless otherwise specified, all text in this document should be blue. In addition to changing the default color of all text in a document, you may wish to simply change the color of a specific section of text. This is fairly easy to do as well. Instead of using the BODY TEXT command, we use the FONT command:

```
<FONT COLOR="red">This is red text</FONT>
```

This, like the other color commands, can be used with any standard color.

There are a wide variety of tags you can use to alter the appearance and behavior of text and images. Just a few others for you to consider would be the <BLINK></BLINK> tags which, as the name implies, causes the text to blink (this is only supported by Netscape and will not work in Internet Explorer). Another example is <STRIKE></STRIKE>, which causes the text to appear with a line through it (a strikethrough). The tags

Appendix **D**

we have covered so far are enough to allow you to accomplish what you need in HTML.

Tables

The next HTML command we are going to examine is the table. You frequently see tables on Web pages and they are a very good way to organize data. You can use the tables with or without a border, and I will explain the various reasons to use one method or the other.

First, I will show you how to create a table with a border:

```
<TABLE BORDER=1>
    <TR>
        <TD>
            <P>This
            <P>Is a
    <TR>
        <TD>
            <P>Table
        <TD>
                <P>With a border
</TABLE>
```

By now, you should be able to recognize that the <TABLE> and </TABLE> tags actually contain the table. Each <TR> tag designates another row in the table. The <TD></TD> create a cell within that row (TD refers to Table Data). Using those three tags you can create a table with any number of rows or columns you wish. Notice that in the first line of this code the BORDER property is set to 1. This means the border has a width and is therefore visible. In some instances you may not want the border to show. Tables can be used simply to hold images and text in relative positions. In cases such as this, you may not wish the border to show. Below is an example of a table whose borders will not show.

```
<P><TABLE BORDER=0 CELLSPACING=0 CELLPADDING=0>
    <TR>
        <TD>
            <P>This
        <TD>
            <P>is a
    <TR>
        <TD>
```

```
            <P>Table
    <TD>
            <P>With no borders or padding
  </TABLE>
```

Notice that BORDER, CELLPADDING, and CELLSPACING are all set to 0. This causes the table itself to not be displayed. However, the contents of the table will display. You should also notice that in both examples I have placed text in each cell.

Lists

It is common to present data in lists. With HTML, you have access to a variety of types of lists. The first we will discuss is the unordered list.

```
<UL>
    <LI> First Item
    <LI> Second Item
</UL>
```

The <UL> and </UL> tags define the code that lies between them as being part of an unordered list. The <LI> tags identify list items. An unordered list item will simply appear as a bullet.

An ordered list is not much different. The <LI> list item stays the same, but the <UL> is going to change somewhat.

```
<OL type = I>
    <LI> First Item
    <LI> Second Item
</OL>
```

The "type =" portion of the tag tells the browser what type of list this is. We used a capital I in our example, which will give you capital roman numerals for your list items.

Here is a table containing all the types of ordered lists and how they appear in your browser.

Type	Result
I	I. First item
	II. Second item

Type	Result
i	i. First item
	ii. Second item
1	1. First item
	2. Second item
a	a. First item
	b. Second item
A	A. Second item
	B. Second item

Marquee

A fascinating item you can add to your Web page is the marquee. A scrolling marquee takes a message or an image and scrolls it across the screen. The basic format is this:

```
<MARQUEE LOOP = INFINITE> Hey this is really cool </MARQUEE>
```

In addition to text, you can place an image in the marquee that you can scroll across the screen like so:

```
<MARQUEE LOOP = INFINITE> <IMG SRC = "mypic.gif"></MARQUEE>
```

You can also change the direction the marquee moves. The <DIRECTION> tag will tell the marquee which direction to scroll to, not from.

```
<MARQEE LOOP = INFINITE DIRECTION = RIGHT>Hey this is a cool marquee
</MARQUEE>
```

You can choose from the following directions: left, right, up, and down. Marquees provide an interesting and relatively easy way to display eye-catching information on your Web page.

Index

Note:

The example files can be downloaded from www.wordware.com/VBNET.